Assessment of Mental Capacity

THIRD EDITION

ASSESSMENT OF MENTAL CAPACITY

A Practical Guide for Doctors and Lawyers

THIRD EDITION

The British Medical Association and the Law Society

The Law Society

ISBN–13: 978–1–85328–778–7

Crown copyright material is reproduced here with the permission of the Controller of HMSO.

First edition 1995
Reprinted in 1997 and 2001
Second edition 2004

This edition published in 2010 by the Law Society
113 Chancery Lane, London WC2A 1PL

Typeset by IDSUK (DataConnection) Ltd
Printed by TJ International, Padstow, Cornwall

FSC
Mixed Sources
Product group from well-managed
forests and other controlled sources
Cert no. SGS-COC-2482
www.fsc.org
© 1996 Forest Stewardship Council

The paper used for the text pages of this book is FSC certified. FSC (the Forest Stewardship Council) is an international network to promote responsible management of the world's forests.

Contents

APPENDICES

Foreword

Before the implementation of the Mental Capacity Act 2005, a case was referred to me that demonstrated the need for greater awareness of the legal tests of capacity and for precise and informative letters from the lawyers requesting such assessments. A caseworker in the Court of Protection gave me a letter from a general practitioner which read:

> "This is to certify that in my opinion Mrs Brown is sufficiently *compos mentis* to understand the nature of any will she should make."

The caseworker asked whether I thought that Mrs Brown had the capacity to make a will, and if she could have permission to instruct her solicitors to draw up a new will.

I was not satisfied with this evidence because the doctor had not explained why Mrs Brown was capable of making a will. Consequently I asked for a second opinion from a specialist in old age psychiatry. This specialist had signed the original medical certificate invoking the jurisdiction of the Court of Protection by confirming that Mrs Brown was incapable, by reason of mental disorder, of managing and administering her property and affairs. He replied:

> "I examined Mrs Brown. . .in the presence of her nephew.
>
> Mrs Brown was unaware of how many sisters or brothers she had and could only remember the name of one brother.
>
> Her short-term memory regarding events of that morning was negligible. She knew her name but did not know where she was presently living, the present year or month. She did however realise that it was cold out and thought it may be winter.
>
> Even her long-term memory was poor. She could remember an address she lived at many years ago, but had no recollection of her recent addresses or even the approximate dates of the Second World War. She did not know her date of birth, who was on the throne, the name of a recent prime minister, and was unable to undertake simple abstract tasks such as counting backwards. She was aware of her husband's death, but not of how long ago it had occurred.
>
> The most generous score on her mental testing would be 2/10, although I feel the only fact she was certain of was her name. Mrs Brown appears to be unaware of her family and any events in her recent past.
>
> Throughout the consultation with her she appeared confused and unable to grasp the meaning of simple requests. I feel she has a gross lack in abilities of reasoning and also in understanding the consequences of her actions. Overall I do not feel she has the capacity to make a will."

Although the specialist had performed various memory tests useful for arriving at a clinical diagnosis, he did not give a diagnosis and he allowed the memory tests to usurp the legal test for ascertaining a person's capacity to make a will. As a result, his report gave no information about Mrs Brown's understanding of what a will is and when it comes into effect, or about her awareness of the extent of her assets.

The purpose of this book is to set out best practice for both professions. It is essential that lawyers who are seeking a medical opinion should provide the medical expert with all the information he or she needs, and give a clear explanation of the relevant legal tests that need to be addressed. It is equally important that doctors, who are asked for an opinion on an individual's capacity to do something, should be aware of the criteria (if any) laid down by the law in relation to that specific transaction.

I was a member of the Working Party of eight people who wrote the first edition, which was published in December 1995. The law and practice relating to mental capacity has progressed by leaps and bounds since then, and frankly the contents of the original edition are barely recognisable in the current one. This is not necessarily a good thing because, in the process of becoming a more exact science, mental capacity has become more complicated, and there is a risk that sooner or later we will be unable to see the wood for the trees. Anyone who has struggled to comprehend the contents of Schedule A1 to the Mental Capacity Act 2005, which was inserted by the Mental Health Act 2007 and relates to the Deprivation of Liberty Safeguards, will appreciate and share my concerns in this respect.

A major milestone was the decision in 2002 in *Masterman-Lister* v. *Brutton & Co.*, which hived off the capacity to litigate from the capacity to manage one's property and affairs generally. The judge, Mr Justice Wright, expressly referred to previous editions of this book and approved its contents. Since then, there have been half a dozen cases analysing the capacity to make a decision on a variety of discrete aspects of the litigation process in personal injury claims. Other significant milestones have been the Mental Capacity Act 2005, which came fully into force on 1 October 2007, and the publication of the Code of Practice to that Act, chapters 3 and 4 of which, thanks to the close involvement of Penny Letts in both publications, have drawn heavily on the contents of earlier editions of this work.

Hopefully these developments in the legislation, case law, professional training, and the dissemination of good practice in the Code of Practice and books such as this will continue to improve awareness of capacity issues among health and legal practitioners, as well as other professionals who may need to carry out assessments of mental capacity.

Denzil Lush
Senior Judge of the Court of Protection
October 2009

Preface

The first two editions of *Assessment of Mental Capacity* have established this book as an indispensable guide for professionals working with people who lack, or who may lack, the capacity to make some decisions or to take actions on their own behalf. Although initially written with a medical and legal audience in mind, the practical, jargon-free approach has helped the book to find a wider readership. Covering a range of issues including: capacity to consent to medical treatment, capacity to make a will, and capacity to form intimate personal relationships, those earlier editions set out the legal and practical issues where decisions had to be made on behalf of adults who lacked capacity to make those decisions for themselves. They also contained a key section on the process of assessing capacity and the factors that needed to be taken into account.

The introduction to the second edition published in 2004 raised the question of legal reform. At the time, decision making in this area was governed by the common law, which was widely held to be fragmented, complex and out of date. That earlier edition drew attention to the Law Commission's successive consultations on the legal framework for decision making and raised the possibility of legal change. That change became a reality during 2007 when the Mental Capacity Act 2005, which incorporates many of the common law's legal and ethical insights, came fully into force in England and Wales.

This new third edition of *Assessment of Mental Capacity* from the BMA and the Law Society is fully updated to take into account the impact of the Mental Capacity Act and continues to offer practical, jargon-free advice. Although designed to be of use to doctors and lawyers, it will prove invaluable to anyone working with, or involved in, the affairs of adults who lack the capacity to make specific decisions. In addition to the core topics covered in the first edition it sets out the main features and principles of the Mental Capacity Act 2005, addresses legal innovations such as Lasting Powers of Attorney in relation to health and welfare decisions, and looks at crucial safeguards where the care or treatment of adults lacking capacity could amount to a deprivation of liberty.

During the updating of this book, it was increasingly apparent that significant social changes were taking place that were of immediate relevance. The combination of an ageing population with an increased sensitivity to the rights and needs of adults with mental health problems or learning disabilities has given new and urgent attention to the legal issues surrounding mental capacity. The Mental Capacity Act has itself further raised awareness of the legal and ethical challenges in this area. Written by experts from a variety of disciplines, and combining practical advice with a thorough grounding in the new legal framework, this new edition of *Assessment of Mental Capacity* is a vital companion to this complex and challenging area of law and medical practice.

The law is stated as at 1 November 2009.

Penny Letts and Julian Sheather
November 2009

Acknowledgements

THIRD EDITION (2009)

The Law Society would like to thank the Medical Ethics Department of the British Medical Association for the opportunity to publish the third edition of this book and Denzil Lush for kindly agreeing to write the foreword.

We would also like to thank the following people for giving freely of their time to review the manuscript and for their invaluable contributions to the text:

Dr JS Bamrah
Ms Veronica English, British Medical Association
Dr Jan Wise

The British Medical Association's Medical Ethics Committee

The Law Society's Mental Health and Disability Committee

Julie Burton, Julie Burton Law
Nigel Eastman (Professor of Law and Ethics, St George's, University of London)
Sophy Miles, Miles and Partners
Camilla Parker, Mental Health and Human Rights Consultant
Paula Scully, Derbyshire County Council
Pauline Thompson, Policy Consultant, Age Concern and Help the Aged
Susan Thompson, Beachcroft LLP

Court of Protection

Denzil Lush, Senior Judge, Court of Protection
Gordon R. Ashton, District Judge and Nominated Judge of the Court of Protection

Law Commission

Tim Spencer-Lane, Policy Advisor, Mental Health and Disability, Law Society (currently on secondment to the Law Commission)

The Official Solicitor

Alistair Pitblado, Official Solicitor to the Senior Courts
Beverley Taylor, Senior Healthcare and Welfare Lawyer

SECOND EDITION (2004)

Managing Editor

Penny Letts

Editorial staff

Veronica English
Jenny McCabe
Gillian Romano-Critchley
Ann Sommerville

Contributors

Gordon R. Ashton
Penny Letts
Peter Rowlands
Edward Solomons
Jonathan Waite

Reviewers

Anthony Harbour
Denzil Lush
The British Medical Association's Medical Ethics Committee
The Law Society's Mental Health and Disability Committee

FIRST EDITION (1995)

Contributors

Nigel Eastman
Michael Hinchcliffe

Penny Letts
Denzil Lush
Steven Luttrell
Lydia Sinclair
Ann Sommerville

Membership of the Assessment of Mental Capacity Working Party for the first edition (1993–1995)

James Birley
Nigel Eastman
J Stuart Horner
Penny Letts
Denzil Lush
Lydia Sinclair
Ann Sommerville
David Watts

About the authors

The following authors, editor and contributors have updated the text of this third edition of *Assessment of Mental Capacity*.

AUTHORS

The British Medical Association is a membership organisation that looks after the professional and personal needs of doctors practising in all branches of medicine in the UK. Its Medical Ethics Committee debates medical ethics, medical law, and the relationship between the medical profession, the public and the state. The BMA's Medical Ethics Department answers ethical enquiries from doctors and publishes guidance on a wide range of issues, including: consent, confidentiality and treatment of incapacitated adults.

The Law Society is a membership organisation that represents solicitors qualified in England and Wales practising both at home and internationally. The Society protects and promotes the interests of the profession by providing advice, training, products and services to its members; developing new legal markets; and influencing law and policy through representation activities. The Society's Mental Health and Disability Committee reviews and promotes improvements in law, and practice and procedure affecting elderly people and those with mental or physical disabilities.

GENERAL EDITOR

Penny Letts is an independent policy consultant and trainer specialising in mental health, mental capacity and disability law. She was Law Society Policy Advisor on Mental Health and Disability matters from 1987–2001, a member of the Mental Health Act Commission from 1995–2004, and Specialist Advisor to the Joint Parliamentary Scrutiny Committee on the Mental Capacity Bill in 2002–03. Penny has written widely on mental health and mental capacity issues including: a substantial part of the *Mental Capacity*

Act 2005 Code of Practice and the *Making Decisions* series of booklets (DCA). She is also a contributor to the *Elderly Client Handbook* (Law Society, 2004), *Mental Capacity: The new law* (Jordans, 2006) and *Court of Protection Practice 2009* (Jordans, 2009)

CONTRIBUTORS

Alexander Ruck Keene is a barrister at 39 Essex Street, who is instructed by individuals (including on behalf of the Official Solicitor), NHS bodies and local authorities before the Court of Protection. He assisted the Office of the Public Guardian and the Court of Protection in developing the procedures for handling applications concerning deprivation of liberty following April 2009, spent three months in Strasbourg at the European Court of Human Rights, and is a contributor to *The Law of Human Rights* 2nd edition (OUP, 2009).

Fenella Morris is a barrister at 39 Essex Street. She is regularly instructed in cases concerning the health, welfare and finances of incapable adults and has appeared in a number of leading cases, including *JE* v. *DE and Surrey County Council*. She is co-author of *Mental Capacity: A guide to the new law* 2nd edition (Law Society, 2008).

Dr Julian Sheather is ethics manager at British Medical Association. His particular interests lie in public health ethics, mental health, consent and mental capacity. Julian is the Ethics Department's lead on child protection and health and human rights. He is a co-author of *Medical Ethics Today* and is a regular contributor to the *British Medical Journal* and *The Journal of Medical Ethics*. Julian is a member of the British Medical Journal's Ethics Committee, the Institute of Medical Ethics and the advisory board of BIOS at the LSE. He also lectures widely both nationally and internationally on a range of topics in medical ethics.

Victoria Butler-Cole is a barrister at 39 Essex Street. She is regularly instructed by family members, local authorities and the Official Solicitor in cases concerning best interests decisions, community care, and mental health in the High Court and the Court of Protection. She contributed to the JUSTICE briefing on the Mental Health Bill and is a contributing author to *The Law of Human Rights* 2nd edition (OUP, 2009). She was previously Assistant Director of the Nuffield Council on Bioethics.

Table of cases

Table of statutes

Table of statutory instruments

Table of European legislation

PART I

Introduction

CHAPTER 1

The law, practice and this book

1.1 MENTAL CAPACITY AND THE LAW

Capacity is the ability to do something. In a legal context it refers to a person's ability to do something, including making a decision, which may have legal consequences for that person, or for other people. Capacity can be the pivotal issue in balancing the right to autonomy in decision-making and the right to protection from harm.

Doctors and lawyers have common responsibilities to ensure the protection of people who lack capacity to decide specific matters for themselves and to promote the autonomy and choices of those who can regulate their own lives. The careful assessment of whether individuals have or lack capacity to make particular decisions is essential to the protection of their rights. Doctors, lawyers and other professionals will be responsible for carrying out assessments of capacity. Effective communication, both between any professionals involved and with the person being assessed, is vital. This book sets out to aid communication, in particular between doctors and lawyers, and to clarify the legal framework within which assessment of capacity takes place.

Background

The issue of capacity took on increased importance in England and Wales in the lead up to, and coming into effect of, the Mental Capacity Act 2005. As indicated in previous editions of this book, reform of the law relating to mental capacity was a long and protracted process, starting in 1989 with a five-year inquiry by the Law Commission which published its final report, including a draft Bill, in 1995.[1] The Government undertook further

3

consultation,[2] leading to a policy statement[3] and eventual publication in 2003 of a second Draft Mental Incapacity Bill.[4] The draft Bill was subject to pre-legislative scrutiny by a Joint Parliamentary Select Committee which made a number of recommendations for improvements.[5] The Joint Committee gave the following reasons why new legislation was necessary:

- the inadequacies of the (then) common law to safeguard those who lack capacity;
- the need to promote awareness and good practice in dealing with those lacking capacity;
- the Government's duty to fulfil human rights obligations towards those lacking capacity;
- the Government's commitment to promote non-discrimination in respect of people lacking capacity; and
- the need to achieve a better balance between autonomy and protection for those who are unable to make decisions.

This process of consultation and scrutiny finally resulted in the Mental Capacity Act 2005 (the 'MCA') which came fully into effect on 1 October 2007. At long last, there is now statutory provision to clarify and govern the making of decisions by and on behalf of people who may lack capacity to make specific decisions for themselves.

The MCA defines what it means to lack capacity and sets out a new integrated jurisdiction for the making of personal welfare decisions, health-care decisions and financial decisions on behalf of people lacking capacity to make such decisions. It also includes provisions to promote and encourage autonomy by ensuring that people are given all appropriate help and support to enable them to make their own decisions where possible, enabling them to prepare in advance for future lack of capacity and maximising their participation in any decision-making process.

This book has been fully updated to take account of the changes introduced by the MCA and to consider the impact of the MCA on other areas of decision-making outside the scope of the Act. The way in which the courts have interpreted issues relating to capacity, both before and after implementation of the MCA is also discussed. Uniquely, the aim of this book is to help doctors and lawyers reach a common understanding of the requirements of the law in all areas where an assessment of capacity may be needed. It is important that both professions work within their own areas of professional expertise but cooperate with each other in the interests of their clients.

1.2 HOW TO USE THIS BOOK

This book sets out to provide a useful resource and tool for the health and legal professions. It is intended to be a source of information appropriate to the assessment of mental capacity in a variety of contexts. Some repetition in the text is unavoidable and is indeed desirable since it is expected that health and legal professionals will refer to the sections which are relevant to a particular client rather than read the book from cover to cover.

Part I begins with a description of the purpose of the book and an explanation of the limits of its coverage. It continues with an outline of important professional and ethical issues for health and legal professionals which arise from a consideration of mental capacity.

Part II provides an outline of the key principles and concepts underpinning the legal framework of the MCA, looking at the statutory definition and test of capacity and how decisions should be made on behalf of people lacking capacity. It also considers the overlapping legislation affecting children and young people and some specific decisions excluded from the MCA. Other legal principles relevant to the assessment of capacity are also described.

Part III examines the legal tests of capacity which apply to various decisions or activities that an individual may wish to undertake (e.g. making a will or getting married). In order for any person to be judged mentally capable of undertaking a particular action, they must meet legal requirements set by the MCA or by the courts. Different requirements apply to different types of decisions. Lawyers often seek medical opinions when they are asked to advise, or act on behalf of, a client whose mental capacity to make specific decisions is in doubt. Lawyers who ask doctors to assess a person's capacity should always make clear the activity or transaction in which the person intends to engage or the decision that the person expects to make, as well as the law's requirements in this respect. **Part III**, by clarifying the legal requirements for a number of activities or decisions, is primarily intended as a reminder to lawyers and to help doctors who have been asked to conduct an assessment of a person's capacity. References to statute and case law are given where appropriate.

Medical practitioners also have to assess an individual's mental capacity to clarify whether medical treatment can proceed without the patient's consent. Whether an apparent consent or refusal of treatment is legally valid is discussed in **Chapter 13** and specific safeguards relating to medical research are considered in **Chapter 14**, both aimed primarily at health professionals.

Chapter 15 discusses the legal safeguards that must (since April 2009) apply to people who lack capacity to consent to their care or treatment who are being looked after in a hospital or care home in conditions which constitute a deprivation of their liberty. This will be of particular interest to health and social care professionals who are involved in applying these safeguards, as well as to lawyers who may be asked to advise people affected by them, and representatives and advocates appointed under these safeguards.

Part IV deals with the medical practicalities of assessing capacity. **Chapter 16** sets out the accepted practice for carrying out assessments of capacity and will be familiar to practitioners who regularly work in the mental health field. It is primarily intended to assist health professionals who only occasionally encounter a request for an assessment of capacity to be carried out. **Chapter 17** aims to help lawyers direct their requests for a medical opinion appropriately and to be aware of the steps involved in a medical assessment.

Please note that when referring to the person lacking capacity we have chosen to adopt the plural 'they/them/their' to avoid using either just the masculine or feminine or, potentially more confusing, a combination of both.

1.3 INTERFACE WITH MENTAL HEALTH LAW

Mental health legislation and mental capacity legislation have very different aims. The Mental Health Act 1983 provides powers for the detention and treatment of a person with a mental disorder, if necessary without that person's consent. It is primarily concerned with the reduction of risk both to the patient and to others, using compulsion where necessary. By contrast, mental capacity legislation seeks to enable and support people to make their own decisions wherever possible. The principles of the MCA ensure that decisions made on behalf of someone lacking capacity must reflect that person's best interests and should restrict that person as little as possible. In practice there are circumstances where mental health and mental capacity legislation may be applicable to the same person and sometimes choices must be made as to which legal framework should be used.

The Mental Health Act 1983 and the Mental Capacity Act 2005 are different legal instruments with different powers and safeguards. The MCA makes it clear that where a patient who lacks capacity to consent is already detained and being given treatment for mental disorder under Part 4 of the Mental Health Act 1983, the Mental Health Act takes priority and 'trumps' the provisions of the MCA. However, decisions relating to treatment that are not covered by the relevant parts of the Mental Health Act 1983, such as treatment for physical disorders, are covered by the MCA. Similarly, people who are detained in hospital under the Mental Health Act and who also lack capacity to make financial or other types of decisions may be subject to the provisions of the MCA.

The Mental Health Act 2007 amended both the Mental Health Act 1983 and the MCA. The amendments to the MCA provide safeguards for people lacking capacity to consent and whose care and treatment involves a deprivation of liberty within the meaning of Article 5 of the European Convention on Human Rights (ECHR) (see **Chapter 15**). To comply with Article 5(1) of the ECHR, any deprivation of liberty must be properly authorised 'in accordance with a procedure prescribed by law'. For people with mental disorders who have to be deprived of their liberty, healthcare and other professionals will need to decide whether detention under the Mental Health Act or the new deprivation of liberty safeguards (DoLS) under the MCA will be more appropriate.

Where an individual lacks capacity to consent to treatment for mental disorder, and it is reasonable and possible to do so, professionals should generally apply the provisions of the MCA, since it is likely to be less restrictive of a person's human rights and freedom of action. However, there may be circumstances when the more formal safeguards provided under the Mental Health Act may be more appropriate. The Code of Practice accompanying the MCA[6] suggests that consideration may need to be given to using mental health legislation where, for example:

- It is not possible to give the person the care or treatment they require without doing something that will deprive them of their liberty. The DoLS will usually apply to those for whom mental health legislation is not appropriate, such as those living in a care home (see **Chapter 15**).
- The person needs treatment that cannot be given under the MCA, such as where the person has made a valid and applicable advance decision to refuse the proposed treatment or part of it (see **Chapter 13**).
- The person may need to be restrained in a way that is not permitted under the MCA (see **Chapter 13**).
- It is not possible to assess or treat the person safely or effectively without using compulsory powers.
- The person may lack capacity in some areas but retains the capacity to refuse a vital part of the treatment and has done so.

As a result of amendments made to the Mental Health Act 1983 by the Mental Health Act 2007, a number of powers under the 1983 Act depend on the patient's mental capacity to make the relevant decision. For example, non-emergency electro-convulsive therapy (ECT) cannot be given to a patient who has capacity to consent to such treatment and refuses. Furthermore, community patients under supervised community treatment (SCT) with capacity can only be given treatment in the community with their consent and those who refuse must be recalled to hospital in order to be given treatment without their consent. Community patients without capacity to consent (who have not been recalled) can be given treatment if a donee of a health and welfare Lasting Power of Attorney, a deputy or the Court of Protection consents to the treatment on their behalf.

Further discussion of the detail of mental health legislation is beyond the scope of this book. Guidance on the use and operation of the Mental Health Act 1983 can be found in the Code of Practice[7] accompanying that Act.

1.4   SCOPE OF THIS BOOK

What is covered?

Law and medical practice in England and Wales

This book deals with the legal position in England and Wales regarding the legal rights and treatment of adults (defined in the MCA as people aged 16 years and over) who may lack mental capacity to make specific decisions for themselves. The focus is on the MCA itself and other areas of the civil law affecting the private rights of citizens. It also indicates the relationship between the law and accepted medical practice and looks in particular at the impact of the MCA on relevant areas of practice.

Information for doctors and lawyers

The book brings together information for health and legal professionals on the interpretation of the law as it affects the concept of capacity to make decisions in various situations and the role of both professions in the assessment of capacity. Pointers are also given for good practice in the assessment of mental capacity.

Outside the scope of this book

Children

The legal position of children under 16 years is different and is beyond the scope of this book. The BMA has published separate guidance for doctors on all aspects of healthcare for children and young people.[8] The Law Society's Children Panel has a membership of solicitors who have been assessed as competent to represent children in all legal proceedings (see **www.lawsociety.org.uk**).

However, apart from a few exceptions (indicated where relevant) the main provisions of the MCA described in this book also apply to young people aged 16–17 as they apply to adults aged 18 years and over. The ways in which the MCA applies to children and young people are described in **Chapter 3**, including the complexities that arise in relation to the assessment of capacity.

Jurisdictions outside England and Wales

The book deals with the law in England and Wales. It does not deal with other parts of the UK.

In Scotland, statutory guidance has been published on the Adults with Incapacity (Scotland) Act 2000, which became law in April 2001 and introduced a statutory framework for decision-making for people with impaired capacity.[9] The BMA has issued separate guidance for doctors on the requirements in Scotland for the assessment of capacity and the treatment of adults who lack capacity to consent.[10]

In Northern Ireland, decision-making in this area is covered by common law, although at the time of writing, the Northern Ireland Assembly was consulting on reform of mental health and capacity law.[11]

The criminal law

The book sets out the legal provisions relating to the civil law (those areas of law concerning the private rights of citizens). It does not cover aspects of the criminal law, except for one specific area. **Chapter 12** deals with the provisions in the criminal law relating to protection of vulnerable people from sexual abuse, which may arise in the context of consent to sexual relationships. Other issues such as a defendant's 'fitness to plead' or the need for an 'appropriate adult' to be present during police questioning are not considered.

Further information for lawyers advising and representing mentally disordered people who are the subject of criminal investigation or proceedings is available from the Law Society.[12]

The MCA does, however, create the criminal offence of ill-treatment or neglect of an incapacitated adult. The Law Society has published a commentary on all the provisions of the MCA.[13]

Physical incapacity

This book does not consider specific issues arising from a person's physical incapacity. Separating issues arising from a person's lack of physical or mental capacity is not always straightforward – for example, when considering the fitness to drive of a person with dementia, both physical and mental impairment may be present. Also, severe physical disabilities may affect a person's ability to communicate their wishes or decisions. Where physical incapacity inhibits communication, every effort should be made to assist the person to communicate, but where this is not possible, the same considerations in assessing capacity will apply as to those with mental disabilities. The MCA makes it clear that when an individual is unable to communicate a decision by any means they will be treated as if they lack capacity to make that decision.

Direct payments

Direct payments allow local authorities to make cash payments to service users who have been assessed as having an eligible need, so that they can buy their own services directly in order to meet that need. Where such a person lacks capacity to consent to direct payments or make the necessary arrangements, then the payment can be made to a 'suitable person'.[14] This book does not consider specific issues relating to a person's mental capacity to agree to direct payments.

Mental Health Act 1983

The interface between the Mental Health Act 1983 and the MCA is discussed briefly in **1.3** above. Further consideration of the detail of mental health legislation is beyond the scope of this book.

1.5 FURTHER ADVICE

Assessing, advising or treating people who may lack capacity to make relevant decisions are complex matters, often giving rise to professional or ethical dilemmas in both medical and legal practice. Some key issues affecting both professions are discussed in **Chapter 2**, but further advice may be needed when considering an individual case. The British Medical Association and the Law Society offer guidance on ethical issues to their members. Doctors can contact the Ethics Department of the BMA and solicitors can telephone the Ethics Helpline operated by the Solicitors Regulation Authority. Guidance is also available from bodies such as the Ministry of Justice, the Office of the Official Solicitor, the Office of the Public Guardian and the Department of Health (see **Appendix I** and **Appendix J**).

NOTES

1. Law Commission (1995) *Mental Incapacity* (Law Com No 231), TSO.
2. Lord Chancellor's Department (1997) *Who decides? Making decisions on behalf of mentally incapacitated adults* (Cm 3803), TSO.
3. Lord Chancellor's Department (1999) *Making decisions: the Government's proposals for making decisions on behalf of mentally incapacitated adults* (Cm 4465), TSO.
4. Draft Mental Incapacity Bill 2003 (Cm 5859-I), TSO.
5. Joint Committee on the Draft Mental Capacity Bill (2003) *Report of the Joint Committee on the Draft Mental Incapacity Bill*, Vol I (HL Paper 198-I, HC 1083-I), TSO.
6. Department for Constitutional Affairs (2007) *Mental Capacity Act 2005 Code of Practice*, TSO; and Ministry of Justice (2008) *Mental Capacity Act 2005: Deprivation of Liberty Safeguards. Code of Practice to supplement the main Mental Capacity Act 2005 Code of Practice*, TSO. Also available online at **www.publicguardian.gov.uk**.
7. Department of Health (2008) *Mental Health Act 1983 Code of Practice*, TSO. Also available online at **www.dh.gov.uk**.
8. British Medical Association (2000) *Consent, rights and choices in health care for children and young people*, Wiley Blackwell.
9. The Scottish Executive has published codes of practice and other information about the operation of the Act. See **www.scotland.gov.uk/Topics/Justice/law/awi**.
10. British Medical Association (2009) *Medical treatment for adults with incapacity: guidance on ethical and medico-legal issues in Scotland*, BMA. See **www.bma.org.uk/sc/ethics/consent_and_capacity**.
11. Department of Health, Social Services and Public Safety (2009) *A Legislative Framework* for *Mental Capacity and Mental Health Legislation in Northern Ireland.*
12. Carolyn Taylor, Julia Krish, Frank Farnham (2009) *Advising Mentally Disordered Offenders: A practical guide* 2nd edition, Law Society Publishing.
13. Nicola Greaney, Fenella Morris, Beverley Taylor (2008) *Mental Capacity: A guide to the new law* 2nd edition, Law Society Publishing.
14. Health and Social Care Act 2001, s.1A. A 'suitable person' is defined in s.1C as a prescribed representative (s.5B), a deputy appointed by the Court of Protection or donee of a Lasting Power of Attorney (s.5C) or another person the local authority considers suitable.

CHAPTER 2

Professional and ethical issues

2.1 CAPACITY TO INSTRUCT A SOLICITOR

In carrying out legal transactions or conducting litigation on behalf of clients with capacity, lawyers must act on their clients' instructions by identifying clearly their clients' objectives and agreeing with their clients on the steps to be taken.[1] They have a duty to advise their clients of the legal consequences of the action they are proposing to take and any other options available, and clients may change their instructions as a result of receiving legal advice. Ultimately, so long as the client has capacity to give instructions, the lawyer must act on those instructions, or cease to act directly on the client's behalf.[2] Therefore a key question for lawyers is whether the client has capacity to give instructions.

The Mental Capacity Act 2005 (the 'MCA') states that a person must be assumed to have capacity unless it is established that that person lacks capacity. However, solicitors would be acting negligently if they acted on a client's instructions without first satisfying themselves that the client has the requisite level of capacity. Different levels of capacity are required for different transactions, for example different considerations apply to making a will than in conducting personal injury litigation. A solicitor must therefore assess the client's understanding in the context of the relevant legal test of capacity (as set out in **Part III**) and then consider whether the client is able to convey in general terms what they wish the solicitor to do.

This does not mean that the client must be able to understand all the details of the law – it is the role of the lawyer to provide legal advice. It is also possible

11

that the client may be clear about some aspects of a legal transaction or proceedings while lacking capacity to deal with others. The Court of Appeal has stressed 'the issue-specific nature' of the test of capacity, describing the process as follows:

> . . . the requirement to consider the question of capacity in relation to the particular transaction (its nature and complexity) in respect of which the decisions as to capacity fall to be made. It is not difficult to envisage claimants in personal injury actions with capacity to deal with all matters and take all 'lay client' decisions related to their actions up to and including a decision whether or not to settle, but lacking capacity to decide (even with advice) how to administer a large award.[3]

This 'issue-specific' approach has been given statutory codification by the MCA, which stresses that an assessment of capacity must be made in relation to the specific decision in question at the particular time the decision needs to be made.

In the same way, lawyers must consider the client's capacity to give instructions in respect of each particular transaction at the time a decision needs to be made. If there is doubt about a client's capacity, it is advisable for the lawyer to seek a medical opinion. It will be necessary to explain to the doctor the relevant legal test of capacity and ask for an opinion as to how the client's medical condition may affect their ability to make the decision in question. However, it is for the solicitor to assess whether the client has the required level of capacity, using the medical opinion and other relevant evidence to inform the assessment.

If the solicitor considers that a client lacks capacity to give instructions, the solicitor should, in some circumstances, decline to act on the client's behalf.[4] However, clients should not be left 'high and dry' and action should be taken to protect their interests.[5] Solicitors must always act in the best interests of their clients and do their best for them.[6] Depending on the circumstances of the case, special procedures may be used to enable a solicitor to act on behalf of a client lacking capacity. For example, the solicitor may be able to put in place safeguards to protect the client's financial affairs, acting on the instructions of a family member or attorney (see **Chapter 5**) or may continue to conduct legal proceedings on the client's behalf by acting through a litigation friend (see **Chapter 8**) or the Official Solicitor (see **Appendices E** and **F**).

2.2   CONFIDENTIALITY

Carrying out an assessment of capacity may require doctors and lawyers to share information about the personal circumstances of the person being assessed. Yet doctors, lawyers and other professionals are bound by a duty of confidentiality towards their clients, imposed through their professional ethical codes and reinforced by law.[7]

The Data Protection Act 1998 (the 'DPA') also regulates practice in this area. The DPA provides individuals with a number of important rights to ensure that personal information and in particular, sensitive personal information (such as health information) is processed fairly and lawfully. Processing includes holding, recording, using and disclosing information. The DPA applies to all forms of media, including paper and images. It requires that all data processing must be 'fair' and 'lawful'. This means that all patients including those who lack capacity must know when and what information about them is being processed. The processing itself must be lawful and this includes meeting common law confidentiality obligations, which are likely to require patient consent (or the consent of a nominated proxy) to be obtained. The DPA also requires organisations that wish to process identifying information to use the minimum of information necessary and to retain it for only as long as it is needed for the purpose for which it was originally collected.

As a general principle, personal information may only be disclosed with the client's consent, even to close relatives or 'next of kin'. However, the courts have confirmed there are circumstances when disclosure is necessary in the absence of consent:

> The decided cases very clearly establish: (i) that the law recognises an important public interest in maintaining professional duties of confidence; but (ii) that the law treats such duties not as absolute but as liable to be overridden where there is held to be a stronger public interest in disclosure.[8]

In relation to people who lack capacity to consent to (or refuse) disclosure, a balance must be struck between the public and private interests in maintaining confidentiality and the public and private interests in permitting, and occasionally requiring, disclosure for certain purposes. Some guidance has been offered in the case of *R (on the application of A S)* v. *Plymouth City Council and C*, which concerned an application for disclosure of social services records to the mother (and nearest relative) of a young adult with learning disabilities who was subject to local authority guardianship under the Mental Health Act 1983. In allowing limited disclosure to the mother, Lady Justice Hale (as she then was) said:

> [The young adult's] interest in protecting the confidentiality of personal information about himself must not be underestimated. It is all too easy for professionals and parents to regard children and incapacitated adults as having no independent interests of their own: as objects rather than subjects. But we are not concerned here with the publication of information to the whole wide world. There is a clear distinction between disclosure to the media with a view to publication to all and sundry and disclosure in confidence to those with a proper interest in having the information in question.[9]

A similar balancing act must be carried out by professionals seeking or undertaking assessments of capacity. It is essential that information concerning the person being assessed, which is directly relevant to the decision in question, is made available to ensure that an accurate and focused assessment can take place. Every effort must first be made to obtain the person's consent to disclosure by providing a full explanation as to why this is necessary and the risks and consequences involved. If the person is unable to consent or refuse, relevant disclosure (of the minimum necessary to achieve the objective of assessing capacity) may be permitted where this is in the person's best interests. However, this does not mean that everyone has to know everything.

Chapter 16 of the MCA Code of Practice[10] provides advice on access to information about individuals lacking capacity to consent to disclosure. The Code states at para. 16.8 the relevant factors as to whether someone else might be able to see information relating to an individual who lacks capacity, which include:

- whether the person requesting the information is acting as an agent, such as a court appointed deputy or attorney for the person who lacks capacity;
- whether disclosure is in the best interests of the person who lacks capacity; and
- what type of information has been requested.

Specific guidance for lawyers and doctors is given in the following sections.

Lawyers

There is a general principle that a solicitor (and the solicitor's firm) is under a duty to:

> . . . keep the affairs of clients and former clients confidential except where disclosure is required or permitted by law or by your client (or former client).[11]

The duty of confidentiality extends to all confidential information about a client's affairs, irrespective of the source of the information, and subject only to limited exceptions in the absence of the client's specific consent.[12] There is no specific exception which permits informing a doctor about the contents of a client's will, for example, or the extent of the client's property and affairs, without first having obtained express consent from the client.

However, there have been decisions in cases involving wills in which disclosure (with the client's approval) may be expected. In *Kenward* v. *Adams* the judge stated that there is a 'golden if tactless rule' (see **4.5** and **6.5**) that:

> . . . when a solicitor is drawing up a will for an aged testator or one who has been seriously ill, it should be witnessed and approved by a medical practitioner, who ought to record his examination of the testator and his findings . . . (and) that if there was an earlier will it should be examined and any proposed alterations should be discussed with the testator.[13]

Any solicitor who cannot obtain from the client consent to the disclosure of confidential information, or has not obtained consent in advance in anticipation of the need for disclosure, would be advised to seek the advice of the Solicitors Regulation Authority (see **Appendix I**).

Doctors

Doctors are bound by a professional duty to maintain the confidentiality of personal health information unless the patient gives valid consent to disclosure, or, if the patient is incapable of giving consent, the doctor believes disclosure to be in that person's best interests. Exceptionally, confidential information can be disclosed without consent where the public interest outweighs the interest in maintaining confidentiality. Difficult decisions may arise if relatives, carers or the patient's lawyer approach the doctor for a medical report on an individual whose capacity to consent is in doubt, but the patient refuses to be assessed (this is discussed in **2.4** below) or else agrees to assessment but not to disclosure of the results. The statutory body for doctors, the General Medical Council, recognises that there are some exceptional circumstances when disclosure of confidential information can be made without consent in the best interests of a person lacking capacity to consent (see **13.7**).

As mentioned above, general guidance on sharing information about a person who lacks capacity can be found in chapter 16 of the MCA Code of Practice. More detailed ethical guidance on confidentiality and disclosure of health information, which draws together guidance from professional and regulatory bodies, is available from the BMA.[14]

2.3 CREATING THE RIGHT ENVIRONMENT FOR ASSESSING CAPACITY

Detailed guidance on the practical aspects of assessing capacity is given in **Part IV** and further advice is given in the MCA Code of Practice, in particular chapters 3 and 4 (see **Appendix B**). The following pointers may be helpful to both doctors and lawyers when trying to create the right environment and optimise the conditions for assessing capacity:[15]

- Try to minimise anxiety or stress by making the person feel at ease.
- If the cause of the incapacity can be treated, the doctor should, in so far as possible, treat it before the assessment of capacity is made.
- If the person's capacity is likely to improve, wait until it has improved. Obviously, if the assessment is urgent it may not be possible to wait.
- Be aware of any medication which could affect capacity (e.g. medication which causes drowsiness). Consider delaying the assessment until any negative effects of medication have subsided.
- If there are communication or language problems, consider enlisting the services of a speech therapist or a translator, or consult family members on the best methods of communication.

- Be aware of any cultural, ethnic or religious factors which may have a bearing on the person's way of thinking, behaviour or communication.
- Choose the best time of day for the examination. Some people are better in the morning; others are more alert in the afternoon or early evening.
- Be thorough, but keep the assessment within manageable bounds time-wise to avoid tiring or confusing the client.
- Avoid obtrusive time-checking. It should be possible, without too much discernible eye movement, to keep a check on the time.
- If more than one test of capacity has to be applied, try to do each assessment on a different day, if possible.
- Choose the best location. Usually, someone will feel more comfortable in their own home than in, say, a doctor's surgery or a lawyer's office.
- Try and ensure that there are no obstructions between you and the client which could hinder the development of a relationship of equals: for example consider the height and positioning of the chairs.
- So far as it is within your control, make sure that the temperature in the room is comfortable and that the lighting is soft and indirect, but sufficiently bright for easy eye contact and interpretation of expression and to allow you to study any relevant documentation.
- Consider whether or not a third party should be present. In some cases the presence of a relative, friend or other person (such as an advocate or attorney) could reduce anxiety. In others, their presence might actually increase anxiety. In some cases a third party might be a useful interpreter. In others, they could be intrusive.
- Try and eliminate any background noise or distractions, such as the television or radio, or people talking.
- If possible, make sure that other people cannot overhear you and that others will not interrupt you either from within or outside the room: for example, by telephone.
- Be sensitive towards other disabilities, such as impaired hearing or eyesight, which could mislead you into assuming that a person lacks capacity.
- Speak at the right volume and speed. Try to use short sentences with familiar words. If necessary, accompany your speech with slightly exaggerated gestures or facial expressions and other means of non-verbal communication.
- If necessary, provide verbal or visual aids to stimulate and improve the person's memory.
- If carrying out more than one test of cognitive functioning, allow a reasonable time for general relaxed conversation between each test so as to avoid any sense of disappointment at failing a particular test.
- If possible, try to avoid subjecting the client to an increasingly demoralising sequence of 'I don't know' answers.
- Take one decision at a time – be careful to avoid making the client tired or confused.

- Don't rush – allow the client time to think things over or ask for clarification, where that is possible and appropriate.
- Some organisations (e.g. BILD, Mencap, Sense and Values into Action) have produced specialised material to support decision-making and decision-makers should consider whether it is appropriate to use it (see **Appendix J**).
- It may be appropriate to provide access to relevant supportive technology.

2.4 REFUSAL TO BE ASSESSED

There may be circumstances in which a person whose capacity is in doubt refuses to undergo an assessment of capacity or refuses to be examined by a doctor. It will usually be possible to persuade someone to agree to an assessment if the consequences of refusal are carefully explained. For example, it should be explained to people wishing to make a will (see **Chapter 6**) that the will could possibly be challenged and held to be invalid after their death, while evidence of their capacity to make a will would prevent this from happening. Similarly, a Lasting Power of Attorney (see **5.3**) could be challenged without evidence of the donor's capacity, with the result that the attorney chosen by the donor may be unable to act. Or it may not be possible to pursue legal proceedings unless the court is satisfied that a party to the proceedings has capacity (see **Chapter 8**). The solicitor may also have to decline to act directly or at all on the person's behalf if there are doubts about the person's capacity to give instructions, indicating the need for special arrangements to be made (see **2.1**).

If the client appears to lack capacity to lack capacity to consent to or refuse assessment, it will normally be possible for an assessment to proceed so long as the person is compliant and this is considered to be in the person's best interests (see **2.5** and **Chapter 3**). In some circumstances, if the person is, or is likely to be, the subject of an application to the Court of Protection, it may be possible for the Court of Protection Special Visitor to carry out the assessment (see **Appendix C**). However, in the face of an outright refusal, no one can be forced to undergo an assessment of capacity. Entry to a person's home cannot be forced in such cases and a refusal to open the door to the doctor may be the end of the matter. Other evidence of capacity (or lack of it) may need to be used, such as letters written by them or witness evidence of their actions or behaviour. Where there are serious concerns about the person's mental health, an assessment under the Mental Health Act 1983 may be warranted but only where it is believed that detention in hospital for assessment or treatment for mental disorder may be necessary.

2.5 PEOPLE ASSESSED AS LACKING CAPACITY

The 'best interests' principle

Both lawyers and doctors need to appreciate that if an individual is judged to lack capacity to make the decision in question, any act or decision taken on that person's behalf must be in that person's best interests. The principle of best interests was firmly established under the common law and is now enshrined in statute in the MCA, which includes a checklist of factors which must be taken into account when determining someone's best interests. The principles in MCA, s.1 must also be considered (see **Chapter 3** for details).

The Mental Capacity Act Code of Practice

The MCA is accompanied by a statutory Code of Practice (Code)[16] providing guidance to anyone using the Act's provisions, including anyone involved in assessing capacity, as well as those involved in caring for or working with people who may lack capacity to make particular decisions.

The MCA imposes a duty on certain people to 'have regard to' any relevant guidance in the MCA Code of Practice when acting in relation to a person lacking capacity.[17] The specified people are those acting in one or more of the following ways (as described in other chapters of this book):

- as an attorney acting under a Lasting Power of Attorney (see **Chapter 5**);
- as a deputy appointed by the court (see **Appendix C**);
- as a person carrying out research under the MCA (see **Chapter 14**);
- as an Independent Mental Capacity Advocate (see **Chapter 3**);
- in applying the deprivation of liberty safeguards (see **Chapter 15**);
- in a professional capacity; and /or
- for remuneration.

The statutory duty to have regard to the Code therefore applies to those exercising formal powers or duties under the MCA (attorneys and deputies), and to professionals (including lawyers, doctors, health and social care professionals) and others acting for remuneration (such as paid carers). There is no duty to 'comply' with the Code – it should be viewed as guidance on good practice rather than instruction. However, the specified people must be able to demonstrate that they are familiar with the Code, and if they have not followed relevant guidance contained in it, they will be expected to give cogent reasons why they have departed from it.[18]

The MCA also confirms that a provision of the Code, or a failure to comply with the guidance set out in the Code, can be taken into account by a court or tribunal where it appears relevant to a question arising in any criminal or civil proceedings.[19] There is no liability for breach of the Code itself, but compliance or non-compliance may be a factor in deciding the issue of liability for breach of some other statutory or common law duty. This may apply to anyone using the MCA's provisions, since they are obliged to act in accordance with the principles of the MCA, which includes acting in the best interests of a person lacking capacity, as described in **Chapter 3**.

2.6   SUMMARY OF POINTS FOR DOCTORS

The following paragraphs give a brief summary of the issues doctors should be aware of when carrying out an assessment of capacity.

In many situations where a judgement about capacity has to be made a doctor's opinion will be obtained. A general practitioner (GP), consultant, other hospital doctor or prison or police doctor may be approached to provide this. If the medical practitioner is not routinely involved in assessing capacity, the practical steps outlined in **Part IV** may provide a helpful guide. Assessment requires some knowledge of the person, including their ethnicity, cultural or religious values and social situation. There is a legal presumption of capacity unless the contrary is shown and assumptions about capacity should not be made merely on the basis of the person's age, appearance, condition or behaviour. In most cases, more than a brief interview and reading of other medical reports is necessary.

Capacity is ultimately a legal concept (see **Part II**). The doctor must assess the person's capacity in relation to whatever activity that person is attempting to carry out. The understanding required for each decision will depend on the complexity of the information relevant to the decision and the legal test to be applied. Doctors who are asked to give an assessment of an individual's capacity must be clear about the relevant legal test (see **Part III**) and should ask a lawyer to explain it, if necessary. For decisions covered by the MCA (financial, healthcare and personal welfare decisions) anyone involved in assessing capacity must have regard to the guidance given in the MCA Code of Practice (see **Appendix B**).

Every person is entitled to privacy and confidentiality (see **2.2** above) but if the doctor does not know the individual it may be necessary to seek views from others with professional and personal knowledge of that person and knowledge of the specific decision in question. For example, assessment of whether someone has capacity to make financial decisions in managing their property and financial affairs depends partly on the decisions which need to be made and the amounts and complexity of the assets involved. A doctor who is asked to provide a medical report in such a case needs some knowledge of the person's assets and the skills required to administer them.

When asked to assess a person with a learning disability, doctors should not rely solely on prior reports giving an estimated 'mental age' but must ensure that a current assessment is made. Statements of a person's mental age may be misleading if they do not reflect the person's experience and the context for the particular decision. Assessments of capacity should be regularly reviewed to take account of changing circumstances or fluctuations in the person's condition.

In some circumstances, health professionals may be asked to witness a patient's signature to a legal document. By witnessing the document, it may be inferred that the doctor or nurse is confirming the patient's capacity to enter into the legal transaction effected by the document, rather than merely indicating that the witness has seen the patient sign the document. Doctors and nurses should be clear as to what they are being asked to do. (See **4.5** on witnessing documents.)

2.7 SUMMARY OF POINTS FOR LAWYERS

The following paragraphs provide a summary of useful points for solicitors to consider when acting for a person who may lack capacity to make specific decisions.

In carrying out legal transactions or conducting litigation on behalf of a client with capacity to make the decisions involved, a solicitor must act on their client's instructions. Ultimately, so long as the client has capacity to give instructions, the solicitor must act on those instructions, or cease to act directly on the client's behalf. Before taking action on behalf of a client, the solicitor must assess the client's capacity in order to be satisfied that the client has the capacity to give instructions in relation to the transaction or decision in question (see **2.1**).

There is a legal presumption of capacity unless the contrary is shown. Whether a client has capacity to make a particular decision is a matter of law, to be determined by applying the correct legal test. Different levels of capacity are required for different activities. If there is doubt about a client's mental capacity, it is advisable for the lawyer to seek a medical opinion. Medical practitioners should be asked to give an opinion as to the client's capacity in relation to the particular activity or decision in question, rather than a general assessment of the client's mental condition. In order to do this, the solicitor has a responsibility to explain to the doctor the relevant legal test of capacity (see **Part III**). It should not be assumed that doctors automatically understand what is being asked of them.

It is important to choose a doctor who has the skills and experience to carry out the particular assessment. This may be the person's GP in situations where familiarity with and personal knowledge of the patient may be helpful. In some cases, a specialist with expertise in the patient's particular medical condition may be preferable. **Chapter 17** provides further information.

A doctor's assessment assumes more weight in borderline cases or those at risk of challenge, which together form the majority of cases upon which doctors and lawyers need to liaise. The most obvious cases of incapacity, such as when a person is unconscious or has very severe learning disabilities, are less likely to require detailed medical confirmation. Similarly, where the person is demonstrably capable of dealing with the matter in hand, medical assessment is superfluous. Fluctuating capacity presents particular difficulties and medical evidence is likely to be essential to demonstrate a person's capacity to take action during a lucid interval (see **4.2**).

Capacity can be enhanced by the way explanations are given, by the timing of them or by other simple measures discussed in this book. It can be impaired by fatigue, pain, anxiety or unfamiliar surroundings. Yet doctors are constantly working under constraints of time or location and other limitations, including perhaps their own preconceptions or prior reports from others about the extent of a person's capacity. Their training also emphasises the concept of promoting the patient's health interests in all circumstances. It is therefore important to ask doctors to assess what the person is actually capable of deciding at the time when the decision needs to be made, not whether the decision is sensible or wise.

NOTES

1. Solicitors Regulation Authority (2009) *Solicitors Code of Conduct 2007* (June 2009 Edition), Law Society Publishing. See Rule 2.02.
2. Ibid: Rule 2.01 and the guidance to Rule 2, in particular paras. 6, 8 and 10.
3. *Masterman-Lister* v. *Brutton & Co and Jewell & Home Counties Dairies* [2002] EWCA Civ 1889, CA at 27.
4. Solicitors Regulation Authority (2009) *Solicitors Code of Conduct 2007* (June 2009 Edition), Law Society Publishing. See Rule 2.01 and the guidance to Rule 2, para. 10. An exception is the representation of patients before the First-tier Tribunal (Mental Health) and the Mental Health Review Tribunal for Wales. See Law Society (2009) *Representation before Mental Health Tribunals Practice Note – 13 August 2009*, Law Society. Available online at **www.lawsociety.org.uk**.
5. Solicitors Regulation Authority (2009) *Solicitors Code of Conduct 2007* (June 2009 Edition), Law Society Publishing. Rule 2.01 and the guidance to Rule 2, para. 6(a)(iii). The guidance refers to 'special circumstances' which apply when dealing with a client who lacks capacity as defined in the MCA, but gives no further details.
6. Ibid. Rule 1.04 and the guidance to Rule 1, para. 8.
7. European Convention on Human Rights, Article 8; Data Protection Act 1998.
8. *W* v. *Egdell* [1990] Ch 359 at 419e.
9. *R (on the application of A S)* v. *Plymouth City Council and C* [2002] EWCA Civ 388 at 49.
10. Department of Constitutional Affairs (2007) *Mental Capacity Act 2005 Code of Practice*, TSO. Available at **www.publicguardian.gov.uk.**
11. Solicitors Regulation Authority (2009) *Solicitors Code of Conduct 2007* (June 2009 Edition), Law Society Publishing. Rule 4.01 and associated guidance.
12. Ibid. Guidance to Rule 4.01, paras. 3 and 9–19.
13. *Kenward* v. *Adams* (1975) *The Times*, 29 November 1975.
14. British Medical Association (2008) *Confidentiality and Disclosure of Health Information Tool Kit,* British Medical Association. Available online alongside other guidance related to confidentiality at **www.bma.org.uk/ethics/confidentiality**.

15. This list was originally devised by Denzil Lush, a contributor to the first edition of this book and now Senior Judge of the Court of Protection. It was influential in framing the guidance in the MCA Code of Practice (see **Appendix B**).
16. See note 10 above. See also Ministry of Justice (2008) *Mental Capacity Act 2005: Deprivation of Liberty Safeguards. Code of Practice to supplement the main Mental Capacity Act 2005 Code of Practice*, TSO. Available online at **www.public-guardian.gov.uk**.
17. Mental Capacity Act 2005, s.42(4).
18. This is based on the House of Lords judgment in *R* v. *Ashworth Hospital Authority (now Mersey Care NHS Trust) ex parte Munjaz* [2005] UKHL 58.
19. Mental Capacity Act 2005, s.42(5).

PART II

Legal principles

The Mental Capacity Act 2005: capacity and best interests

3.1   THE LEGAL FRAMEWORK

In England and Wales, the law in relation to adults who lack the capacity to make decisions on their own behalf is laid down in the Mental Capacity Act 2005 (the 'MCA'). The MCA, supported by the accompanying MCA Code of Practice (the 'Code')[1] issued by the Lord Chancellor, provides a comprehensive legal framework for the making of decisions on behalf of adults who may lack capacity to make specific decisions for themselves. The legal framework set out in the MCA is based on two fundamental concepts: lack of capacity and best interests. This chapter describes how the MCA defines and applies those concepts.

The MCA applies to all personal welfare decisions, healthcare decisions and financial decisions taken on behalf of people who permanently or temporarily lack capacity to make those decisions for themselves. All professionals working with adults who lack, or who may lack, capacity to make such decisions need to be familiar with the underlying principles and main provisions of the Act and must also have regard to the MCA Code of Practice.

The MCA confirms the previous common law position that capacity is function-specific, relating to each particular decision at the time the decision needs to be made, and many of the MCA's provisions are based on relevant principles and procedures previously established by the common law.

In particular, the MCA has established the common law principle of 'best interests' as the legal basis for anyone (family member, carer or professional) who is acting or making decisions on behalf of a person who lacks capacity to make those decisions for themselves. The MCA sets out a checklist of factors which must always be taken into account when determining someone's best interests (see **3.6**).

While the MCA has enshrined in statute existing best practice (as described in earlier editions of this book) and former common law principles, it has also introduced into the law several new provisions, including:

- the ability to nominate substitute decision-makers in relation to health and welfare decisions (in addition to financial decisions) under a Lasting Power of Attorney (LPA);
- the development of a new Court of Protection with extended powers;
- safeguards when adults who lack capacity to consent to their participation are enrolled in certain forms of research; and
- the deprivation of liberty safeguards.

These provisions are described in the following chapters, so far as they are relevant to the assessment of capacity.

The sections of the MCA that contain the principles and preliminary matters (ss.1–6) are reproduced in **Appendix A** of this book. The chapters of the Code of Practice most relevant to making an assessment of capacity (chapters 2, 3 and 4) are reproduced in **Appendix B**.

3.2 THE STATUTORY PRINCIPLES

The MCA starts with a statement of guiding principles setting out the values that underpin the legal requirements in the Act and govern all decisions made and actions taken under its powers. Where confusion arises about how aspects of the MCA should be implemented, it will be helpful to refer to these statutory principles. Actions or decisions that clearly conflict with the principles are unlikely to be lawful, although there may be occasions on which the principles are in tension with each other, and some balancing will be required.

The five statutory principles, as set out in MCA, s.1, are:

1. **A person must be assumed to have capacity unless it is established that he lacks capacity.**
   The starting point for assessing a person's capacity to make a particular decision is always the presumption that the individual has capacity. Where there is doubt, the burden of proof is generally on the person who is seeking to establish a lack of capacity and the matter is decided according to the usual civil standard, the balance of probabilities.[2]

2. **A person is not to be treated as unable to make a decision unless all practicable steps to help him to do so have been taken without success.**
   People must be supported and encouraged to make their own decisions wherever possible. Chapter 3 of the MCA Code of Practice (see **Appendix B**)

gives detailed guidance on a range of practicable steps which may assist in maximising a person's decision-making capacity, although the relevance of the various steps suggested will vary depending on the particular circumstances.

3. **A person is not to be treated as unable to make a decision merely because he makes an unwise decision.**

   This principle confirms the common law right of a person to make decisions which others may consider to be unwise.[3] Some caution may need to be applied in operating this principle in practice. While an unwise decision should not, by itself, be sufficient to indicate lack of capacity, it may be sufficient to raise doubts as to the person's capacity, for example if the decision is out of character. What matters is the ability to make the decision, not the outcome.

4. **An act done, or decision made, under this Act for or on behalf of a person who lacks capacity must be done, or made, in his best interests.**

   This establishes 'best interests' as the single criterion to govern all actions or decision-making affecting people who lack capacity to make specific decisions for themselves. Further details on the meaning and determination of best interests are set out in MCA, s.4 (see **3.6** below).

5. **Before the act is done, or the decision is made, regard must be had to whether the purpose for which it is needed can be as effectively achieved in a way that is less restrictive of the person's rights and freedom of action.**

   Where there is more than one course of action or a choice of decisions to be made, all possible options or alternatives should be considered (including whether there is a need for any action or decision at all). Other options need only be considered so long as the desired purpose of the action or decision can still be achieved. Since the decision-maker is only required to 'have regard to' this principle, an option which is not the least restrictive alternative may be chosen if this is in the best interests of the person lacking capacity.

In assessing capacity, the first three of these principles are particularly important. A decision that someone lacks capacity is not to be made lightly. The starting point is the presumption that people do not lack capacity, even when they make unwise choices, and all practicable steps must first be taken to help them make the decision in question before they are assessed as lacking capacity.

Chapter 3 of the MCA Code of Practice contains many suggestions to facilitate decision-making (see also the checklist at **2.3**). The Code also sets out a list of questions that should be asked before carrying out an assessment of capacity:[4]

- Does the person have all the relevant information they need to make the decision?
- If they are making a decision that involves choosing between alternatives, do they have information on all the different options?

27

- Would the person have a better understanding if information was explained or presented in another way?
- Are there times of day when the person's understanding is better?
- Are there locations where they may feel more at ease?
- Can the decision be put off until the circumstances are different and the person concerned may be able to make the decision?
- Can anyone else help the person to make choices or express a view (for example, a family member or carer, an advocate or someone to help with communication)?

3.3   DEFINITION OF MENTAL CAPACITY

Capacity refers to the ability that a person possesses to make specific decisions or to take actions that influence their life, ranging from a simple decision about what to have for breakfast, to far-reaching decisions about investments or serious medical treatment.

The MCA stipulates that people should not be labelled 'incapable' simply on the basis that they have been diagnosed with a particular condition, or because of any preconceived ideas or assumptions about their abilities due, for example, to their age, appearance, condition or any aspect of their behaviour.[5] Rather it must be shown that they lack capacity for each specific decision at the time that decision needs to be made. Individuals retain the legal right to make those decisions for which they continue to have capacity.

Section 2(1) of the MCA states that:

> . . . a person lacks capacity in relation to a matter if at the material time he is unable to make a decision for himself in relation to the matter because of an impairment of, or a disturbance in the functioning of, the mind or brain.

Capacity is therefore decision-specific and time-specific and the inability to make the decision in question must be because of 'an impairment of, or a disturbance in the functioning of, the mind or brain'. Loss of capacity can be partial or temporary and capacity may fluctuate. It is essential that an assessment of capacity is based on the individual's ability to make a specific decision at the time it needs to be made, and not their ability to make decisions in general. It would be wrong to say that someone lacks capacity; rather, the person may lack capacity to make a particular decision at a particular time.

3.4   THE TEST OF CAPACITY

The definition of capacity in the MCA therefore imposes a test of capacity with two parts:

1. Does the individual have an impairment of, or a disturbance in the functioning of, their mind or brain (for example, a disability, condition or trauma that affects the way their mind or brain works)? If so,

2. Does the impairment or disturbance cause the person to be unable to make a specific decision at the time it needs to be made?

The impairment or disturbance does not need to be permanent, and can also include (but is not limited to) conditions associated with some forms of mental illness, dementia, significant learning disabilities, the long-term effects of brain damage, physical or medical conditions that cause confusion, drowsiness or loss of consciousness, concussion following a head injury, and the symptoms of alcohol or drug use.

Section 3 of the MCA defines what it means to be unable to make a decision. In deciding whether the impairment or disturbance causes the person to be unable to make a decision, four factors must be considered:[6]

1. **Does the person understand the information relevant to the decision to be made?**
    The information relevant to a decision includes information about the reasonably foreseeable consequences of deciding one way or another, or of failing to make the decision. An explanation of all relevant information must have been given to the person using the means of communication that is most appropriate for their particular circumstances.
2. **Can the person retain that information in their mind?**
    Retaining information for even a short time may be adequate in the context of some decisions – it will depend on what is necessary for the decision in question. Aids to recollection such as notes, pictures, photographs and voice recorders may be helpful.
3. **Can the person use or weigh that information as part of the decision-making process?**
    An apparently irrational or unwise decision is not necessarily proof that an individual has failed to use or weigh relevant information, but it may trigger the need for a more detailed assessment, particularly if the decision is out of character. The focus must be on the process of decision-making (for example, whether the person can weigh up any risks involved) not the outcome. The person may be assisted in that process by professional advice or support from family or friends.
4. **Can the person communicate the decision?**
    Where an individual cannot communicate their decision in any way, by talking, using sign language or any other means, the Act states that the individual is unable to make a decision for themselves. Examples include people who are unconscious or in a coma or those with a rare condition sometimes referred to as 'locked-in syndrome' who are conscious, yet totally unable to communicate.

If an impairment or disturbance in the person's mind or brain is causing them to be unable to do any of the four things set out above, then they do not have capacity to make the decision in question.

Assessing capacity will not always be straightforward, particularly if a person has fluctuating capacity or where some capacity is demonstrable but its extent is uncertain. Detailed practical advice about the assessment of mental capacity is given in **Part IV** of this book.

3.5 WHO ASSESSES CAPACITY?

The person who wishes to make a decision on behalf of another who lacks capacity is responsible for assessing that person's capacity. The more serious the decision, the more formal the assessment of capacity is likely to be. Where appropriate, it might be advisable to refer to a psychiatrist or psychologist for a second opinion. In a healthcare setting the doctor or healthcare professional proposing the particular treatment or medical procedure is responsible for assessing capacity. For legal transactions, solicitors are responsible for assessing their clients' capacity to instruct them. If in doubt the solicitor should request an opinion from a doctor or other professional with experience in assessing capacity.

The MCA requires that any assessment that a person lacks capacity must be based on a 'reasonable belief' backed by objective reasons. This requires taking reasonable steps to establish that the person lacks capacity to make the decision in question.[7] Professionals should keep careful records of the steps they have taken and their reasons for believing that the person lacks capacity to make that particular decision.

Where there are disputes about whether a person lacks capacity and these cannot be resolved using more informal methods, the Court of Protection can be asked for a declaration about the person's capacity (see **Appendix C**).

3.6 BEST INTERESTS

Where someone lacks capacity to make a particular decision, the MCA establishes 'best interests' as the criterion for any action taken or decision made on that person's behalf. In view of the wide range of decisions and actions covered by the Act and the varied circumstances of the people affected by its provisions, the concept of best interests is not defined in the MCA. Instead, MCA, s.4 sets out a 'checklist' of common factors which must be considered when determining what is in a person's best interests. The checklist can be summarised as follows:

1. **Equal consideration and non-discrimination**
    The person determining best interests must not make assumptions about someone's best interests merely on the basis of their age or appearance, condition or an aspect of their behaviour.

2. **All relevant circumstances**

   Try to identify all the issues and circumstances relating to the decision in question which are most relevant to the person who lacks capacity to make that decision.

3. **Regaining capacity**

   Consider whether the person is likely to regain capacity (e.g. after receiving medical treatment). If so, can the decision wait until then?

4. **Permitting and encouraging participation**

   Do whatever is reasonably practicable to permit and encourage the person to participate, or to improve their ability to participate, as fully as possible in any act done or any decision affecting them.

5. **The person's wishes, feelings, beliefs and values**

   Try to find out the views of the person lacking capacity, including:

   - The person's past and present wishes and feelings – both current views and whether any relevant views have been expressed in the past, either verbally, in writing or through behaviour or habits.
   - Any beliefs and values (e.g. religious, cultural, moral or political) that would be likely to influence the decision in question.
   - Any other factors the person would be likely to consider if able to do so (this could include the impact of the decision on others).

6. **The views of other people**

   Consult other people, if it is practicable and appropriate to do so, for their views about the person's best interests and to see if they have any information about the person's wishes, feelings, beliefs or values. But be aware of the person's right to confidentiality – not everyone needs to know everything. In particular, it is important to consult:

   - anyone previously named by the person as someone to be consulted on the decision in question or matters of a similar kind;
   - anyone engaged in caring for the person, or close relatives, friends or others who take an interest in the person's welfare;
   - any attorney of a Lasting or Enduring Power of Attorney made by the person;
   - any deputy appointed by the Court of Protection to make decisions for the person.

   For decisions about serious medical treatment or a change of residence and where there is no one who fits into any of the above categories, the NHS body or the local authority involved has a duty to appoint an Independent Mental Capacity Advocate (IMCA), who must be consulted before any decision is made.[8]

7. **Life sustaining treatment**

   Where the decision concerns the provision or withdrawal of life-sustaining treatment (defined in the MCA as being treatment which a person providing healthcare regards as necessary to sustain life[9]), the person determining whether the treatment is in the best interests of someone who lacks capacity to consent must not be motivated by a desire to bring about the individual's death.[10]

Not all the factors in the best interests 'checklist' will be relevant to all types of decisions or actions, but they must still be considered if only to be disregarded as irrelevant to that particular situation. Neither the person's own views (past or present) nor the views of those consulted (including family or close friends) will be determinative, but must be weighed up alongside other factors.[11] Any option which is less restrictive of the person's rights or freedom of action must also be considered, so long it is in the person's best interests. Detailed guidance on determining best interests is given in chapter 5 of the MCA Code of Practice.

3.7 APPLICATION AND EXCLUSIONS

The MCA's core principles and the two-stage test apply to the assessment of capacity in the situations covered by the MCA: financial, healthcare and welfare decisions which may need to be made for an individual by someone else. The MCA Code of Practice states that the common law may continue to apply in other situations where capacity may need to be assessed, for example: making a will, making a gift, entering into a contract, carrying out litigation and marrying.[12]

While some common law tests of capacity continue to be relevant (as described in **Part III**) there remains some uncertainty about the extent to which the MCA test of capacity will replace common law tests in contexts outside the scope of the MCA. However, the High Court has confirmed that the correct approach is to apply the MCA test for capacity in deciding whether a person has capacity to conduct litigation in proceedings to which the Civil Procedure Rules apply,[13] since those Rules have subsequently been amended to conform with changes brought about by the MCA.

Even where the MCA does not strictly apply to the assessment of capacity, it will be prudent to have reference to its requirements and to the MCA Code of Practice, since they provide a thorough and comprehensive approach to lack of capacity derived from the common law.

Children and young people

The MCA applies to adults (defined as aged 16 years and over) who may lack capacity to make specific decisions, leaving matters concerned with the care and welfare of children and young people to be resolved under other legislation (most notably the Children Act 1989) and the common law. However, some overlap is inevitable, particularly for young people aged 16–17. Some complexities also arise in relation to the assessment of capacity (or competence) of children and young people to make specific decisions affecting them.

Children aged under 16

The MCA does not generally apply to children aged under 16, except in two specific circumstances:

- the MCA allows the Court of Protection to make decisions about the management of property and financial affairs of children under 16 who are likely still to lack the capacity to make such decisions after they turn 18,[14] and
- the criminal offences of ill-treatment or wilful neglect of a person lacking capacity apply regardless of the victim's age.[15]

In these cases, capacity will have to be assessed with reference to the MCA, as in the case of adults.

Where welfare or healthcare decisions are required of a child aged under 16, any disputes may be resolved by the family courts under the Children Act 1989. In such cases, the common law test of *Gillick* competence applies: i.e. whether the child has sufficient maturity and intelligence to understand the nature and implications of the proposed treatment.[16] *Gillick* competence is a 'developmental concept' reflecting the child's increasing development to maturity, so that a child will not lose or acquire competence on a day-to-day or week-by-week basis.[17] The understanding required for different treatments or decisions may vary, depending on the nature of the decision in question.

Young people aged 16 or 17

The main provisions of the MCA apply to adults, which includes young people aged 16 years or over. The starting point for assessing whether a young person aged 16 or 17 has capacity to make a specific decision is therefore the test of capacity in the MCA, having regard to the MCA principles. However, there may be circumstances where 16–17-year-olds who are unable to make a decision for themselves will not be covered by the provisions of the MCA.

A young person may be unable to make a decision either:

- because of an impairment of, or disturbance in the functioning of, their mind or brain (they lack capacity within the meaning of the MCA); or
- for reasons of immaturity (due to the person's age, they are unable to make the decision in question).

Young people aged 16 and 17 are presumed to have capacity to consent to surgical, medical or dental treatment.[18] If a young person suffers from an impairment of, or a disturbance in the functioning of, the mind or brain which may affect their ability to make a particular healthcare decision, an assessment of capacity under the MCA will be required, notwithstanding the presumption that the young person has capacity.

However, if there is no such impairment or disturbance, the MCA will not apply if it can be established that the young person's inability to make a decision is because:

- they do not have the maturity to understand fully what is involved in making the decision (i.e. they lack *Gillick* competence); or
- the lack of maturity means that they feel unable to make the decision for themselves (for example, where particularly complex or risky treatment is proposed, they may be overwhelmed by the implications of the decision).[19]

In cases where the MCA applies, decisions about a young person's care or treatment may be made under the provisions of the MCA in the person's best interests (see **Chapters 11** and **13**), without the need to obtain parental consent (although those with parental responsibility should generally be consulted).

The Court of Protection may become involved in decisions about medical treatment where there is a disagreement between the young person and the treating health professionals, or in decisions about welfare matters, for example if the young person's parents do not appear to be acting in the best interests of the young person. The MCA makes provision for the transfer of cases affecting anyone under 18 from the Court of Protection to the children's courts and vice versa. The choice of court will depend on the particular circumstances and what is the most appropriate way of dealing with the matter in question.[20]

Particular complexities may arise concerning the care and treatment of children and young people with mental disorder, involving some interaction between the Mental Health Act 1983, the MCA and legislation relating to children. The Department of Health has issued specific guidance for professionals working with children, young people and families in children and adolescent services (CAMHS), adult mental health services and children's services.[21] The Mental Health Act Code of Practice also provides guidance on the treatment of children under the Mental Health Act 1983.[22]

Decisions excluded from the MCA

The MCA Code of Practice states that there 'are certain decisions which can never be made on behalf of a person who lacks capacity to make those specific decisions. This is because they are either so personal to the individual concerned, or governed by other legislation'.[23] These excluded decisions are set out in the MCA,[24] and are summarised under the sub-headings below.

Family relationships

Nothing in the MCA permits a decision to be made on someone's behalf on the following:

- consent to marriage or a civil partnership;
- consent to have sexual relations;
- consent to a decree of divorce on the basis of two years' separation;
- consent to the dissolution of a civil partnership;
- consent to a child being placed for adoption or the making of an adoption order;
- discharge of parental responsibility for a child in matters not relating to the child's property; or
- consent under the Human Fertilisation and Embryology Act 1990.

Mental Health Act matters

Where a person who lacks capacity to consent is detained in hospital under the Mental Health Act 1983 and is being given medical treatment under the provisions of Part 4 of that Act, nothing in the MCA authorises anyone to:

- give the person treatment for mental disorder; or
- consent to the person being given treatment for mental disorder.

In other words, the consent to treatment provisions and safeguards in Part 4 of the Mental Health Act 1983 will 'trump' the MCA's provisions in relation to treatment for mental disorder of patients liable to be detained under the 1983 Act.

However, amendments have been introduced into the MCA by the Mental Health Act 2007 to take account of the new provisions in the amended 1983 Act relating to electro-convulsive therapy (ECT) for patients under 18 years[25] and the treatment of patients subject to the new Community Treatment Orders (CTOs) for whom attorneys or deputies with relevant powers may consent to treatment on their behalf.

A brief summary of aspects of the interface between mental health and mental capacity legislation is given in **Chapter 1** (see **1.3**).

Voting rights

The MCA does not permit a decision on voting (at an election for any public office or at a referendum) to be made on behalf of a person who lacks capacity to vote (see **Chapter 10** on capacity to vote).

Unlawful killing or assisting suicide

For the avoidance of doubt, it is made clear in the MCA that the Act does not affect the law relating to unlawful killing such as euthanasia, murder, manslaughter or assisted suicide.[26]

NOTES

1. Department of Constitutional Affairs (2007) *Mental Capacity Act 2005 Code of Practice*, TSO (available at **www.publicguardian.gov.uk**); and Ministry of Justice (2008) *Mental Capacity Act 2005: Deprivation of Liberty Safeguards. Code of Practice to supplement the main Mental Capacity Act 2005 Code of Practice*, TSO. Available online at **www.dh.gov.uk**.
2. Mental Capacity Act 2005, s.2(4).
3. *Bird* v. *Luckie* (1850) 8 Hare 301.
4. Department of Constitutional Affairs (2007) *Mental Capacity Act 2005 Code of Practice*, TSO. Paragraph 4.36.
5. Mental Capacity Act 2005, s.2(3).
6. Ibid: s.3(1).
7. Ibid: s.5(1); and Department of Constitutional Affairs (2007) *Mental Capacity Act 2005 Code of Practice*, TSO. Paragraphs 4.44–4.45 of the Code provide guidance on 'reasonable belief' and the possible steps to take to establish a lack of capacity (see **Appendix B**).
8. Sections 35–41 of the Mental Capacity Act 2005 established the Independent Mental Capacity Advocate (IMCA) service to provide a statutory right to advocacy services for particularly vulnerable people who lack capacity to make certain serious decisions (see **www.dh.gov.uk**).
9. Mental Capacity Act 2005, s.4(10).
10. Ibid: s.4(5).
11. In *Re S and S (Protected Persons), C* v. *V* [2009] WTLR 315, the Court of Protection considered the weight to be given to the wishes and feelings of the person lacking capacity in an application to the court. Further guidance is given in *Re M, ITW* v. *Z, M and Others* [2009] EWHC 2825 (Fam).
12. Department of Constitutional Affairs (2007) *Mental Capacity Act 2005 Code of Practice*, TSO. Paragraphs 4.32 and 4.33.
13. *Saulle* v. *Nouvet* [2007] EWHC 2902 (QB).
14. Mental Capacity Act 2005, s.18(3).
15. Ibid: s.44.
16. *Gillick* v. *West Norfolk and Wisbech Area Health Authority* [1986] 1 AC 112.
17. *Re R (A Minor) (Wardship: Consent to medical treatment)* [1992] 1 FLR 190 at 200.
18. Family Law Reform Act 1969, s.8(1).
19. Department of Constitutional Affairs (2007) *Mental Capacity Act 2005 Code of Practice*, TSO. Paragraph 12.13.
20. Mental Capacity Act 2005, s.21; and Mental Capacity Act 2005 (Transfer of Proceedings) Order 2007 (SI 2007/1899).
21. National Institute for Mental Health in England (2009) *The Legal Aspects of the Care and Treatment of Children and Young People with Mental Disorder: A guide for professionals*, National Mental Health Development Unit. (Available online at **www.nmhdu.org.uk**) In particular, Chapter 2 deals with the principles and concepts involved in assessing the ability of children and young people to make decisions for

themselves. (NMHDU has taken over some of the activities previously carried out by NIMHE.)

22. Department of Health (2008) *Mental Health Act 1983 Code of Practice,* TSO. Available online at **www.dh.gov.uk,** see chapter 36.

23. Department of Constitutional Affairs (2007) *Mental Capacity Act 2005 Code of Practice*, TSO. Paragraph 1.9.

24. Mental Capacity Act 2005, ss.27–29.

25. Electro-convulsive therapy (ECT) can be provided for patients aged 16–17 years under the Mental Capacity Act 2005, s.5 if that is in their best interests and does not amount to a deprivation of liberty, and a Second Opinion Appointed Doctor considers ECT to be appropriate.

26. Mental Capacity Act 2005, s.62. However, in *R (Purdy)* v. *DPP* [2009] UKHL 45, it was held that the prohibition of assisted suicide in the Suicide Act 1961, s.2(1) interfered with the claimant's right under Article 8 of the ECHR to respect for private life (her personal autonomy and right to self-determination) in respect of a person with capacity to make such a decision who wished to be helped to travel to a country where assisted suicide was lawful.

CHAPTER 4

The legal principles: capacity and evidence

4.1 Capacity and the role of the courts
4.2 Capacity and the law of evidence
4.3 Solicitors instructing doctors
4.4 Doctors receiving instructions from solicitors
4.5 Witnessing documents

4.1 CAPACITY AND THE ROLE OF THE COURTS

Whether a person has or lacks capacity to do something is a question that must generally be decided by reference to the framework set out in the Mental Capacity Act 2005 (the 'MCA)' (see **Chapter 3**). Some common law tests of capacity may require additional considerations, for example in relation to testamentary capacity (see **Chapter 6**). In some cases, it may ultimately be a question for a court to answer. Where a court becomes involved, the final decision rests with the judge, although evidence from a wide range of sources (including the views of family members, of care home staff, a solicitor, health or social care professionals or other expert witnesses) may be of assistance in enabling a court to arrive at its conclusions.[1]

In practice doctors, solicitors, social workers and carers make decisions about capacity every day of the week and very few cases ever get as far as a court. Nevertheless, the courts retain their overall jurisdiction in these matters.[2] By making a decision on capacity, anyone with authority over an individual can deprive that person of some civil rights and liberties enjoyed by most adults and safeguarded by the Human Rights Act 1998.[3] Alternatively, such a decision could permit the person lacking capacity to do something, or carry on doing something, whereby harm or serious prejudice could result to either the person lacking capacity or to others.

Doctors and lawyers should always bear in mind that if they conclude someone has or lacks capacity to make a decision or enter into a transaction, they might have to justify to a court their reasons for that conclusion. It is helpful therefore to know what effect an opinion as to someone's capacity could have on the individual concerned. For example, it could restrict, protect, or empower them.

If a case does go to court, the judge has to:

- decide what the background facts are;
- apply the law to those facts; and
- come to a decision as to the person's capacity to make the decision in question.

Others involved in making decisions about capacity might find it useful to follow the same steps.

4.2   CAPACITY AND THE LAW OF EVIDENCE

Presumption of capacity

To keep any investigation of the facts within manageable bounds, courts apply various rules of evidence. These are based on conclusions (presumptions) which must, or may, be drawn from particular facts. Presumptions are either irrebuttable or rebuttable:

- If a presumption is irrebuttable, it is not open to challenge and the court must arrive at a particular conclusion, regardless of any evidence to the contrary.
- If a presumption is rebuttable, the court has to assume that certain facts are true until the contrary is proved. The most well known rebuttable presumption is the presumption of innocence: that anyone charged with a criminal offence is presumed to be innocent until proved to be guilty.

One important rebuttable presumption that applies to mental capacity is the presumption of capacity, now enshrined as one of the statutory principles of the MCA.[4] An adult is presumed to have the mental capacity to make a particular decision, until the contrary is proved. The burden of proof rests on those asserting incapacity.

Since capacity must always be assessed in relation to a specific task at a particular time, it may need to be reviewed frequently. The MCA Code of Practice explains that it is important to review capacity from time to time, as people can improve their decision-making capabilities. Someone with an ongoing condition may become able to make some, if not all, decisions. The Code states that:

> . . . capacity should always be reviewed:
> - whenever a care plan is being developed or reviewed,
> - at other relevant stages of the care planning process, and
> - as particular decisions need to be made.[5]

Prior to the implementation of the MCA it was considered that there was also a presumption of continuance, i.e. once it has been proved that someone lacks capacity, this state of affairs is presumed to continue until the contrary is proved. However, as the legal approach to capacity has moved towards issue-specific assessments, and there is increased recognition in the MCA of the importance of promoting autonomous decision-making, it is questionable whether this presumption would still be upheld by the courts. Therefore a possible alternative approach is to say that when an individual has been assessed as lacking capacity in relation to a particular decision at a particular time, it may be easier to show that the individual lacks capacity in relation to the same or a similar decision at another time.

Lucid intervals or fluctuating capacity

The presumptions of capacity and continuance tend to suggest that a person is either constantly capable or constantly incapable. Capacity can fluctuate, however, and an intermittent state of capacity is known at law as a 'lucid interval' or 'fluctuating capacity'. Generally speaking, a deed or document signed by someone who lacks capacity is void and of no effect. But if it is signed during a lucid interval it may be valid. This will almost certainly need to be confirmed by medical evidence. When dealing with someone who has fluctuating capacity, it is important to remember that it may be possible to put off the decision until the person has the capacity to make it.

The burden of proof

Generally, if someone alleges something, that person has to prove it. In cases involving mental capacity the burden of proof is affected by the operation of the presumption of capacity. So the burden of proof is on the person who alleges that someone lacks capacity (because capacity is presumed until the contrary is proved). As noted above, where someone has been shown to lack capacity in relation to a particular decision, it may be easier to discharge the burden of proof in relation to a subsequent similar decision.

The standard of proof

Those on whom the burden of proof rests must prove their case to a particular standard. There are two standards of proof:

- 'beyond reasonable doubt', which only applies in criminal proceedings; and
- 'the balance of probabilities', which applies in civil proceedings.

In deciding whether or not someone has capacity to enter into a particular transaction or make a particular decision, the standard of proof is the civil standard, the balance of probabilities (now confirmed by the MCA).[6] In practical terms this is the most important rule of evidence in assessing capacity. Having decided what the facts are, and having applied the law to those facts, the assessor must then decide whether on balance the individual is more likely to have capacity, or more likely to lack capacity to do something.

Character evidence and similar fact evidence

In criminal cases, evidence about a person's character or past events which are similar to those under consideration may only be admitted in certain circumstances, in an effort to avoid unfair prejudice to a defendant. In civil cases, however, a person's psychiatric history is usually highly relevant to the question of capacity and is therefore almost always admissible.

The court may also take into account other witness or documentary evidence which is relevant to the person's capacity to take the decision in question. For example, in the *Masterman-Lister*[7] case (see also **5.5**) the court gave detailed consideration to Mr Masterman-Lister's diaries, letters and computer documents. In the more recent case of *Saulle* v. *Nouvet*[8] the court took into account witness statements and oral evidence from family members as well as home videos of Mr Saulle. The court must however be 'alive to the fact that [it is] ... investigating ... capacity not outcomes, although of course outcomes can often cast a flood of light on capacity'.[9]

Opinion evidence and expert evidence

In court proceedings witnesses are usually confined to stating the facts – what they have seen or heard – and are not permitted to express their own opinions. An exception is made in the case of expert witnesses who are entitled not only to say what they have seen and heard but also to express the opinion they formed as a result.

There is no formal definition as to what constitutes expertise. In general, people will be treated as experts if they have devoted time and attention to the particular branch of knowledge involved, or if they have had practical experience of it and, in some cases, if they have acquired a reputation for being skilled in it.

Whether or not it is justifiable, the law tends to regard registered medical practitioners in relevant fields as de facto experts on mental capacity, and therefore considers them entitled to express an opinion as to whether a person is or was capable of understanding the nature and effects of a particular transaction. The Court of Appeal has confirmed that in almost every case where a court is required to make a decision as to capacity, it needs medical evidence to guide it, although this will not necessarily be given greater weight than other relevant evidence.[10]

Before the MCA came into effect, not all doctors had a sufficient level of knowledge or expertise to determine issues of capacity,[11] but training leading up to and following implementation of the MCA may have improved the situation. In giving an opinion on capacity, doctors should set out their qualifications and experience which may have a bearing on their expertise in assessing capacity and on applying the MCA and the MCA Code of Practice. The BMA issues guidance for doctors who act or are considering acting as expert witnesses.[12]

The weight of evidence

Whether or not the burden of proof is discharged depends on the weight and value which the judge attaches to the various strands of evidence. This involves weighing up the credibility or reliability of the evidence, and ultimately comes down to deciding which version of events is more likely to be correct. Although the courts attach a great deal of weight to medical evidence, one doctor's opinion may not be shared by another, and it is not unprecedented for a judge to favour the evidence of someone who is not even medically qualified. For example, in the case of *Birkin* v. *Wing*[13] the judge preferred the evidence of a solicitor, who considered that the client was mentally capable of entering into a particular contract, to that of a doctor who said that the client lacked capacity.

4.3 SOLICITORS INSTRUCTING DOCTORS

Solicitors asking a doctor to provide medical evidence as to whether or not a client has capacity to make a particular decision should bear in mind the following points.

*   It cannot automatically be assumed that all doctors are experts in these matters (see **Chapter 17**).
*   The quality of the doctor's evidence depends heavily on the quality of the instructions given to the doctor.
*   Be clear about the specific capacity that needs to be assessed, for example: capacity to enter into a contract; capacity to marry; capacity to create a Lasting Power of Attorney; or capacity to make a decision about finances or property (see **Part III**).
*   Inform the doctor about the legal test to be applied, including the impact of the MCA.
*   Explain the legal test in simple language that an ordinary intelligent person, but someone who is not a qualified lawyer, will be able to understand.
*   Let the doctor have all the relevant information needed to reach an informed opinion. For example, if an application is being made to the Court of Protection for the appointment of a financial deputy, the doctor needs to know something about the client's property and affairs in order to assess whether or not that client lacks capacity to make decisions about such property and affairs (but see **2.2** on confidentiality).

- Make sure that the doctor is aware that the standard of proof is the balance of probabilities, rather than beyond reasonable doubt.
- Remind the doctor that their opinion on the client's capacity is open to challenge (and as a courtesy the doctor should be informed if the matter is likely to be contentious, without giving the impression that a lower standard of care will suffice in a non-contentious case).
- Wherever possible avoid asking for simultaneous assessments of a client's capacity for a variety of different transactions. For example, where a client is in the early stages of dementia it would be unreasonable to expect the doctor to assess in one examination whether the client is capable of making a will, creating a lasting power of attorney, making a lifetime gift, and consenting to medical treatment, since the assessment must be made in relation to each decision at the time the decision needs to be made.

4.4 DOCTORS RECEIVING INSTRUCTIONS FROM SOLICITORS

Doctors assessing capacity at the request of a solicitor should bear the following points in mind.

- Guidance for doctors who have limited experience in assessing capacity is given in **Chapter 16**, but doctors should decline instructions from solicitors if they feel that they have insufficient knowledge or practical experience to make a proper assessment of capacity.
- If necessary, more information should be requested from the solicitor. Do not automatically assume that the solicitor is an expert in these matters or has passed on all relevant details.
- If necessary, further information should be requested regarding:
  - details of the test of capacity that the law requires, with an explanation of that test in simple language that an ordinary intelligent person who is not legally qualified can understand;
  - why a medical opinion is being sought and what effect the opinion might have on the patient or client;
  - the person's property, affairs or family background if they are relevant to the particular type of capacity to be assessed;
  - whether the matter is likely to be contentious or disputed (but doctors should not be pressurised into making a decision merely because it will please the solicitor or the person's family or one faction of the person's family).

- Wherever possible, keep reports specific, rather than general. Remember that:
  - a laconic opinion lacking detail, diagnosis and reasons is likely to be of little value in terms of evidence;

- the opinion could deprive the individual of the autonomy that most adults enjoy to make decisions about their own affairs;
- the opinion could allow the individual to do something or to carry on doing something which could be extremely prejudicial to the individual or somebody else;
- the opinion could affect the availability of certain financial benefits or services;
- doctors can be called on by a court to give an account of the reasons for arriving at a particular opinion.

4.5   WITNESSING DOCUMENTS

Medical professionals, especially those working in hospitals, are often reluctant to witness a patient's signature on a document. This is understandable because, more often than not, the professional status of a doctor or nurse is being invoked in order to lend authority to a transaction.

In the section on capacity and the law of evidence (**4.2** above) a distinction was drawn between ordinary witnesses and expert witnesses:

- Ordinary witnesses are expected merely to state what they have seen or heard. When it comes to witnessing a signature on a document, an ordinary witness simply states that the document was signed by a person in their presence.
- Expert witnesses are in a different position, because they are invited not only to say what they have seen or heard but also to express an opinion.

As was mentioned earlier, the law tends to regard medical practitioners as de facto experts on mental capacity. So when a doctor witnesses someone's signature on a document, there is an inference that the doctor considered the patient to have the requisite capacity to enter into the transaction effected by the document. If doctors are not confident about the person's capacity, or have not assessed it formally, they should decline to act as witnesses. They must also decline to act as witnesses if they are likely to benefit personally.

When medical evidence should be obtained (the 'golden rule')

Obtaining medical evidence about a person's capacity is sometimes required by the law, while in other cases, it is merely desirable or a matter of good practice. There are particular circumstances, however, where the courts have strongly advised that a doctor should witness a person's signature, thereby providing medical evidence as to the person's capacity. For example, in 1975 in *Kenward* v. *Adams*[14] the judge laid down what he called 'the golden if tactless rule' that, where a will has been drawn up for an elderly person or for someone who is seriously ill, it should be witnessed or approved by a medical practitioner. The judge assumed that the doctor would not only make a formal assessment of capacity but also record their examination and findings. The need to observe this 'golden rule' was repeated in 1977 in *Re Simpson*[15] and restated in *Buckenham* v. *Dickinson*[16] (in 1997) in which the solicitor was criticised for failing to follow the 'golden rule'.

In the more recent case of *Cattermole* v. *Prisk* (in 2006), the court observed[17]:

> This 'golden rule' provides clear guidance as to how, in relevant cases, disputes can be avoided or minimised (with the material relevant to the determination of the dispute contemporaneously recorded and preserved). The 'golden rule' is not itself a touchstone of validity and is not a substitute for the established tests of capacity.

Medical professionals therefore need to be clear about what they are being asked to do. It is recommended that, in cases where there is any doubt about a patient's capacity to enter into a particular transaction, they should only witness the patient's signature on a document when:

- they have formally assessed the patient's capacity;
- they are satisfied that, on the balance of probabilities, the patient has the requisite capacity to enter into the transaction effected by the document;
- they make a formal record of their examination and findings.

Some NHS Trusts reportedly prohibit their staff from witnessing legal documents. In such cases, the health professional should take advice from the Trust before acting as a witness.

NOTES

1. *Richmond* v. *Richmond* (1914) 111 LT 273; *Martin Masterman-Lister* v. *(1) Jewell (2) Home Counties Dairies* [2002] EWHC 417 (QB); and *Martin Masterman-Lister* v. *Brutton & Co* [2002] EWCA Civ 1889; [2002] Lloyds Rep Med 239.
2. See for example: *Re MB (Medical Treatment)* [1997] 2 FLR 426; *R (on the application of Wilkinson)* v. *Broadmoor Special Hospital Authority and others* [2002] 1 WLR 419; *Re B (Adult: Refusal of Medical Treatment)* [2002] 2 All ER 449; *Masterman-Lister* v. *(1) Jewell (2) Home Counties Dairies* [2002] EWHC 417; and *Masterman-Lister* v. *Brutton & Co* [2002] EWCA Civ 1889.
3. The Human Rights Act 1998, which came into effect in October 2000, incorporates into UK law the bulk of the substantive rights set out in the European Convention on Human Rights (ECHR).
4. Mental Capacity Act 2005, s.1(2).
5. Department of Constitutional Affairs (2007) *Mental Capacity Act 2005 Code of Practice*, TSO. Paragraph 4.29.
6. Mental Capacity Act 2005, s.2(4).
7. *Masterman-Lister* v. (1) *Jewell (2) Home Counties Dairies* [2002]; and *Masterman-Lister* v. *Brutton & Co* [2002] EWCA Civ 1889.
8. *Saulle* v. *Nouvet* [2007] EWHC 2902 (QB).
9. *Masterman-Lister* v. *Brutton & Co* [2002] EWCA Civ 1889 at 54.
10. Ibid: at 29.
11. Jackson E and Warner J (2002) 'How much do doctors know about consent and capacity?' *Journal of the Royal Society of Medicine*, 2002, 95 (12): 601–3.

12. British Medical Association (2007) *Expert witness guidance. British Medical Association*; and British Medical Association (2005) *Guidance for doctors preparing professional reports and giving evidence in court*, British Medical Association.
13. *Birkin* v. *Wing* (1890) 63 LT 80.
14. *Kenward* v. *Adams* (1975) *The Times*, 29 November 1975.
15. *Re Simpson (Deceased), Schaniel* v. *Simpson* (1977) 121 SJ 224.
16. *Buckenham* v. *Dickinson* [1997] CLY 661. In this case, it was acknowledged that failure to observe the 'golden rule' would not invalidate the will.
17. *Cattermole* v. *Prisk* [2006] 1 FLR 693, at 699. The 'golden rule' was also considered in some detail in *Scammell and Scammell* v. *Farmer* [2008] EWHC 1100 (Ch), at 117–123.

PART III

Legal tests of capacity

CHAPTER 5

Capacity to deal with financial affairs

5.1   TYPES OF POWERS OF ATTORNEY

A power of attorney is a deed by which one person (the donor) gives another person (the attorney) the authority to act in the donor's name and on their behalf. Historically that power could only be exercised in respect of the donor's property and financial affairs. However, following the coming into force of the Mental Capacity Act 2005 (the 'MCA'), an attorney can be granted the power to make decisions concerning the health and/or welfare of the donor (see **Chapter 13**).

A power of attorney can be specific or general. If it is specific, the attorney only has the authority to do the things specified by the donor in the power. If it is general, the attorney has the authority to do anything that the donor can lawfully do by an attorney. The law imposes certain restrictions on what actions a donor can delegate to an attorney. For example, an attorney cannot execute a will on the donor's behalf, nor act in situations which require the personal knowledge of the donor (such as acting as a witness in court). Therefore under a general power of attorney, the attorney only has the authority to do what the donor can lawfully delegate to someone else.

There are three types of powers of attorney:

- an Ordinary Power of Attorney, which ceases to have effect if the donor becomes mentally incapable;

- a Lasting Power of Attorney ('LPA'), which continues to operate after a donor has become mentally incapable, provided that it is registered with the Office of the Public Guardian;
- an Enduring Power of Attorney ('EPA'), which is similar in broad terms to an LPA for property and financial affairs. Following implementation of the MCA, an EPA can no longer be created but, as discussed below, those made before 1 October 2007 will continue to be valid and will therefore be of relevance for practitioners for some years to come.

5.2 ORDINARY POWERS OF ATTORNEY

The test of capacity which a person must satisfy in order to make a power of attorney is that the donor understands the nature and effect of what they are doing. An Ordinary Power of Attorney (one which is not 'enduring' or 'lasting') tends to be used as a temporary expedient. For example, where the donor is going abroad for several months and needs someone to look after various legal or financial transactions during their absence. The historic view is that the capacity required to create an ordinary power of attorney is co-existent with the donor's capacity to do the act which the attorney is authorised to do. If there is any doubt as to the donor's capacity to do the act in question, it would be advisable for the donor to create a lasting power rather than an ordinary power, so long as the donor has the requisite capacity to do so.

5.3 LASTING POWERS OF ATTORNEY

Lasting Powers of Attorney ('LPAs') became available in England and Wales on 1 October 2007, when the MCA came into force. They replace EPAs, and while there are many similarities between EPAs and LPAs, there are also significant differences:

- LPAs can cover health and welfare decisions (see **Chapter 13**), unlike EPAs which are restricted to property and financial affairs.
- LPAs can be registered at any time and must be registered before they are used, (unlike EPAs, which must be registered when the donor is or is becoming incapable of managing their property and affairs) (see **5.5**);
- attorneys acting under an LPA (referred to as 'donees' in the MCA) have a legal duty to act in accordance with the principles set out in the MCA[1] and to have regard to the MCA Code of Practice. Apart from those who are acting in a professional capacity, EPA attorneys have no such statutory duties, though they may have a duty at common law to act in the donor's best interests;

- LPAs allow donors to appoint replacement attorneys if their chosen attorney is unable to act, whereas EPAs do not.

The MCA provides that donors can choose more than one person to make different kinds of decisions. For instance, a donor may wish to grant an LPA in favour of one person for the purposes of managing the donor's property and financial affairs, and a separate LPA in favour of another person for purposes of making decisions affecting the donor's welfare.[2] The MCA also allows the donor to appoint two or more attorneys and to specify whether they should act:

- jointly (i.e. always act together);
- jointly and severally (either together or independently); or
- jointly in respect of some matters and jointly and severally in respect of others.

Only adults aged 18 or over can make an LPA. The relevant prescribed form must be used.[3] There are separate forms for health and welfare LPAs and those dealing with property and affairs. The MCA and associated regulations[4] set down a number of requirements that must be satisfied before an LPA can be validly acted upon, including:

- the donor must sign a statement saying that they have read the prescribed information as to the nature and effect of an LPA (or that somebody has read it to them) and that they want the LPA to apply when they no longer have capacity;
- the document must name people (not any of the attorneys) who the donor wishes to be told about an application to register the LPA, or it should say that there is no one they wish to be told;
- the attorney(s) must sign a statement saying that they have read the prescribed information and that they understand their duties (in particular the duty to act in the donor's best interests);
- the document must include a certificate completed by an independent third party (called the 'certificate provider'), confirming that:[5]

  - in their opinion, the donor understands the LPA's purpose and the scope of the authority under it;
  - nobody used fraud or undue pressure to trick or force the donor into making the LPA, and that;
  - there is nothing to stop the LPA being created.

A certificate provider must be chosen by the donor and can either be someone who has known the donor personally for at least two years, or be someone who, because of their relevant professional skills and expertise, considers themselves competent to make the judgements required to be able to sign the certificate (see below).

Unless the LPA is registered with the Office of the Public Guardian, it does not take effect[6] and the attorney will have no authority under the power. Once the LPA has been registered by the donor or the attorney, the authority of the attorney will depend on the wording of the LPA.

Unless expressed to the contrary, the attorney under a financial LPA will have the authority to make all decisions about the donor's financial and property affairs, whether or not the donor has capacity. If, however, even after registration the donor has capacity to perform some tasks, such as running a bank account or shopping, then the fact that the power has been registered should not as matter of practice prevent the donor from carrying out these activities.

Conversely, the donor may specify in a financial LPA that it only takes effect upon the loss of capacity of the donor. The MCA Code of Practice (paragraph 7.33) makes clear that it is the donor's responsibility to decide how their capacity should be assessed, and the donor can specify, for instance, that that the LPA only applies if their GP or another doctor confirms in writing that they lack capacity to make specific decisions about property or finances.

Capacity to make a lasting power of attorney

Certificate to confirm understanding

The certificate provider (see above) has an important role to in safeguarding against abuse. The guidance provided by the Office of the Public Guardian[7] states that the certificate provider must confirm that, in their opinion, the donor understands what the LPA is, its contents and the powers it gives the attorney. It also suggests that the certificate provider should discuss with the donor the following topics to establish the donor's capacity and understanding:

- What is your understanding of what is an LPA is?
- What are your reasons for making an LPA?
- Why have you chosen me to be your certificate provider?
- Who have you chosen to be your attorneys?
- Why them?
- What powers are you giving them?
- In what circumstances should the power be used by your attorneys?
- What types of decision would you like them to make, and what (if any) should they not take?
- If there are any restrictions in the LPA, what do you believe they achieve?
- What is the difference between any restrictions and any guidance made in the LPA?
- Have the chosen attorneys provided you with answers to any of these questions?

- Do you have any reason to think they could be untrustworthy?
- Do you know when you could cancel the LPA?
- Are there any other reasons why the LPA should not be created?

Certificate providers should also have in mind the functional and diagnostic tests of capacity set down in the MCA.[8] But the questions the certificate provider is asked to confirm are limited to the donor's understanding of the purpose and scope of the LPA, while other tests of capacity to perform a legal act refer to the nature and effect of the act in question, which arguably require a greater degree of understanding. In practice, it is unlikely the two tests will differ to any significant extent.

Capacity to make an LPA

Until such point as a case is determined by the court with specific reference to the capacity required to grant an LPA, the cases determined under the old EPA regime may continue to be of assistance. In *Re K, Re F*,[9] having stated that the test of capacity to create an Enduring Power of Attorney was that the donor understood the nature and effect of the document, the judge in the case set out four pieces of information which any person creating an Enduring Power of Attorney should understand:[10]

- if such be the terms of the power, that the attorney will be able to assume complete authority over the donor's affairs;
- if such be the terms of the power, that the attorney will be able to do anything with the donor's property which the donor could have done;
- that the authority will continue if the donor should be, or should become, mentally incapable;
- that if the donor should be, or should become, mentally incapable, the power will be irrevocable without confirmation by the Court of Protection.

The decision in *Re K, Re F* has been criticised for imposing too simple a test of capacity to create an enduring power but the simplicity or complexity of the test depends largely on the questions asked by the person assessing the donor's capacity. For example, if the four pieces of basic relevant information described by the judge in *Re K, Re F* were mentioned to the donor, and if the donor was asked 'do you understand this?' in such a way as to encourage an affirmative reply, the donor would probably pass the test with flying colours and, indeed, the test would be too simple. If, on the other hand, the assessor were specifically to ask the donor 'what will your attorney be able to do?' and 'what will happen if you become mentally incapable?' the test would be substantially harder. That such questions susceptible to the answers 'yes' or 'no' may be inadequate for the purpose of assessing capacity to make a power of attorney can also be inferred from the decision in *Re Beaney (deceased)*,[11] confirmed by the Court of Appeal in *Re W (Enduring Power of Attorney)*.[12]

In view of the significant differences between EPAs and LPAs, the criteria set out in *Re K, Re F* relating to capacity to make an EPA may not be directly applicable to LPAs. It has been suggested by one commentator that the criteria would need to be adapted, for example to show that the donor understands the following:[13]

- that the LPA cannot be used until it is registered by the Public Guardian;
- that under a property and affairs LPA, the attorney will, in general, be able to do anything with the donor's property which the donor could have done personally, unless any restrictions have been specified in the LPA;
- that the donor can revoke the LPA at any time while the donor has capacity to do so, without the court having to confirm the revocation;
- that if the donor lacks capacity to make a decision covered by the registered LPA, they could not revoke the power without confirmation by the court;
- the authority conferred by the LPA is subject to the provisions of the MCA, and in particular, s.1 (the principles) and s.4 (best interests).

In addition to the matters set out above, the donor must also be able to understand the reasonably foreseeable consequences of making or not making the LPA or of making it in different terms or appointing different people.[14]

Although the legislation does not require that a certificate be completed by a medical practitioner, where the donor is of borderline capacity it is advisable that the certificate be completed by a doctor or other relevant professional, who should record their findings. Alternatively the certificate provider should obtain the views of a medical practitioner or other expert and record their findings.[15] Guidance for medical practitioners on the procedures to be followed in such circumstances is provided in **4.4**. Solicitors instructed to draw up an LPA on behalf of a client must first be satisfied that the client has the required capacity, assisted by a medical opinion where necessary. A Practice Note on this topic has been issued by the Law Society.[16]

Registration of an LPA

Unless the LPA is registered with the Office of the Public Guardian, it does not take effect. The application for registration can be made either by the donor or the attorney(s). Unless the Court of Protection provides otherwise, notification must first be given to the donor or attorney(s) (whoever is not the applicant for registration) and to the person(s) named by the donor in the LPA instrument as being entitled so such notification.

The prescribed form for notification[17] makes it clear that the donor and any person notified have a right to object to registration (within five weeks of the date of the notice). There are no specified grounds for objection by donors. Named persons or attorneys may either object to the Public Guardian on factual grounds (for example, because either the donor or an attorney is bankrupt or has died) or to the Court of Protection on the following grounds prescribed in the Regulations:[18]

- one or more of the requirements for the creation of an LPA have not been met;
- the power has been revoked or has otherwise come to an end;
- fraud or undue pressure was used to induce the donor to create the power;
- the donee has behaved, is behaving, or proposes to behave in a way that:
  - contravenes or would contravene his authority; or
  - is not or would not be in the donor's best interests.

Capacity to revoke a lasting power of attorney

Until an application for registration has been made, the donor may revoke a power of attorney at any time. If the donor does so, but the attorney believes the donor lacks the capacity to revoke the power, the attorney can apply for registration of the power. The donor may then object to the registration on the ground that the power is no longer valid, and the court must decide whether this ground for objection is established. However, if the donor has destroyed the LPA document, it is not possible to apply for registration.

Even where the LPA has been registered, it can be revoked at any time when the donor has capacity to do so.[19] Unlike the position that prevailed in respect of an EPA, the Court of Protection no longer has to confirm the revocation. However, in cases of doubt an application may be made to the Court for a declaration as to whether the LPA has in fact been revoked by the donor.[20] The Court will need to consider whether the donor has (or had) capacity to revoke the LPA at the relevant time. It is likely that the Court will adopt the same approach as it previously took to applications made to revoke EPAs,[21] in which it required evidence that the donor knew:

- who the attorney(s) are;
- what authority the attorney(s) have;
- why it is necessary or expedient to revoke the power;
- what the foreseeable consequences of revoking the power are.

5.4 ENDURING POWERS OF ATTORNEY

Enduring Powers of Attorney ('EPAs') became available in England and Wales in March 1986, when the Enduring Powers of Attorney Act 1985 came into force. After the coming into force of the MCA on 1 October 2007, an EPA can no longer be created, but EPAs made prior to that date remain valid.[22]

Unless the EPA specifically states that it will not come into force until the donor is mentally incapacitated (which is rare), the power is 'live' from the moment it is executed (i.e. signed and witnessed) by the donor and attorney. In other words, the attorney could act under it straight away and can continue to act, even though the donor may still be perfectly capable of looking after their own property and affairs. If the EPA is not registered with the Office of the Public Guardian, the donor and the attorney have what is known as concurrent authority. Both of them can manage and administer the donor's property and affairs.

An attorney acting under an EPA must apply to the Office of the Public Guardian for the registration of the power if the attorney has reason to believe that the donor is, or is becoming mentally incapable of managing and administering their property and affairs[23] (see **5.5** below).

The donor and the donor's closest relatives must be informed of the attorney's intention to register the power. There is a statutory list of relatives who must be notified.[24] Both the donor and any of the relatives have the right to object to the registration of the power, for example, if they believe that the donor is not yet incapable of managing their own affairs, or that the power may be invalid because it has been revoked by the donor. Once the power has been registered by the Office of the Public Guardian, the donor and the attorney no longer have concurrent authority. Only the attorney has the authority to manage and administer the donor's property and affairs. If, however, even after registration the donor has capacity to perform some tasks, such as running a bank account or shopping, the fact that the power has been registered should not as matter of practice prevent the donor from carrying out these activities.

Capacity to make an enduring power of attorney

Since EPAs can no longer be made, the question of capacity to make an EPA is only relevant where someone is retrospectively challenging the validity of an EPA. The issues are similar, but not identical, to those applicable to determining capacity to make a LPA (see **5.3**). In particular the criteria set out in *Re K, Re F* (see **pages 53–54**) must be satisfied to confirm the donor's understanding of the nature and effect of the EPA.

Capacity to revoke an enduring power of attorney

Until an application for registration has been made, the donor may revoke an EPA at any time. If the donor does so, but the attorney believes the donor lacks the capacity to revoke the power, the attorney can apply for registration of the power. The donor may then object to the registration on the ground that the power is no longer valid, and the court must decide whether this ground for objection is established. However, if the donor has destroyed the EPA documents, it cannot be registered. After registration, no revocation of an EPA by the donor is valid unless and until the Court of Protection confirms the revocation.

There have been no reported decisions on the capacity to revoke an EPA. According to Lush and Rees the evidence which the Court requires in order to be satisfied that the donor has the necessary capacity to revoke the power is as follows, whereby the donor should know:[25]

- who the attorney(s) are;
- what authority the attorney(s) have;
- why it is necessary or expedient to revoke the power;
- what the foreseeable consequences of revoking the power are.

In practice, where the donor of a registered EPA wishes to revoke it, the attorney often disclaims (that is, gives notice to the Public Guardian) that they wish to cease acting as attorney. The court must then decide whether the donor has capacity to resume management of their own affairs, or whether a deputyship order or some other order should be made in respect of the donor.

5.5   CAPACITY TO MANAGE PROPERTY AND AFFAIRS

The question as to the capacity of a person to manage property and affairs will arise in three subtly different contexts:

- Where a judge sitting other than as a judge in the Court of Protection is considering whether a person has capacity to manage their property and affairs (e.g. in the context of litigation, discussed further in **Chapter 8**). The courts have made it clear that, in these circumstances, judges should apply the common law test for capacity, rather than consider themselves formally bound to follow the statutory test set down in the MCA.[26] However, for most practical purposes, it appears likely that judges in this situation will adopt the same approach to the question of capacity as is set down in the MCA.
- Where a person who has not previously made an LPA or an EPA lacks capacity within the meaning of the MCA of making financial decisions and thus becomes incapable of managing and administering their property and affairs. In these circumstances, it may be necessary for someone to apply to the Court of Protection for an order setting out how the person's affairs may be dealt with.[27] Where long-term management of property and affairs is required it is likely that the Court will appoint a deputy with authority to deal with the day-to-day management of the person's affairs, working to a fund management plan approved by the Court. An outline of the powers and procedures of the Court of Protection and the role of deputies is to be found at **Appendix C**.

● Where a person who made a valid EPA before 1 October 2007 now ceases to be capable of managing and administering their property and affairs. This will trigger the attorney's duty to register the EPA with the Office of the Public Guardian.

5.6 PROPERTY AND AFFAIRS DEPUTIES

If a person who has not previously made an EPA or LPA is found to lack capacity within the meaning of the MCA of making financial decisions, and is thus incapable of managing and administering their property and affairs, some formal arrangements may need to be made to authorise someone else to deal with those affairs. In most cases, the Court of Protection is likely to appoint a 'property and affairs deputy'. Deputies are, in broad terms, the equivalent to receivers previously appointed under Part VII of the Mental Health Act 1983. Receivers appointed before the MCA came into effect are treated under the new regime as property and affairs deputies appointed by the Court of Protection.

The deputy could be a family member or a professional, as decided by the Court. The Court must be satisfied that appointing a deputy is in the person's best interests and the court order will set out the extent of the deputy's powers (which should be as limited in scope and duration as is practicable in the circumstances). The deputy can only make decisions that the person lacks capacity to make, and must always act in the person's best interests and in accordance with the MCA principles (see **Chapter 3**). Deputies are supervised by the Office of the Public Guardian (see **Appendix C**) and may be required to submit accounts or other reports on how they are dealing with the person's property and affairs.

The common law test for incapacity to manage property and affairs

The leading common law case remains that of *Martin Masterman-Lister* v. *(1) Jewell (2) Home Counties Dairies* (in the High Court)[28] and *Martin Masterman-Lister* v. *Brutton & Co* (in the Court of Appeal).[29] This confirmed the 'issue-specific nature' of the test of capacity, which must be considered in relation to the particular transaction (including its nature and complexity) under consideration. A distinction was drawn between capacity to manage day-to-day affairs, capacity to deal with the complexities of personal injury litigation, and capacity to manage a large award of damages.

In personal injury actions, however, it is necessary to focus first on the person's ability to participate in the litigation rather than the whole of their affairs (see **Chapter 8**) and then to consider separately the person's capacity to manage any award of damages:

It is not difficult to envisage claimants . . . with capacity to deal with all matters and take all 'lay client' decisions related to their actions up to and including a decision whether or not to settle, but lacking capacity to decide (even with advice) how to administer a large award.[30]

Capacity to manage property and affairs under the MCA

Assessing a person's capacity to manage and administer their property and affairs must be by reference to the particular person and their particular circumstances, in relation to each decision about property and affairs at the time that decision needs to be made. The test of capacity to be applied is that set out in the MCA[31] (see **Chapter 3**). The test requires the presence of an impairment of, or disturbance in the functioning of, the mind or brain that causes the person to be unable to understand information relevant to the decision, retain it and use or weigh the information as part of the process of making the decision in question. The MCA Code of Practice suggests that where the impairment or disturbance is ongoing or long-term, this may be relevant to an assessment of the person's capacity to manage their property and affairs generally.[32]

Where an application is made to the Court of Protection for authority to make financial decisions on a person's behalf, the Court will require evidence that the person lacks capacity to make the decision (or decisions) in question. Such evidence, in applying the test in MCA,[33] is provided on Court of Protection Form COP3 'Assessment of Capacity' (see **Appendix G**). This form may be helpful when applying the statutory test of capacity in other situations.

A person's capacity to make financial decisions depends largely on the value and complexity of their property and affairs and the extent to which that person may be vulnerable to exploitation. It has been held that property and affairs 'means business matters, legal transactions, and other dealings of a similar kind'.[34] It does not include personal matters such as where to live or decisions about medical treatment.

Given the absence of specific provisions in the Code of Practice governing the assessment of capacity to manage property and affairs, it is suggested the following checklist should be adopted (this checklist was set out in the first edition of this book in the common law context and was endorsed by Mr Justice Wright in the High Court decision in *Masterman-Lister*).[35]

Checklist

The checklist is not intended to be exhaustive or authoritative, but gives some indication of the wide range of information which may be needed in order to make a proper assessment of a person's understanding of that information and hence, their capacity to manage their property and affairs.

The extent of the person's property and affairs

The extent of the person's property and affairs would include an examination of:

- income and capital (including savings and the value of the home), expenditure, and liabilities;
- financial needs and responsibilities;
- whether there are likely to be any changes in the person's financial circumstances in the foreseeable future;
- the skill, specialised knowledge, and time it takes to manage the affairs properly and whether the impairment of, or disturbance in the functioning of, the person's mind or brain is affecting the management of the assets;
- whether the person would be likely to seek, understand and act on appropriate advice where needed in view of the complexity of the affairs.

Personal information

Personal information about the patient might include:

- age;
- life expectancy;
- psychiatric history;
- prospects of recovery or deterioration;
- the extent to which capacity could fluctuate;
- the condition in which the person lives;
- family background; family and social responsibilities;
- any cultural, ethnic or religious considerations;
- the degree of backup and support the person receives or could expect to receive from others.

A person's vulnerability

Other issues should be considered with the following questions.

- Could inability to manage the property and affairs lead to the person making rash or irresponsible decisions?
- Could inability to manage lead to exploitation by others – perhaps even by family members?
- Could inability to manage lead to the position of other people being compromised or jeopardised?

In *Masterman-Lister* Mr Justice Wright held that 'while [the above questions] are plainly proper and appropriate questions to ask, they have to be answered, in my view, in the light of the other guidance set out in the checklist'. Subsequent cases have indicated that such questions may indeed be relevant. In *Mitchell* v. *Alasia*,[36] Cox J relied on qualities such as impulsiveness and volatility when deciding that the claimant was, by reason of his mental disorder, incapable of managing and administering his own affairs. And in *Lindsay* v. *Wood*, Stanley Burnton J observed that:

> When considering the question of capacity, psychiatrists and psychologists will normally wish to take into account all aspects of the personality and behaviour of the person in question, including vulnerability to exploitation.[37]

Capacity to manage property and affairs in the context of enduring powers of attorney

As part of the legacy of the old EPA regime, it is necessary to note that the old test of capacity to manage property and affairs survives in part into the new regime of the MCA, falling for consideration only where:

(a)   a person has made a valid EPA; and
(b)   that EPA has not been registered.

Attorneys acting under an EPA must register it with the Public Guardian when they have reason to believe that the donor is or is becoming mentally incapable (see **5.4** above). In this context, 'mentally incapable' means that the donor 'is incapable by reason of mental disorder within the meaning of the Mental Health Act 1983, of managing and administering his property and affairs'.[38]

For the purposes of registering an EPA, 'mental disorder' is defined as 'mental illness, arrested or incomplete development of the mind, psychopathic disorder and any other disorder or disability of the mind'.[39] It is perhaps worth noting that almost anyone satisfying the test for mental incapability in this context would also satisfy the test for lack of capacity under the MCA.

5.7   CAPACITY TO CLAIM AND RECEIVE SOCIAL SECURITY BENEFITS

There is a statutory mechanism through which social security benefits may be claimed on behalf of people lacking capacity to manage their own affairs. This procedure, called appointeeship, is normally used when an incapacitated person has limited assets and income only from benefits or pensions, and there is no need for more formal procedures.

Appointeeship

If a person is entitled to social security benefits, but is considered to be incapable of claiming and managing them, the Secretary of State for Work and Pensions can appoint an individual aged 18 or over (known as an 'appointee') to:

• exercise any rights and duties the claimant has under the Social Security Acts and Regulations. For example: claiming benefits; informing the relevant agency of the Department for Work and Pensions (DWP) of any change in the claimant's circumstances; and appealing against the decision of a decision-maker in a DWP agency;

- receive any benefits payable to the claimant;
- deal with the money received on the claimant's behalf in the interests of the claimant and their dependants.

An appointee may be appointed by the Secretary of State where:

- a person is, or is alleged to be, entitled to benefit, whether or not a claim for benefit has been made by him or on his behalf;
- that person is unable for the time being to act;
- no deputy has been appointed by the Court of Protection (or receiver appointed under Part VII of the Mental Health Act 1983 but treated as being a deputy appointed by the Court of Protection) with power to claim or, as the case may be, receive benefit on the person's behalf.[40]

The test of capacity is therefore that the person is 'for the time being unable to act'. The phrase is not defined in Regulations, but internal guidance for decision-makers published by the DWP suggests that people may be unable to act 'for example, because of senility or mental illness'.[41] The DWP agency will usually arrange for a visiting officer to visit the person to make an independent assessment of their ability to manage their financial affairs and, more specifically, their ability to understand how to make and manage a claim to benefit. Further guidance states that 'the visiting officer must assess whether the customer shows comprehension of the rights and responsibilities of making the claim.'[42]

Some decisions of the former Social Security Commissioners (now judges of the Upper Tribunal) have considered the claimant's capacity, mainly in relation to the level of the claimant's understanding when making a claim which resulted in overpayment, but there are no formal legal criteria which specify the capacity required.[43] It has been suggested that in order to have the capacity to claim, receive and deal with benefits, an individual should be able to:

- understand the basis of possible entitlement (presumably with advice where necessary);
- understand and complete the claim form;
- respond to correspondence relating to social security benefits;
- collect or receive the benefits;
- manage the benefits in the sense of knowing what the money is for;
- choose whether to use it for that purpose and if so, how.[44]

The application for the appointment of an appointee, which is usually completed by the person applying to be appointed to this role, states 'You may be asked to produce medical evidence of the claimant's inability to manage his own affairs.'[45] There is no standard form of medical certificate, however, and in the majority of cases, medical evidence is not required.

The Secretary of State can revoke an appointment at any time, and there is no right of appeal to a tribunal against the Secretary of State's refusal to appoint a particular individual as appointee or against the revocation of such an appointment. At the time of writing the DWP is developing a system for monitoring appointeeships, in order to comply with its obligations under the UN Convention.[46]

Appointees have no authority to deal with the claimant's capital. If the claimant has savings or capital which needs to be applied or invested, an application should be made to the Court of Protection for directions as to how to proceed. It is unlikely that an appointee would need to apply to the Court of Protection if they held a 'reasonable sum' of accrued savings from unspent pension or benefits. The Court has indicated that it would regard a reasonable sum as being equivalent to one month's accommodation costs, and around £500 cash float to meet unforeseen emergencies.

5.8   PROTECTION FROM FINANCIAL ABUSE

People who are, or are becoming, incapable of dealing with their own financial affairs are particularly vulnerable to abuse, which can range from outright fraud to inadvertent mishandling of money by attorneys or appointees who are not fully aware of what they can or cannot do.

Professional advisers have an important role to play in protecting incapacitated people from the risk of abuse, particularly at the time of assessing capacity.

When carrying out an assessment of capacity to make a financial decision or to manage property and affairs, professionals must act in accordance with the MCA and the guidance in the Code of Practice (see **Chapter 3** and **Appendix B**). The following checklist may also be helpful to professional advisers in assessing risk and guarding against possible abuse:[47]

- Never express an opinion on a person's capacity to make a decision without first seeing the person for that purpose.
- Make sure the correct test of capacity is applied in relation to the particular transaction being considered, taking account of the individual circumstances, and in particular, the vulnerability of the person being assessed.
- Be careful of mistaking the person's ability to express a choice (such as who should be the attorney) for the ability to understand the nature and effect of a particular transaction (such as making an LPA).
- In assessing the ability to understand information relevant to a decision, make sure the person is aware of and able to appreciate not only the benefits, but also the risks involved in the particular transaction.
- Always give reasons for deciding why a person has or does not have the required degree of understanding.

The Public Guardian has a statutory duty to deal with representations (including complaints) made about the actions of an attorney acting under a registered EPA or LPA, or a deputy appointed by the Court of Protection.[48] Anyone wishing to raise concerns should contact the Compliance and Regulation Unit of the Office of the Public Guardian (OPG). There is a dedicated phone line for reporting concerns: 020 7664 7734. The OPG can investigate the actions of a deputy or attorney and can also refer concerns to other relevant agencies. When it makes a referral, the OPG will make sure that the relevant agency keeps it informed of the action it takes.[49] The OPG can also make an application to the Court of Protection if it needs to take possible action against an attorney or deputy.

In addition to this specific duty, the OPG has a general responsibility for safeguarding vulnerable adults and has issued guidance on possible indicators of causal factors of abuse.[50] Where concerns are raised that are outside the Public Guardian's jurisdiction (e.g. in relation to unregistered EPAs or appointeeships) the OPG must refer them to the correct agency so that the concern is addressed.

NOTES

1. Mental Capacity Act 2005, s.1. See **Appendix A**.
2. Ibid: s.10(4).
3. Available from the Office of the Public Guardian (**www.publicguardian.gov.uk**). The LPA forms were revised in 2009 and the new forms prescribed in the Lasting Powers of Attorney, Enduring Powers of Attorney and Public Guardian (Amendment) Regulations 2009 (SI 2009/1884) must be used after 1 October 2009.
4. Lasting Powers of Attorney, Enduring Powers of Attorney and Public Guardian Regulations 2007 (SI 2007/1253) as amended by SI 2009/1884.
5. Mental Capacity Act 2005, Sched. 1, para. 2(1)(e).
6. Ibid: s.9(2)(b) and Sched. 1.
7. Office of the Public Guardian (2009) *Evidence for people who went to make a Lasting Power of Attorney for property and financial affairs guide for certificate providers and witnesses.* The Office of the Public Guardian. See Chapter 4. Available online at **www.publicguardian.gov.uk**.
8. The statutory test of capacity in ss.2 and 3 of the Mental Capacity Act 2005, having regard to the principles in s.1. (See also **Chapter 3**.)
9. *Re K, Re F* [1988] 1 All ER 358.
10. Ibid: 363d–f.
11. *Re Beaney (deceased)* [1978] All ER 595.
12. *Re W (Enduring Power of Attorney)* [2001] 1 FLR 832, paras. 23 and 25.
13. Adapted from: Denzil Lush (2009) *Cretney and Lush on Lasting and Enduring Powers of Attorney* 6th edition, Jordan Publishing, p.35.
14. Mental Capacity Act 2005, s.3(4).
15. *Kenward* v. *Adams* (1975) *The Times*, 29 November 1975.
16. Law Society (2009) *Lasting Powers of Attorney Practice Note – 24 September.* The Law Society. Available online at **www.lawsociety.org.uk**.
17. Form LPA001 Notice of intention to apply for registration of a Lasting Power of Attorney. Available online at **www.publicguardian.gov.uk**.

18. Lasting Powers of Attorney, Enduring Powers of Attorney and Public Guardian Regulations 2007 (SI 2007/1253), reg.15.
19. Mental Capacity Act 2005, s.13(2).
20. Ibid: s.22(2)(b).
21. Lush D and Rees D (2009) *Heywood and Massey: Court of Protection Practice*, Sweet and Maxwell, para. 4–031.
22. The Enduring Powers of Attorney Act 1985 was repealed by the Mental Capacity Act 2005, but in respect of EPAs which remain valid after 1 October 2007 the relevant provisions were largely re-enacted in Sched. 4 to the Mental Capacity Act 2005. The Court will have regard to the principles of the Mental Capacity Act 2005 when determining questions arising under pre-existing EPAs. See *Re J (Enduring Power of Attorney)* [2009] EWHC 436 (Ch), in which the principle of encouraging autonomy enshrined in the Mental Capacity Act 2005 was expressly cited in determining the validity of an EPA.
23. Mental Capacity Act 2005, Sched. 4, paras. 4(1) and (2).
24. Ibid: Sched. 4, para. 6.
25. Lush D and Rees D (2009) *Heywood and Massey: Court of Protection Practice*, Sweet and Maxwell, para. 4–031.
26. In the matter of *MM (an adult)* [2007] EWHC 2003 (Fam) at paras. 79–80; and *Saulle* v. *Nouvet* [2007] EWHC 2902.
27. Mental Capacity Act 2005, ss.16(1)(b) and 16(2)(b).
28. *Martin Masterman-Lister* v. *(1) Jewell (2) Home Counties Dairies* [2002] EWHC 417 (QB).
29. *Martin Masterman-Lister* v. *Brutton & Co* [2002] EWCA Civ 1889.
30. Ibid: at 27.
31. The statutory test of capacity in ss.2 and 3 of the Mental Capacity Act 2005, taking account of the principles in s.1. (See also **Chapter 3**.)
32. Department of Constitutional Affairs (2007) *Mental Capacity Act 2005 Code of Practice*, TSO. Paragraphs 4.28–4.30.
33. The statutory test of capacity in ss.2 and 3 of the Mental Capacity Act 2005, taking account of the principles in s.1. (See also **Chapter 3**.)
34. *F* v. *West Berkshire Health Authority* [1989] 2 All ER 545, 554d.
35. *Martin Masterman-Lister* v. *(1) Jewell (2) Home Counties Dairies* [2002] EWHC 417 (QB) at 25.
36. *Mitchell* v. *Alasia* [2005] EWHC 11 (unreported).
37. *Lindsay* v. *Wood* [2006] EWHC 2895 (QB) at 18.
38. Mental Capacity Act 2005, Sched. 4, para. 23(1).
39. Note that this is the old definition of mental disorder under s.1 of the Mental Health Act 1983, prior to its amendment by the Mental Health Act 2007.
40. Social Security (Claims and Payments) Regulations 1987 (SI 1987/1968), reg.33.
41. Department for Work and Pensions. *Decision makers guide*, Department for Work and Pensions, para. 02440. Updated regularly online, see **www.dwp.gov.uk**.
42. Department for Work and Pensions (2008) *Agents, Appointees, Attorneys and Deputies Guide,* Department for Work and Pensions, para. 5171. See **www.dwp.gov.uk**.
43. See for example the following reported decisions of the Social Security Commissioners: R(A) 1/95; R(IS) 14/96; R(IS) 5/00. See **www.osscsc.gov.uk**.
44. Lavery R and Lundy L (1994) 'The social security appointee system'. *Journal of Social Welfare Law*. 1994, 16:313–27:316.
45. Department for Work and Pensions Form BF56 'Application for appointment to act on behalf of someone else'. See **www.dwp.gov.uk**.
46. United Nations Convention on the Rights of the Persons with Disabilities and its Optional Protocol 2006. See **www.un.org/disabilities.**

47. This checklist has been adapted from: Lush D 'Managing the financial affairs of mentally incapacitated persons in the United Kingdom and Ireland' in Jacoby R and Oppenheimer C (2002) *Psychiatry in the elderly* 3rd edition, Oxford University Press.
48. Mental Capacity Act 2005, s.58(1)(h).
49. Office of the Public Guardian (2008) *Protocol for joint work between the Office of the Public Guardian and Local Authorities for Safeguarding Vulnerable Adults,* Office of the Public Guardian. See **www.publicguardian.gov.uk**.
50. Office of the Public Guardian (2008) Safeguarding Vulnerable Adults Policy, Office of the Public Guardian, Appendix 1. See **www.publicguardian.gov.uk**.

Capacity to make a will

6.1 INTRODUCTION

A will is a document in which the maker (called the 'testator' if he is a man; and the 'testatrix' if she is a woman) appoints an executor to deal with their affairs when the person dies, and describes how the person's estate is to be distributed after death. The maker of a will must be aged 18 or over. A will comes into operation only on the maker's death. Until then the person can revoke the will or make a new one at any time, provided that they still have the capacity to do so. The making of a new will normally revokes any previous will, provided the person making the will had the capacity to do so (see **6.7** on capacity to revoke a will).

Someone who dies without leaving a valid will is said to die 'intestate'. The person responsible for sorting out an intestate's affairs is called an administrator, and that person has a duty to distribute the estate to the intestate's relatives in the shares set out in the Administration of Estates Act 1925 (as amended).

About 10 per cent of the wills made in England and Wales are home-made, handwritten or typed by the person making it, usually on a pre-printed form bought at a stationers or Post Office. In most cases however, people ask a solicitor to prepare a will for them.

Solicitors instructed to prepare a will must first be satisfied that the client has the required capacity (see **6.2**), assisted by a medical opinion where necessary (see **6.5**). The solicitor discusses the client's circumstances; advises them of the various options; prepares a draft will based on these discussions; and sends a copy of the draft to the client for approval. The draft is then approved or amended, and the will prepared in readiness for executing (signing) in the presence of a witness.

The degree of understanding which the law requires a person making a will to have is commonly known as 'testamentary capacity'. People making a will should have testamentary capacity both when they give instructions to a solicitor for the preparation of the will (or, in the case of a home-made will, when they write or type it), and when they execute, or sign, the will.

6.2   TESTAMENTARY CAPACITY: THE POSITION AT COMMON LAW

The leading case on testamentary capacity is *Banks* v. *Goodfellow*.[1] In this case the testator, John Banks, was a bachelor in his 50s who lived with his teenaged niece, Margaret Goodfellow. He had paranoid schizophrenia and was convinced that a grocer (who was, in fact, dead) was pursuing and persecuting him. In 1863, with his solicitor's assistance, he made a short and simple will leaving his entire estate (15 houses) to Margaret. He died in 1865 and Margaret inherited the estate.

Nobody would have questioned the validity of this will were it not for the fact that Margaret died shortly after coming into her inheritance. She was under age and unmarried, and the 15 properties passed to her half-brother, who was not related to John Banks. The will was contested by various members of the Banks family on the grounds that, when he made the will, John had lacked testamentary capacity because of his paranoid delusions. The court held that partial unsoundness of mind, which has no influence on the way in which a testator disposes of his property, is not sufficient to make a person incapable of validly disposing of his property by will.[2] So John Banks's will was valid.

The Lord Chief Justice set out the following criteria for testamentary capacity:

> It is essential . . . that a testator shall understand the nature of the act and its effects; shall understand the extent of the property of which he is disposing; shall be able to comprehend and appreciate the claims to which he ought to give effect; and, with a view to the latter object, that no disorder of mind shall poison his affections, pervert his sense of right, or prevent the exercise of his natural faculties – that no insane delusion shall influence his will in disposing of his property and bring about a disposal of it which, if the mind had been sound, would not have been made.[3]

The first three elements (understanding the nature of the act, its effects, and the extent of the property being disposed of) involve the will-maker's understanding. In other words, the will-maker's ability to receive and evaluate information which may possibly be communicated by others. The final test (being able to comprehend the claims to which they ought to give effect) goes beyond understanding and requires the person making the will to be able to distinguish and compare potential beneficiaries and arrive at some form of judgment. A person making a will can, if mentally capable, ignore the claims of relatives and other potential beneficiaries.

Everyone has the right to be capricious, foolish, biased or prejudiced, and it is important to remember that when someone's capacity is being assessed it is the ability to make a decision (not necessarily a sensible or wise decision) that is under scrutiny. In the case of *Bird* v. *Luckie* the judge specifically remarked that although the law requires a person to be capable of understanding the nature and effect of an action, it does not insist that the person behaves 'in such a manner as to deserve approbation from the prudent, the wise, or the good'.[4]

It is not clear how far a solicitor or doctor can assist in enhancing the capacity of someone who is making a will. An explanation in broad terms and simple language of relevant basic information about the nature and effect of the will is probably in order. Within reason, it may also be appropriate to remind the person making the will of the extent of their assets. But the final test, being able to comprehend and appreciate the claims to which they ought to give effect, is one that the person must pass unaided. There is a substantial body of judicial authority which insists that 'unquestionably, there must be a complete and absolute proof that the party who had so formed the will did it without any assistance'[5] and that 'a disposing mind and memory is one able to comprehend, of its own initiative and volition, the essential elements of will-making . . . merely to be able to make rational responses is not enough, nor to repeat a tutored formula of simple terms'.[6]

6.3 THE MENTAL CAPACITY ACT 2005

A solicitor or doctor considering whether a person has testamentary capacity must now also have regard to the provisions of the Mental Capacity Act 2005 (see **Chapter 3**). The common law tests set out above will continue to be of considerable assistance, particularly in relation to the final element of the test of 'comprehending and appreciating the claims to which he ought to give effect'. The test in the MCA has been held to be a 'modern restatement' of the test in *Banks* v. *Goodfellow*.[7] Note also that the principle in *Bird* v. *Luckie* is also enshrined in the MCA, which expressly provides that a person is not to be treated as unable to make a decision merely because he makes an unwise decision.[8]

As regards the extent to which a person's testamentary capacity may be enhanced, the MCA confirms the principle that a person 'is not to be treated as unable to make a decision unless all practicable steps to enable him to do so have been taken without success'.[9] If and to the extent that it is not already spelled out in the common law tests, the MCA provides that the solicitor or doctor should also consider whether the testator understands the likely effects of making the will or not making the will at this time or deciding to make a different will.[10]

It is important to note, however, that, at least in respect of wills made before the coming into force of the MCA on 1 October 2007, the courts will approach the question of testamentary capacity without reference to the MCA, but rather by the common law test set out above.[11] This may have relevance as regards the burden of proof in respect of establishing the validity of the will, since under the MCA the onus is on the person alleging lack of testamentary capacity, while at common law, the position was different. This point was reaffirmed in the case of *Perrins* v. *Holland* where the will in question was made before the MCA came into effect, when Mr Justice Lewison commented:[12]

> However, there are six points that I should make. First, since the test is a common law test it is capable of being influenced by contemporary attitudes. Second, our general understanding of impaired mental capacity of adults has increased enormously since 1870. Third, we now recognise that an adult with impaired mental capacity is capable of making some decisions for himself, given help. Thus fourth, we recognise that the test of mental capacity is not monolithic, but is tailored to the task in hand: *Hoff* v. *Atherton* [2005] WTLR 99, 109. Fifth, contemporary attitudes toward adults with impaired capacity are more respectful of adult autonomy. Sixth, even the traditional test must be applied in the context of the particular testator and the particular estate. A testator with a complex estate and many potential beneficiaries may need a greater degree of cognitive capability than one with a simple estate and few claimants.

6.4 SUPERVENING INCAPACITY

Occasionally a person becomes ill, or their condition deteriorates, between giving instructions for the preparation of a will and executing it. In these circumstances, if the will has been prepared strictly in accordance with the instructions given, it may still be valid even though, when it is executed, the person merely recalls giving instructions to the solicitor and believes that the will being executed complies with those instructions. This rule was set out in *Parker* v. *Felgate*.[13]

This case concerned a 28-year-old widow, Mrs Compton, who suffered from glomerulonephritis, or Bright's disease. In July 1882 she consulted her solicitor about making a new will. She wanted to leave £500 to her father, £250 to her brother, and the rest of her estate (about £2,500) to Great Ormond Street Hospital. During August she experienced extreme renal failure. The will was drawn up on the basis of the earlier instructions, and it was signed by someone else in her presence and at her direction, as the law permits. Four days later Mrs Compton died. Her father and brother, who would have benefited on her intestacy, contested the will on the ground that she lacked testamentary capacity when the will was executed.

The judge held that in a case of this nature, three questions must be asked:

1. When the will was executed, did she remember and understand the instructions she had given to her solicitor?
2. If it had been thought advisable to stimulate her, could she have understood each clause of the will when it was explained to her?
3. Was she capable of understanding, and did she understand, that she was executing a will for which she had previously given instructions to her solicitor?

These questions should be asked in the order of priority listed above, and if the answer to any one of them is 'yes' the will shall be valid. On the evidence in this particular case the jury answered 'no' to the first two questions, and 'yes' to the third, and accordingly Mrs Compton's will was valid and Great Ormond Street Hospital got its legacy.

The *Parker* v. *Felgate* rule was recently upheld in the case of *Perrins* v. *Holland*, where it was clarified that:[14]

> . . . in a case in which the principle in *Parker v Felgate* is applied it is not necessary to prove knowledge and approval of the will, provided that (a) the testator believes that it gives effect to his instructions and (b) it does in fact do so.

The same principle applies when the person making a will has written or typed it and that person's condition deteriorates between preparing the will and executing it.[15]

6.5   THE NEED FOR MEDICAL EVIDENCE: THE 'GOLDEN RULE'

According to the courts there is a 'golden rule' that a solicitor, when drawing up a will for an elderly person or someone who is seriously ill, should try to ensure that the will is witnessed or approved by a medical practitioner[16] (see **4.5**). It has been held that this rule 'provides clear guidance as to how, in relevant cases, disputes can be avoided, or minimised (with the material relevant to the determination of the dispute contemporaneously recorded and preserved)'.[17]

When a medical practitioner witnesses a will, there is a strong inference that the doctor has made a formal assessment and reached the conclusion that the person has the requisite capacity to make a will (see **4.5**).

It is important to note, however, the golden rule has been categorised as guidance and is not 'of itself a touchstone of validity',[18] nor a substitute for the established tests of capacity and of knowledge and approval.

The medical practitioner should record their examination and findings and, where there is an earlier will, it should be examined and any proposed alterations should be discussed with the person. Doctors should not be involved in an assessment of capacity to make a will, or act as witness to a will, in which they are named as a beneficiary.

Where medical opinion is sought on an assessment as to testamentary capacity, this is best achieved by careful instructions to the doctor. There is a sample letter of instruction in **Appendix H**, setting out the relevant issues.

6.6   CHECKLIST

The following checklist covers what is meant by 'understanding the nature of the act and its effects', 'understanding the extent of the property being disposed of' and being 'able to comprehend and appreciate the claims to which a person making a will ought to give effect'. It is not intended to be either authoritative or exhaustive, but to give an indication of the issues which the will-maker must be able to understand, depending on their individual circumstances. For the first three elements considered below the test of capacity involves the person's ability to receive and evaluate information which may be communicated by others, such as a solicitor. The final element of the test requires the person to exercise choice.

The nature of the act of making a will

People making a will should understand that:

- they will die;
- the will shall come into operation on their death, but not before;
- they can change or revoke the will at any time before their death, provided they have the capacity to do so.

The effects of making a will

People making a will should understand and where necessary make choices in regard to:

- who should be appointed as executor(s) (and perhaps why they should be appointed);
- who gets what under the will;
- whether a beneficiary's gift is outright or conditional (for example, where the beneficiary is only entitled to the income from a lump sum during their lifetime, or is allowed to occupy residential property for the rest of the beneficiary's life);
- that if they spend their money or give away or sell their property during their lifetime, the beneficiaries might lose out;
- that a beneficiary might die before them;

72

- whether they have already made a will and, if so, how and why the new will differs from the old one;
- the reasonably foreseeable consequences of making or not making a will at this time.

The extent of the property

It is important to note that the judge in *Banks* v. *Goodfellow*[19] used the word 'extent', rather than value. Practical difficulties can arise when the investments of the person making the will are managed by somebody else and there are no recent statements or valuations. In these cases solicitors should apply a reasonableness test to any estimate the person making the will gives about the extent of their wealth.

People making a will should understand:

- the extent of all the property owned solely by them;
- the fact that certain types of jointly owned property might automatically pass to the other joint owner, regardless of anything that is said in the will;
- whether there are benefits payable on their death which might be unaffected by the terms of their will (e.g. insurance policies and pension rights);
- that the extent of their property could change during their lifetime;
- whether they have any debts and how these are to be paid.

The claims of others

People making a will should be able to comprehend and appreciate the claims to which they ought to give effect. While they have the right to ignore these claims, even to the extent of being prejudiced or capricious, they must be able to give reasons for preferring some beneficiaries and, perhaps, excluding others. For example possible beneficiaries:

- may already have received adequate provision from the person;
- may be financially better off than others;
- may have been more attentive or caring than others;
- may be in greater need of assistance because of their age, or physical or mental disabilities.

6.7 CAPACITY TO REVOKE A WILL

When a will is revoked it is cancelled and will no longer come into effect on its maker's death. A will can be revoked in three ways:

- If the person who made it subsequently gets married, the will is automatically revoked by operation of law, unless it was specifically made in contemplation of that marriage (capacity to consent to marriage is discussed in **11.4**). If a person who lacks testamentary capacity marries (thereby revoking a previous will) it may be necessary to apply to the Court of Protection for the making of a statutory will (see **6.8**).

- Making a will or signing a document which expressly states that the earlier will is revoked. In this case the usual rules on testamentary capacity apply.
- With the intention of revoking the will, the maker personally burns, tears or destroys it, or authorises somebody else to burn, tear or destroy it in the maker's presence.

The capacity required to revoke a will by destroying it was considered in the case of *Re Sabatini*.[20] In June 1940 Mrs Ruth Sabatini executed a will in which she left a few legacies to various friends and relatives, and the rest of her estate to her favourite nephew, Anthony. On 16 September 1965 she tore up this will. On 24 November 1965 she was diagnosed as suffering from Alzheimer's disease. She died in May 1966, aged 91. If the will had been validly revoked, Mrs Sabatini would have died intestate, and the whole of her estate (worth just over £50,000) would have been distributed among eight nephews and nieces, each getting an equal share. Since the original 1940 will had been destroyed, Anthony applied for probate of a carbon copy which would give him legal authority to deal with his aunt's estate according to that will. He realised that the burden was on him to prove that his aunt was not of sound mind, memory, and understanding when she tore up her will. He produced compelling medical evidence to support his case.

The barrister representing the other seven nephews and nieces put forward the argument that a lower standard of capacity, a lesser degree of concentration, was acceptable when a will is destroyed, and that a person who was incapable of making a new will might understand that a beneficiary had become unworthy of their inheritance and wish to deprive the beneficiary of it by tearing up the will and dying intestate. The judge rejected this argument, and said that as a general rule an individual must have the same standard of mind and memory and the same degree of understanding when destroying a will as when making one. Taking all the evidence in this case, and regarding the events of 16 September in the light of what had happened before and Mrs Sabatini's condition afterwards, the only possible conclusion was that the destruction of her will was not 'a rational act rationally done'. She did not have the capacity to revoke her will, and the carbon copy of the 1940 will was accepted for the purpose of granting probate.

The *Sabatini* case establishes that a person who intends to revoke their will must be capable of:

- understanding the nature of the act of revoking a will;
- understanding the effect of revoking the will (this might even involve a greater understanding of the operation of the intestacy rules than is necessary for the purpose of making a will, although there is no direct authority on the point and it would be extremely difficult to prove retrospectively);

- understanding the extent of their property;
- comprehending and appreciating the claims to which they ought to give effect.

6.8 STATUTORY WILLS

If someone lacks capacity to make a valid will for themselves, an application can be made to the Court of Protection for what is known as a statutory will (or a codicil) to be drawn up and executed on the person's behalf.[21]

The court requires evidence of lack of testamentary capacity, applying the test of capacity in the MCA[22] (see **Chapter 3**). In addition to information about the extent of the person's property and affairs, the Court will require information as to the person's state of mind and health, their current and future care needs, their ability to have their wishes and feelings to be taken into account, their life expectancy and so forth.[23]

In the majority of cases, applications for a statutory will are likely to be made by an attorney appointed under an LPA with authority to deal with the person's property and affairs, or by a deputy appointed by the Court of Protection to make financial decisions for the person. However, it is no longer a prerequisite that the person must be shown to be incapable of managing and administering their property and affairs, merely that they lack capacity to make a valid will for themselves.[24]

Conversely, the fact that a person falls under the jurisdiction of the Court of Protection (either in relation to their property and affairs or their welfare), or has an attorney or deputy acting on their behalf, does not necessarily mean that the person lacks testamentary capacity. If the person has testamentary capacity a solicitor can be instructed and the will drawn up under the direction of the Court of Protection.

In *Re (P)*,[25] it was held that the old guidance given by the Court Protection prior to the coming into force of the MCA was no longer to be followed.[26] Mr Justice Lewison held that, in line with the approach to be taken generally under the MCA, the goal of the inquiry in making a statutory will is to work out what is in the person's best interests, rather than what the person might be expected to have done. In order to make that determination, it is necessary to adopt the same structured approach to determining the person's best interests as would be adopted in other circumstances (see **3.6**). In particular it is necessary to have regard to the to person's past and present wishes.[27]

NOTES

1. *Banks* v. *Goodfellow* (1870) LR 5 QB 549.
2. For a recent example of this, see *Hoff* v. *Atherton* [2004] EWCA Civ 1554, [2004] All ER (D) 314 (Nov) in which the testator suffered from mild to moderate dementia but the court was still satisfied that he had testamentary capacity.

3. *Banks* v. *Goodfellow* (1870) LR 5 QB 549 at 565.
4. *Bird* v. *Luckie* (1850) 8 Hare 301.
5. *Cartwright* v. *Cartwright* (1793) 1 Phill Ecc 90, 101.
6. *Leger* v. *Poirier* [1944] 3 DLR 1, 11–12.
7. *Scammell and Scammell* v. *Farmer* [2008] EWHC 1100 (Ch): para. 24. The MCA Code of Practice makes specific reference to this test at para. 4.32 and also states at para. 4.33 that the Act does not replace the common law tests. See **Appendix B**.
8. Mental Capacity Act 2005, s.1(4).
9. Ibid: s.1(3).
10. Ibid: s.3(4).
11. *Scammell and Scammell* v. *Farmer* [2008] EWHC 1100 (Ch), paras. 25–29.
12. *Perrins* v. *Holland and Anor* [2009] EWHC 1945 (Ch) at para. 40.
13. *Parker* v. *Felgate* (1883) 8 PD 171. A recent application of this rule is *Clancy* v. *Clancy* [2003] EWHC 1885 (Ch).
14. *Perrins* v. *Holland and Anor* [2009] EWHC 1945 (Ch) at para. 52.
15. *In the Estate of Wallace: Solicitor of the Duchy of Cornwall* v. *Batten* [1952] TLR 925.
16. See: *Kenward* v. *Adams* (1975) *The Times*, 29 November 1975; and *Buckenham* v. *Dickinson* [1997] CLY 661.
17. *Cattermole* v. *Prisk* [2006] 1 FLR 693 at 699.
18. Ibid: at 699.
19. *Banks* v. *Goodfellow* (1870) LR 5 QB.
20. *Re Sabatini* (1970) 114 SJ 35.
21. Mental Capacity Act 2005, s.18(1)(i).
22. The statutory test of capacity in ss.2 and 3 of the Mental Capacity Act 2005, taking account of the principles in s.1. (See also **Chapter 3**.)
23. The information required by the Court, and the procedures to be followed in are set out in Practice Direction 9F – Applications relating to statutory wills, codicils, settlements and other dealings with P's property (Supplements Part 9 of the Court of Protection Rules 2007 (SI 2007/1744), r.71).
24. Mental Capacity Act 2005, s.16(1)(b).
25. *Re P* [2009] EWHC 163 (Ch).
26. In particular, the guidance contained in *Re D(J)* [1982] Ch 237 in which the court set out principles to be adopted in coming to a 'substituted judgment' as to what the patient would have done.
27. To satisfy s.4(6) of the Mental Capacity Act 2005.

Capacity to make a gift

7.1   INTRODUCTION

It is not uncommon for people (especially older people) to give away some or most of their assets to others, usually to their children or grandchildren. Often a gift is made to reduce the amount of tax payable on their death, and the law regards tax avoidance – as distinct from tax evasion – as an entirely legitimate exercise. Sometimes a gift is made for other reasons: perhaps to prevent assets falling into the hands of creditors on bankruptcy, or to enable the giver to claim social security benefits, or to be funded by a local authority if the person has to go into a care home. Parliament has anticipated most of these schemes and the relevant legislation usually contains lengthy anti-avoidance provisions which could render such gifts ineffective. The Law Society has also published a Practice Note on the subject of gifts of assets.[1]

Anyone who is asked to assess whether a person has capacity to make a gift should:

(a)   not let the underlying purpose or motive affect the assessment, unless it is so perverse as to cast doubt on capacity; and
(b)   be satisfied that the giver is acting freely and voluntarily, and that no one is pressurising the person into making a gift.

A professional who is the likely recipient should not be involved in an assessment of capacity to make a gift.

7.2   THE TEST OF CAPACITY: THE COMMON LAW

The most important case on capacity to make a gift is *Re Beaney (Deceased)*.[2]
In this case a 64-year-old widow with three grown up children owned and lived
in a three-bedroom semi-detached house. Her elder daughter lived with her. In
May 1973, a few days after being admitted to hospital suffering from advanced
dementia, the widow signed a deed of gift transferring the house to her elder
daughter. The widow died intestate the following year. Her son and younger
daughter applied successfully to the court for a declaration that the transfer of
the house was void and of no effect because their mother was mentally incapable of making such a gift. The judge in the case set out the following criteria
for capacity to make a lifetime gift:

> The degree or extent of understanding required in respect of any instrument is rel-
> ative to the particular transaction which it is to effect . . . Thus, at one extreme, if
> the subject-matter and value of a gift are trivial in relation to the donor's other
> assets, a low degree of understanding will suffice. But, at the other, if its effect is to
> dispose of the donor's only asset of value and thus, for practical purposes, to pre-
> empt the devolution of his estate under [the donor's] will or . . . intestacy, then
> the degree of understanding required is as high as that required for a will, and the
> donor must understand the claims of all potential donees and the extent of the
> property to be disposed of.

The judge added that, even where the degree of understanding in making a
gift of lesser value is not as high as that required for a will, the donor must be
capable of understanding that they are making an outright gift and not, for
example, merely transferring property to someone else so that it can be sold.
When someone wishes to make a substantial gift it may also be prudent to
consider whether the donor understands the effect that disposing of the asset
could have on the rest of their life.

7.3   THE MENTAL CAPACITY ACT 2005

A solicitor or doctor considering whether a person has capacity to make a gift
following implementation of the Mental Capacity Act (MCA) 2005 must now
have regard to the provisions of the MCA and the MCA Code of Practice
(see **Chapter 3, Appendix A** and **Appendix B**). While the common law tests set
out above will also continue to be of assistance[3] the test of capacity to make
a gift of money or property is that set out in MCA.[4]

In particular, an unwise decision to give away money or property should
not automatically lead to the conclusion that the person lacks capacity, since
the principle in *Bird* v. *Luckie*[5] that a person is not to be treated as unable to
make a decision because he makes an unwise decision is now enshrined in the
MCA.[6] However, if the decision is 'obviously irrational or out of character'[7]
it may trigger the need for a more thorough assessment of capacity. To the

extent that it is not already spelled out in the common law tests, the MCA provides that the solicitor or doctor must also consider whether the person making the gift understands the likely effects of making it or not making it, or deciding one way or another.[8]

In respect of gifts made before the coming into force of the MCA on 1 October 2007, it is likely the courts will approach the question of capacity without reference to the MCA, but rather by the common law test set out above.[9]

7.4 CHECKLIST

This checklist includes some of the points that may need to be considered in order to establish whether someone has the capacity to make a lifetime gift of a substantial asset. Some elements may involve assessing the person's ability to receive and evaluate information which may possibly be communicated by others, such as a solicitor or other adviser. Others involve the person's ability to exercise personal choice. A lower level of capacity is sufficient where the gift is insignificant in the context of the person's assets as a whole.

The nature of the transaction

People making a gift should understand the following about the nature of the transaction:

- that it is a gift (rather than, say, a loan or a mortgage advance or the acquisition of a stake or share in the recipient's business or property);
- whether they expect to receive anything in return;
- whether they intend the gift to take effect immediately or at some later date (perhaps on death);
- who the recipient is;
- whether they have already made substantial gifts to the recipient or others;
- whether the gift is a one-off, or part of a larger transaction or series of transactions;
- the fact that if the gift is outright they will not be able to ask for the asset to be returned;
- the underlying purpose of the transaction.

The effect of the transaction

People who make a gift should understand the possible effects of the transaction, such as:

- the effect that making the gift will have on their own standard of living in the future, having regard to all the circumstances including their age, life

expectancy, income, financial resources, financial responsibilities and financial needs;
• the effect that receiving the gift may have on the recipient.

The extent of the property

People who make a gift should understand the following about the extent of the property:

• that the subject matter of the gift belongs to them, and that they are entitled to dispose of it;
• the extent (and possibly the value) of the gift in relation to all the circumstances and, in particular, in the context of their other assets.

The claims to which the giver ought to give effect

People who make a gift should be able to comprehend and appreciate the claims of the potential beneficiaries under their will or intestacy. For instance, they must appreciate:

• the effect the gift could have on other beneficiaries;
• why the recipient is more deserving than others (for example, the recipient may be less well-off financially, may have devoted more time and attention to caring for the person, or may be in need of greater assistance because of age or disability);
• whether it is necessary to compensate others, perhaps by making a new will;
• whether there was any bias or favouritism towards the recipient before making the gift.

7.5 GIFTS MADE BY ATTORNEYS

The provisions allowing attorneys to make gifts will vary depending on whether they are acting under Lasting Powers of Attorney (LPAs) (see **5.3**) or Enduring Powers of Attorney (EPAs) (see **5.4**).

Lasting powers of attorney

An attorney under a property and affairs LPA can only make gifts of the donor's money or belongings to people who are related to or connected with the donor (including the attorney) on specific occasions, including:

• births or birthdays;
• weddings or wedding anniversaries;

- civil partnership ceremonies or anniversaries; or
- any other occasion when families, friends or associates usually give presents.[10]

If the donor previously made donations to any charity regularly or from time to time, the attorney can make donations from the person's funds. This also applies if the donor could have been expected to make such payments.[11] But the value of any gift or donation must be reasonable and take into account the size of the donor's estate.

The MCA Code of Practice states:

> The Donor cannot use the LPA to make more extensive gifts than those allowed under section 12 of the Act. But they can impose stricter conditions or restrictions on the attorney's powers to make gifts. They should state these restrictions clearly in the LPA document when they are creating it. When deciding on appropriate gifts, the attorney should consider the donor's wishes and feelings to work out what would be in the donor's best interests. The attorney can apply to the Court of Protection for permission to make gifts that are not included in the LPA.[12]

There is a simplified procedure for making gifts not specified in the LPA which may be used provided the gifts are not disproportionately large and the applicant knows or reasonably believes that there are unlikely to be any objections.[13]

Enduring powers of attorney

An attorney acting on behalf of the donor of an EPA (see **5.4**) has limited authority to make gifts provided that there is nothing in the power itself which prohibits the attorney from making gifts, and 'the value of each gift is not unreasonable having regard to all the circumstances and in particular the size of the donor's estate'.[14]

Attorneys can only make gifts to:

- a charity to which the donor has made gifts, or might be expected to make gifts if they were not mentally disordered;
- any person (including the attorney) who is related to or connected with the donor, provided that the gift is of a seasonal nature, or made on the occasion of a birth or marriage, or on the anniversary of a birth or marriage.

These rules apply regardless of whether the EPA is registered or unregistered, but an attorney cannot make gifts (unless authorised to do so by the Court of Protection) while the power is in the course of being registered. If the EPA is registered and the attorney wishes to make more substantial gifts, or gifts to people who are not related to or connected with the donor, or on an occasion other than a birth or marriage or birthday or wedding anniversary, the attorney should apply for an order of the Court of Protection (see **5.5** and **7.6**). There is a simplified process for making such gifts provided they are not disproportionately large and the applicant knows or reasonably believes that there are unlikely to be any objections.[15]

7.6 GIFTS MADE BY DEPUTIES

There are no specific provisions in the MCA governing the powers of deputies to make gifts or loans or enter into financial transactions in which a gift element is proposed on behalf of the person on whose behalf they are appointed to make financial decisions. The court order appointing the deputy will set out the extent, if any, of the deputy's powers to make gifts or loans (see **Appendix C**). However, if the deputy considers that those powers are insufficient, there is a simplified mechanism by which applications to the Court of Protection can be made for approval of such gifts or transactions, so long as they are not disproportionately large and the applicant knows or reasonably believes that there are unlikely to be any objections.[16]

Most deputies are required to provide some sort of security (for example, a guarantee bond) to the Public Guardian to cover any loss as a result of the deputy's actions, including making unauthorised gifts of the person's money or property.[17]

7.7 RISK OF FINANCIAL ABUSE

People who are (or are becoming) incapable of looking after their own affairs are at particular risk of financial abuse and one of the easiest forms of abuse is the improper gifting of their money or other assets. This may be where vulnerable people are persuaded to give away money or property without being fully aware of the circumstances, or having the capacity to do so, or when people appointed to act on their behalf (such as attorneys, deputies or appointees) abuse their position of trust (see **5.7**). The careful assessment of capacity to make a gift is therefore an important safeguard against financial abuse.

Where medical opinion is sought on an assessment of capacity to make a gift, this is best achieved by careful instructions to the doctor. **Appendix H** is a sample letter of instruction which can be adapted for capacity to make a gift.

NOTES

1. The Law Society (2009) *Making Gifts of Assets Practice Note – 16 July 2009*, Law Society. This Practice Note replaces previous guidance: Law Society (2000) *Gifts of property: implications for future liability to pay for long-term care*, Law Society.
2. *Re Beaney (Deceased)* [1978] 2 All ER 595, 601f–h.
3. The MCA Code of Practice makes specific reference to *Re Beaney* at para. 4.32 and states at para. 4.33 that the Act is in line with the common law tests and does not replace them.

4. The statutory test of capacity in ss.2 and 3 of the Mental Capacity Act 2005, taking account of the principles in s.1. (See also **Chapter 3**.)
5. *Bird* v. *Luckie* (1850) 8 Hare 301.
6. Mental Capacity Act 2005, s.1(4).
7. Department of Constitutional Affairs (2007) *Mental Capacity Act 2005 Code of Practice*, TSO, para. 2.11.
8. Mental Capacity Act 2005, s.3(4).
9. See by analogy to the position in respect of testamentary capacity, *Scammell and Scammell* v. *Farmer* [2008] EWHC 1100 (Ch), paras. 25–29.
10. Mental Capacity Act 2005, s.12(3)(b).
11. Ibid: s.12(2)(b).
12. Department of Constitutional Affairs (2007) *Mental Capacity Act 2005 Code of Practice*. TSO, para. 7.42.
13. Court of Protection *Practice Direction 9D – Applications by currently appointed deputies, attorneys and donees in relation to P's property and affairs* (supplements Part 9 of the Court of Protection Rules 2007 (SI 2007/1744)).
14. Mental Capacity Act 2005, Sched. 4, para. 3(3).
15. Court of Protection *Practice Direction 9D – Applications by currently appointed deputies, attorneys and donees in relation to P's property and affairs* (supplements Part 9 of the Court of Protection Rules 2007 (SI 2007/1744)).
16. Ibid.
17. Mental Capacity Act 2005, s.19(9)(a).

CHAPTER 8

Capacity to litigate

8.1 INTRODUCTION

People who lack capacity to conduct legal proceedings (known as lacking 'capacity to litigate' or 'litigation capacity') may become parties to proceedings in the High Court of Justice, the county courts (civil, family and insolvency) and the Family Proceedings Court, as well as in the Court of Protection (see **Appendix C**). When an adult who lacks litigation capacity or a child is involved in legal proceedings (see also **2.1**), a procedure is needed to enable the proceedings to continue by appointing someone else to give instructions and otherwise conduct the proceedings on their behalf. These procedures are to be found in the relevant rules for the type of proceedings, which are:

- Civil Procedure Rules 1998, Part 21 (CPR);
- Family Proceedings Rules 1991, Part IX (FPR);
- Family Procedure (Adoption) Rules 2005, Part 7 (FP(A)R);
- Insolvency Rules 1986, Part 7, Chapter 7 (IR);
- Court of Protection Rules 2007, Part 17.

This Chapter is concerned with adults who lack capacity to litigate in civil proceedings other than in the Court of Protection. The adult litigant who lacks litigation capacity is referred to in civil, family and adoption proceedings as a 'protected party', and in insolvency proceedings as an 'incapacitated person' (see **8.2**). A child may also in some circumstances be a protected party (for example, in the case of a claim for damages on behalf of a brain injured child who will not be capable of handling the award after reaching the age of 18).

The litigant may also be a 'protected beneficiary' if they will lack capacity to manage any money recovered in the proceedings. The representative in civil and (once the new Family Procedure Rules come into effect in 2010) family proceedings is known as a 'litigation friend'.

The purpose of the various rules is to ensure that:

- adults who lack litigation capacity or children are represented by a suitable adult (a litigation friend);
- compromises and settlements agreed on their behalf are approved by the court;
- if an individual is also deemed to be a 'protected beneficiary', there is supervision of any money recovered in the proceedings.

Substantive decisions which determine how any significant funds recovered or damages awarded will be administered will be taken by the Court of Protection on the basis of its own determinations of capacity at times when they are necessary and in respect of particular decisions. Such decisions may also be made by a deputy appointed by the Court of Protection with the appropriate authority (see **Chapter 5** and **Appendix C**).

Any proceedings involving a child or protected person conducted without such a representative are likely to be invalid and any settlement set aside, unless the court retrospectively gives approval.

Solicitors asked to act on behalf of a protected person should ensure that a suitable person is put forward for appointment as litigation friend (see **8.4**). The appointment is generally made by the court that will hear the proceedings, but it is possible for a person to become a litigation friend without a court order. Care should be taken to select a litigation friend who has no actual or potential conflict of interest with the person who lacks capacity. In most cases, a relative, friend or someone with a close connection with the protected party will act as litigation friend. A deputy already appointed by the Court of Protection may also be appointed to act as litigation friend, and will be entitled to do so in proceedings within the scope of their authority if the Court of Protection has specifically authorised the deputy to conduct legal proceedings on behalf of the protected person. Where there is no suitable person willing and able to act as litigation friend, the Official Solicitor to the Senior Courts will consider accepting appointment, but should first be consulted and his consent obtained. Further information on the role of the Official Solicitor is given in **Appendix E**.

The courts have sought to discourage satellite litigation as to whether a litigation friend is required. Where an application to appoint a litigation friend is made with good reason and is supported by responsible evidence in accordance with the relevant procedural rules, there should be no need for the other party to the litigation to become involved except where that party has a financial interest (e.g. a claim for damages following a brain injury where the amount of damages may be increased if the Court of Protection becomes involved).[1]

8.2   THE TEST OF CAPACITY TO LITIGATE

The common law

The capacity to litigate was considered for the first time in any detail in an English court by Wright J, and subsequently by the Court of Appeal, in *Masterman-Lister* v. *Brutton & Co*,[2] from which the following principles emerged:

1.   Although there is no requirement in CPR Part 21 that a judge should consider medical evidence or be satisfied as to incapacity before a party to civil proceedings is to be treated as a patient (now a protected person), since the implementation of the Human Rights Act 1998 (and in particular Article 6(1) of the European Convention), the court should always, as a matter of practice, at the first convenient opportunity, investigate the question of capacity whenever there is any reason to suspect that it might be absent. This means that, even where the issue does not seem to be contentious, a judge who is responsible for case management will almost certainly require the assistance of a medical report before being able to be satisfied that incapacity exists.

2.   The test to be applied to determine a person's capacity is issue-specific. In relation to capacity to litigate, what has to be considered is whether a party to legal proceedings is capable of understanding, with the assistance of such proper explanation (in broad terms and simple language) from legal advisers and other experts as the case may require, the matters on which their consent or decision was likely to be necessary in the course of those proceedings.[3] If the party has the capacity to understand what is needed to pursue or defend a claim, there is no reason why the law, whether substantive or procedural, should require the interposition of a litigation friend.

3.   Capacity depends on time and context. Accordingly, a decision in one court as to capacity does not bind another court, which has to consider the same issue in a different context. Any medical witness asked to assist in relation to capacity therefore needs to know the particular decision and test of capacity in relation to which his advice is sought.

The Mental Capacity Act 2005

It is suggested in the MCA Code of Practice[4] that the old common law tests of capacity to litigate (as set out above) may still apply, although the Code acknowledges that judges (sitting elsewhere than in the Court of Protection) may decide to adopt the statutory test of capacity in relation to decisions outside of the scope of the MCA if that is appropriate, including for example where the issue is capacity to litigate. However, after the Code was published and at the same time as the MCA came into effect on

1 October 2007, amendments were introduced into the CPR, the FPR and the FP(A)R so as to incorporate the same definition of capacity as applies under the MCA.[5]

The test for lack of capacity to conduct proceedings is therefore the statutory test under the MCA (see **Chapter 3**). However, many of the above principles that evolved under the common law will continue to be of assistance in applying the statutory test in the context of capacity to conduct legal proceedings.

Insolvency proceedings

A broader definition of an 'incapacitated person' was provided for in insolvency proceedings which took into account incapacity due to both mental disorder and physical affliction or disability.[6] From 1 October 2007 following implementation of the Mental Capacity Act 2005 this became:

> Where . . . it appears to the court that a person affected by the proceedings is one who lacks capacity within the meaning of the Mental Capacity Act 2005 to manage and administer his property and affairs either:
>
> 1. by reason of lacking capacity within the meaning of the Mental Capacity Act 2005; or
> 2. due to physical affliction or disability,
>
> special rules apply.

Although a wider definition and different causes of incapacity are accepted in insolvency proceedings compared with other types of litigation, it would appear that the initial qualification of 'lacks capacity within the meaning of the Mental Capacity Act 2005' restricts this to the new statutory definition. However, the approach to assessing the person's mental incapacity (as opposed to physical disability) is assumed to be the same as under the other court rules.

Where a finding of incapacity is made, the court may appoint such person as it thinks fit to appear for, represent or act for the incapacitated person. The appointment may be made either generally or for the purpose of any particular application or proceeding, or for the exercise of particular rights or powers which the incapacitated person might have exercised but for his incapacity.[7]

8.3 APPLYING THE TEST

There is a presumption of capacity so the burden of proof rests on those asserting lack of capacity. If there is clear evidence that the person has been incapacitated for a considerable period (for example following a road accident) then the burden of proof may be more easily discharged, but it remains on whoever asserts lack of capacity to make the decision which now needs to be made in the context of conducting legal proceedings. The test is applied on the balance of probabilities, so it is not necessary to be satisfied beyond reasonable doubt that the person lacks litigation capacity. See **Chapter 4** for an explanation of these legal principles.

When considering whether an individual is incapable of personally conducting legal proceedings the MCA test should be applied (see **Chapter 3**).

All practicable steps must first be taken to help the person make the necessary decisions for themselves. The person should not be held unable to understand information relevant to a decision if they can understand an explanation given in broad terms or simple language, and with the assistance of such proper explanation from legal advisers and other experts as the case may require.[8] If the first element of the test is satisfied but there is doubt about the other, it may be appropriate to ask the court to decide whether the second element is satisfied as a preliminary issue in the legal proceedings. When a person is treated as lacking capacity he is deprived of important rights and there is potential for a breach of the Human Rights Act 1998, yet there is no requirement under the various rules (listed in **8.1**) for a judicial determination of capacity. The final decision as to capacity in respect of the particular legal proceedings rests with the court, which should ensure that the individual concerned is given an opportunity to make representations unless the lack of capacity is beyond doubt, and investigate the question of capacity whenever there is any reason to suspect that it may be absent.

When applying the test of capacity, evidence from the person concerned, whether admitting or denying incapacity, cannot be regarded as being of great weight. Expert evidence will normally be required, which could be from a doctor or psychologist, depending on the type of case and the circumstances of the person alleged to lack capacity. The judge may be assisted by seeing the individual but this may not always be appropriate. If the issue of capacity is contested, medical evidence will be required (especially with respect to the existence and effect of any impairment of, or disturbance in the functioning of, the mind or brain).

Obtaining medical evidence can present real difficulties, especially if the person being assessed refuses to cooperate (see **2.4**). Where there are practical difficulties in obtaining medical evidence the Official Solicitor may be consulted and will try to assist (see **Appendix E**). A doctor who is asked to express an opinion as to whether a person is incapable of bringing or defending court proceedings should be provided with sufficient information as to the extent and nature of those proceedings, as well as the medical background.

In assessing capacity to conduct litigation, it will be particularly important to have regard to the statutory requirement to take all practicable steps to help the individual make a decision, and to provide information in an appropriate manner. If an individual's family, medical advisers and legal advisers can provide clear and straightforward information about the proposed proceedings, it may be possible for the individual to be treated as having litigation capacity, even if, for example, they would not have capacity to manage large sums of money (and would therefore be a 'protected beneficiary' despite not being a 'protected party', although the CPR fail to provide for such a situation).

Finally, it is extremely important to remember that capacity is both issue-specific and time-specific. The former has two consequences:

1. The question of capacity has to be considered in relation to the specific litigation in issue, as Mr Justice Munby put it in *Sheffield City Council* v. *E and another*:[9]

> Someone may have the capacity to litigate in a case where the nature of the dispute and the issues are simple, whilst at the same time lacking the capacity to litigate in a case where either the nature of the dispute or the issues are more complex. In this sense litigation is analogous to medical treatment. Some litigation, like some medical treatment, is relatively simple and risk free. Some litigation, on the other hand, like some medical treatment, is highly complex and more or less risky. Someone may have the capacity to consent to a simple operation whilst lacking the capacity to consent to a more complicated – perhaps controversial – form of treatment. In the same way, someone may have the capacity to litigate in a simple case whilst lacking the capacity to litigate in a highly complex case. Just as medical procedures vary very considerably, so too does litigation.

2. It is necessary to analyse independently whether the person has capacity to make the decision in question and whether they have the capacity to litigate about that decision. Although only in 'unusual circumstances will it be possible to conclude that someone who lacks subject-matter capacity can nonetheless have litigation capacity'[10] the possibility cannot be ruled out, particularly in the case of a person whose impairment is such that they are on the cusp of having subject-matter capacity.

Both of the issue-specific and time-specific nature of capacity were given further consideration in *Saulle* v. *Nouvet*, when Mr Andrew Edis QC, sitting as a Deputy Judge of the High Court, made the following observations:[11]

> . . . the Court must focus on the matters which arise for decision now, and on the Claimant's capacity to deal with them now. I am required not to attempt to foretell the future and provide for situations which may arise when he may have to take some other decision at some other time when his mental state may be different . . . I consider that [Dr X] may well be right when he suggests that there may be times in the future when the Claimant will lack capacity to make particular decisions, and note his concern that if that happens when he does not have the support of his family for any reason, he may not come to the attention of the Court of Protection until it is too late. This is a risk against which the old test for capacity used by the Court of Protection under Part VII of the 1983 [Mental Health] Act used to guard. The modern law is different.

8.4   THE REPRESENTATIVE IN LEGAL PROCEEDINGS

Suitability of representatives

In civil proceedings, the criteria for appointment as litigation friend (other than the Official Solicitor or person authorised by the Court of Protection) are that the person:

- can fairly and competently conduct proceedings on behalf of the child or protected party;
- has no interest adverse to that of the child or protected party;
- (where the child or protected party is a claimant) undertakes to pay any costs which the child or protected party may be ordered to pay in relation to the proceedings, subject to any right to be repaid from the assets of the child or protected party.[12]

The first two requirements also apply to proceedings in the Court of Protection.[13] A certificate of suitability must be filed in the civil and family courts and in the Court of Protection where a person wishes to become a litigation friend without a court order.[14]

8.5   IMPLICATIONS OF INCAPACITY

If significant damages or compensation are to be awarded (for example in a personal injury claim or the distribution of assets on a divorce) then an application should be made to the Court of Protection for the appointment of a deputy if the litigant is a protected beneficiary who lacks capacity to manage these funds.

NOTES

1. *Folks* v. *Faizey* [2006] EWCA Civ 381.
2. See *Masterman-Lister* v. *Jewell & Home Counties Dairies* [2002] EWHC 417; and *Masterman-Lister* v. *Brutton & Co* [2002] EWCA Civ 1889.
3. The person must also be able to make a decision based on that understanding, when qualities such as stability, impulsiveness and volatilily may be relevant (see *Mitchell* v. *Alasia* [2005] EWHC 11.
4. Department of Constitutional Affairs (2007) *Mental Capacity Act 2005 Code of Practice*, TSO, paras.4.32–4.33
5. The High Court has since confirmed in *Saulle* v. *Nouvet* [2007] EWHC 2902 (QB) that the statutory test as set out in the Mental Capacity Act 2005 applies in civil proceedings and in the Court of Protection.
6. For a case which illustrates the problems involved, see *Hunt* v. *Fylde Borough council* [2008] BPIR 1368.
7. Insolvency Rules 1986, rule 7.43(1)–(2).

8. Mental Capacity Act 2005, s.3(2) and *Masterman-Lister* v. *Brutton & Co* [2002] EWCA Civ 1889.
9. *Sheffield City Council* v. *E and another* [2004] EWHC 2808 (Fam) at para. 39. The case was decided before the Mental Capacity Act 2005 came into force, but the approach suggested by Mr Justice Munby would remain applicable today.
10. Ibid: para. 49; see also *The NHS Trust* v. *Miss T* [2004] EWHC 2195 (Fam).
11. *Saulle* v. *Nouvet* [2007] EWHC 2902 (QB) at paras. 51 and 54.
12. Civil Procedure Rules 1998, r.21.4(3).
13. Court of Protection Rules 2007, r.140.
14. Court of Protection Rules 2007, r.143; CPR r.21.5; Family Proceedings Rules 1991 r.9.2.

CHAPTER 9

Capacity to enter into a contract

9.1   INTRODUCTION

It is difficult to generalise about an individual's contractual capacity. Without really being aware of it, most people enter into some sort of contract every day, such as purchasing groceries, buying a bus ticket or train ticket, or depositing clothes at the dry-cleaners. Some general rules apply to each of these contracts, as well as to more complicated written agreements with several pages of small print.

9.2   GENERAL RULES

Prior to the introduction of the Mental Capacity Act 2005 (the 'MCA'), the law relating to contractual capacity was a complex combination of common law and statutory rules from which some general rules have emerged.

Contractual capacity relates to the specific contract at the time that contract is entered into, rather than to contracts in general. This means, for example that a person could have capacity to buy a cinema ticket but not the capacity required to enter into a credit agreement with a mail order firm. The person must be capable of understanding the nature and effects of the specific contract that they are entering into and of agreeing to it.[1] The degree of understanding varies according to the type of agreement or transaction involved.[2] Some contracts require a relatively low degree of understanding (buying a bus ticket), whereas others demand a much higher level of understanding (a complex hire purchase agreement).

The law of contract also requires that the parties must have intended to enter into a contract that is legally binding. In the case of social and domestic arrangements (for example, financial arrangements within the family) there is a presumption that there is no such intention. However, this presumption may be rebutted by evidence to the contrary.

9.3 VOIDABLE CONTRACTS

In dealing with contracts made by people whose mental capacity is in doubt, the courts have had to counterbalance two important policy considerations:

- a duty to protect those who are incapable of looking after themselves; and
- a duty to ensure that other people are not prejudiced by the actions of persons who lack capacity to contract but who appear to have full capacity.

So, people without contractual capacity are bound by the terms of a contract they have entered into, even if it was unfair, unless it can be shown that the other party to the contract was aware of their lack of capacity or should have been aware of this.[3] For example, at some stage a person with hypomania may go on a reckless shopping spree. If the shopkeeper has no reason to suspect that the customer is hypomanic, the customer is bound by the contract. But if the shopkeeper was or should have been aware of the customer's mental state, the contract is voidable, and therefore cannot be enforced.

9.4 NECESSARIES

The Sale of Goods Act 1979

The Sale of Goods Act 1979 imposes a special rule to apply to contracts for 'necessaries'. A person without mental capacity who agrees to pay for goods or services which are necessaries is legally obliged to pay a reasonable price for them. Although the 1979 Act applies to goods, the rule regarding necessaries would also govern the provision of essential services.

The Mental Capacity Act 2005

These rules are now brought together and given statutory force by the MCA.[4] This clarifies that the obligation to pay a reasonable price applies to both the supply of necessary goods and the provision of necessary services to a person lacking capacity to contract for them. Necessaries are defined in the MCA as goods or services which are suitable to the person's condition in life (that is, to their place in society, rather than any mental or physical condition) and their actual requirements at the time of sale and delivery (for example, ordinary drink, food and clothing).[5] The MCA Code of Practice states that the aim of this provision is to make sure that people can enjoy a similar standard of living and way of life to those they had before lacking capacity. For example, the Code suggests that if a person who now lacks capacity previously chose to buy expensive designer clothes, these are still necessary goods, as long as they can still afford them. But they would not be necessary for a person who always wore cheap clothes, no matter how wealthy they were.[6]

Whether something is necessary or not is established in two stages by asking the following questions:

1. Are the goods or services capable of being necessaries as a matter of law?
2. If so, were the goods or services necessaries, given the particular circumstances of the incapacitated person who ordered them?

Case law has established that goods are not necessaries if the person's existing supply is sufficient. So, for instance, a person who buys a pair of shoes would probably be bound to pay for them, but if the same person purchased a dozen pairs, the contract might be voidable at the person's option.

A contract for necessaries cannot be enforced against a person who lacks mental capacity if it contains harsh or onerous terms. The requirement that only a reasonable price is to be paid is an extension of this principle because a reasonable price need not be the same as the agreed or sale price.[7]

9.5   CONTRACTUAL CAPACITY: IMPACT OF THE MENTAL CAPACITY ACT 2005

In relation to contracts for necessary goods and services as provided for under the MCA, the test for capacity to enter into a contract is the standard statutory test as set out in the MCA,[8] since the statutory test applies 'for the purposes of this Act'. This suggests that the MCA statutory test would also apply in relation to capacity to enter into other types of contracts, unrelated to necessaries. The MCA Code of Practice suggests that judges may choose to adopt the statutory test if they consider it to be appropriate,[9] but the issue in relation to contractual capacity has not yet been considered by the courts. Elements of the previous common law approach are in any event present in the new statutory definition, particularly that capacity must be assessed in relation to the specific contract at issue at the time it is entered into.

9.6   DEPUTIES AND ATTORNEYS

A person whose financial affairs are managed by an attorney acting under a registered EPA or LPA (see **Chapter 5**), or by a deputy appointed by the Court of Protection (see **Appendix C**) cannot generally enter into any contract which is inconsistent with the attorney's powers under the EPA or LPA, or the deputy's powers as determined by the Court. Any such contracts are void, unless the person had contractual capacity at the time when entering into it.[10]

A deputy is not permitted to enter into any agreement for the person if the deputy believes that the person does in fact have capacity to make the decision for themselves. Further, deputies are not permitted to carry out contracts and to seek court approval retrospectively – they can only operate within the powers given to them by the Court of Protection. However, the Court of Protection has the power to make orders or give directions or authorities for the carrying out of any contract entered into by a person subject to its jurisdiction.

9.7 CHECKLIST

Solicitors may wish to seek an opinion from a doctor about a client's contractual capacity, either before a contract is agreed, or retrospectively if the validity of a contract is being challenged. The solicitor should identify the specific contract to which the assessment of capacity relates. Different information is required according to the type and complexity of the contract, for example fewer details may be required concerning a contract to purchase double glazing than for a complex agreement to enter into a home income plan. The solicitor needs to provide such details as:

- the identity of the other party to the contract;
- how much the client has to pay or is being paid;
- when the payment will be made or received;
- what is being given or received in exchange;
- any important terms and conditions which affect the client's rights and liabilities;
- the circumstances in which the contract was entered into (place and time of day);
- the method of communication between the parties;
- any opportunity afforded to the client to reconsider the contract.

The doctor should then be asked whether the client has an impairment of, or disturbance in the functioning of, their mind or brain which may affect their understanding of information relevant to the contract. This includes information about the nature and effect of that contract at the time a decision is (or was) required, and whether the person is (or was) able to retain that information, and use or weigh it as part of the process of reaching the decision. Where it is considered that the client was not capable of understanding a contract made previously, which is now being challenged, the doctor should also be asked whether in their opinion, the client's lack of capacity should have been obvious to the other party when the contract was made.

NOTES

1. *Boughton* v. *Knight* (1873) LR 3 PD 64, at 72.
2. *Re Beaney (Deceased)* [1978] 1 WLR 770.
3. *Imperial Loan Company* v. *Stone* [1892] 1 QB 599.
4. Mental Capacity Act 2005, s.7.
5. Ibid: s.7(2), based on the definition in the Sale of Goods Act 1979, s.3(3).
6. Department of Constitutional Affairs (2007) *Mental Capacity Act 2005 Code of Practice*, TSO, para. 6.58.
7. Mental Capacity Act 2005, s.7(1), based on Sale of Goods Act 1979, s.8(3).
8. The statutory test of capacity in ss.2 and 3 of the Mental Capacity Act 2005, taking account of the principles in s.1. (See also **Chapter 3**.)
9. Department of Constitutional Affairs (2007) *Mental Capacity Act 2005 Code of Practice*, TSO, paras. 4.32 and 4.33.
10. Before the Mental Capacity Act 2005 came into effect, any such contracts were automatically voidable, regardless of whether the person has contractual capacity and regardless of whether the other party was aware of the Court of Protection's involvement: *Re Walker* [1905] 1 Ch 160; and *Re Marshall* [1920] 1 Ch 284. However, since the Mental Capacity Act 2005 became law, it is no longer clear whether this line of case law is still applicable.

CHAPTER 10

Capacity to vote

10.1   ENTITLEMENT TO VOTE

The majority of people with mental health problems or learning disabilities have the right to vote in parliamentary and local elections. It is rare for doctors or lawyers to become involved in determining capacity to vote, but better knowledge of the legal position may serve to encourage more people to register and therefore to be able to vote. It is a widely held belief that any degree of learning disability or mental health problem renders a person ineligible to vote. This is not true, but such a belief may result in people with learning disabilities or mental health problems being excluded from the electoral register, which does disqualify them from voting. Encouragement is therefore needed to ensure that their names are entered on the electoral register, and that they are given every opportunity to exercise their right to vote.[1]

The people entitled to vote as electors in parliamentary elections in any constituency, or in local government elections are defined in legislation as those:

- whose name appears on the relevant electoral register;
- who are not subject to any legal incapacity to vote (apart from by virtue of their age);
- who are either Commonwealth citizens or citizens of the Republic of Ireland;
- who are of voting age (aged 18 or over).[2]

The main factors which determine whether a person with a learning disability or a mental disorder can vote are whether the person is:

97

(a)   subject to any legal incapacity to vote; and

(b)   has an address for registration purposes.

10.2   LEGAL INCAPACITY TO VOTE

Legal incapacity to vote was defined in a case in 1874 called *Stowe* v. *Joliffe* as 'some quality inherent in a person, which either at common law, or by statute, deprives him of the status of Parliamentary elector'.[3] This definition still applies today. Case law dating back to the 18th century previously held that the name of an 'idiot' may not appear on the electoral register, and hence such a person was unable to vote. However, the Electoral Administration Act 2006 (s.73) abolished any common law rules regarding the legal incapacity of a person to vote by reason of their mental state. Therefore people will not be subject to a legal incapacity to vote by virtue only of their mental health problems or learning disabilities and are therefore eligible for registration. However, some may lack the mental capacity to vote, which should be assessed at time the person wishes to cast a vote.

There is no definition in either statute or case law of the mental capacity to vote. The common law sets the threshold of understanding quite low, requiring only a capacity to understand in 'broad terms' the nature and effect of voting and an ability to make a choice between candidates.

10.3   ELIGIBILITY FOR REGISTRATION

There are no legal provisions to control the registration as electors of people who have a learning disability or mental health problem and who are living in the community (as opposed to living in a hospital). At present, the decision as to whether a person is registered on the electoral roll is made by the person themselve or, sametimes, by whoever completes the annual canvass form which is sent to all households. This form does not raise questions of mental capacity, so there is no reason why all adults resident in the household should not be included. The final decision as to whether a person's name is included in the electoral roll rests with the Electoral Registration Officer ('ERO') who must consider each case on its merits. If an ERO considers that someone is entitled to be registered as an elector, there is no discretion to omit that person's name from the register unless any legal incapacity to vote can be established.

Guidance issued by the Electoral Commission advises EROs to ensure that persons with learning difficulties or mental health conditions are included in the register of electors.[4] This places the onus on people who wish to object to the inclusion of a name to make their case, rather than requiring people with mental health problems or learing difficulties who may be eligible to vote to use the appeals procedure in order to be registered.

The Political Parties and Election Act 2009 makes provision for a move from the system of household registration towards gradual implementation of individual electoral registration in Great Britain. From 1 July 2010, people will be asked by the ERO to provide, on a voluntary basis, their signature, date of birth and National Insurance Number. The impact of the changes will be monitored by the Electoral Commission to ensure that everyone eligible for registration is included in the electoral register. The Commission will publish a report by July 2014, so that Parliament can then decide whether electors should be required to provide these 'identifiers' in order to register. It is likely that provision will need to be made to ensure that people who may have difficulty providing these 'identifiers' (for example because of a mental health problem or other disability) are not deprived of their right to vote.

Place of residence

The Representation of the People Act 2000, which came into effect in September 2001, introduced changes in electoral procedures and registration intended to make it easier for disabled people to register and to vote. Under previous electoral legislation, people were only able to register if they could establish their place of residence on a specific qualifying date each year. There were special rules relating to the voting rights of patients in 'mental hospitals' (see below) as such hospitals could not be used as a place of residence for the purpose of electoral registration. The Representation of the People Act removed the annual qualifying date, and introduced 'rolling' electoral registration to enable people to be added to (or deleted from) the electoral register at any time of the year.[5]

Both voluntary (informal) and detained patients in mental hospitals (with the exception of those detained as a consequence of criminal activity) may continue to be registered for electoral purposes at their home address. However, if their stay in hospital is so long that they have lost their residence, they may still register as electors by making a 'declaration of local connection' providing a local contact address. This could be:

- the address of the hospital;
- an address where they would be resident if they were not in hospital; or
- an address in the UK where they have lived at any time in the past.[6]

Registration by declaration of local connection is also available to homeless people. It does not apply to detained patients who have been sentenced or rewarded by the courts or transferred to hospital from prison under Part III of the Mental Health Act 1983. These people, along with all sentenced prisoners, are disqualified from voting.[7] It may be that this situation will change in the future, as the European Court of Human Rights has held that a blanket ban on voting rights for prisoners violates the European Convention on Human Rights.[8]

The definition of 'mental hospital' includes any establishment or unit whose main purpose is the reception and treatment of people suffering from any form of mental disorder.[9] This does not include hostels or care homes where the treatment of residents is not the primary purpose. The definition also excludes psychiatric wards of district general hospitals and homes for older people.

It is for EROs to decide which hostels or care homes for older people, for people with mental health problems, or those with learning disabilities, come within the definition of a 'mental hospital'. If necessary they can obtain advice from the Department of Health, Welsh Assembly Government or local Primary Care Trust for NHS homes or hostels, or the Care Quality Commission or Care and Social Services Inspectorate (Wales) for privately run institutions. Hostels or homes which are not 'mental hospitals' should be treated, for electoral purposes, in the same way as any other qualifying address.[10] The Electoral Commission guidance suggests that EROs should consider keeping records of care homes and hostels in their areas in order to obtain information about changes of residents and to give residents and wardens additional advice on the registration process.[11]

10.4 AT THE POLLING STATION

The decision as to whether and how to vote must be made by the electors themselves and cannot be made by any other person on their behalf.[12] Any person whose name appears on the electoral register should be allowed to cast their vote unless, at the polling station on the day of the poll, it appears to the presiding officer that the elector may not have the common law capacity to vote. The presiding officer may put to the elector certain statutory questions permitted by the election rules.[13] The permitted questions are:

- Are you the person whose name appears on the register as . . .?
- Have you already voted?

Although these questions are inappropriate for determining mental capacity, no further questions may be put. If the presiding officer considers that the questions are not answered satisfactorily, they can refuse to issue a ballot paper. If the questions are answered satisfactorily, the person must be allowed to vote.

Electors who are unable to read can ask the presiding officer to help them by marking their votes on the ballot paper, but they must be capable of giving directions to the presiding officer as to how they wish to vote. No one is allowed to accompany an elector into the polling booth or give any other assistance in marking the ballot paper, but some voters with physical disabilities are entitled to assistance from a companion.[14]

10.5 POSTAL AND PROXY VOTING

The Representation of the People Act 2000 extended the provisions for permitting an elector to vote by post or by appointing a proxy to vote on their behalf.[15] These methods of voting are now available either at the time of registration for the period of the register, or before a particular election. EROs are able to explain the procedures and provide the relevant application forms. Anyone on the electoral register can vote by post, which means that no check is made on their capacity when they cast their vote. No definition is given as to the mental capacity required to appoint a proxy, but it is presumed that the elector should have the common law capacity to vote and the ability to choose the person to be appointed. The Electoral Commission considers that a person must have capacity to appoint or to continue to have a proxy, as that can be taken to be a decision on voting.[16]

10.6 CONCLUSION

It is important that patients in hospital and residents in hostels and care homes are aware of their voting rights, and staff should assist them by providing information, declaration forms and absent voting forms. People with mental health problems or disabilities living in the community may require help from their relatives, carers and sometimes their doctors to ensure they are not deprived unnecessarily of this most basic of civil rights.

NOTES

1. The Joint Committee on Human Rights has drawn attention to the 'significant barriers' faced by people with learning disabilities, particularly those in care homes, in registering and exercising their right to vote: JCHR *A Life like Any other? Human Rights of Adults with Learning Disablities* HL Paper 40-1, HC 73-1, paras 264-273.
2. Representation of the People Act 1983, ss.1–2 (as amended by Representation of the People Act 2000, s.1(1)).
3. *Stowe* v. *Joliffe* [1874] LR9 CP 750.
4. Electoral Commission (2008) *Managing electoral registration in Great Britain: guidance for Electoral Registration Officers*, The Electoral Commission, Part B, para. 5.3.
5. Representation of the People Act 1983, s.4(6) (as amended by Representation of the People Act 2000, s.1(2)).
6. Representation of the People Act 1983, s.7 (as amended by Representation of the People Act 2000, s.4).
7. Representation of the People Act 1983, s.3A (as inserted by Representation of the People Act 2000, s.2).
8. *Hirst* v. *United Kingdom (No.2)* (2006) 42 EHRR 41.
9. Representation of the People Act 1983, s.7(6) (as amended by Representation of the People Act 2000, s.4).

10. Electoral Commission (2008) *Managing electoral registration in Great Britain: guidance for Electoral Registration Officers*, The Electoral Commission, Part B, para. 5.9.
11. Electoral Commission (2008) *Managing electoral registration in Great Britain: guidance for Electoral Registration Officers*, The Electoral Commission, Part E, para. 3.11.
12. Mental Capacity Act 2005, s.29.
13. Representation of the People Act 1983, Schedule 1 – Parliamentary Election Rules, Rule 35; Local Elections (Principal Areas) (England and Wales) Rules 2006 (SI 2006/3304).
14. Representation of the People Act 2000, s.13 (amended the Parliamentary Election Rules to make it easier for disabled people to vote). See also: Representation of the People (England and Wales) Regulations 2001 (SI 2001/341), reg.12.
15. Representation of the People Act 2000, s.12.
16. Electoral Commission (2008) *Managing electoral registration in Great Britain: Guidance for Electoral Registration Officers*, The Electoral Commission, Part B, para. 5.10.

CHAPTER 11

Capacity and personal relationships

11.1   RIGHT TO FORM RELATIONSHIPS

Every person has fundamental rights which may not be infringed unless there are special and widely agreed grounds justifying such an infringement. Respect for individual rights in those matters which people can decide for themselves is embodied in national and international agreements. For example, the United Nations Declaration on Human Rights of 1948 articulates the rights of adults to freedom and equal treatment. Also, the European Convention on Human Rights, incorporated into UK law under the Human Rights Act 1998, states:

> Everyone has the right to respect for his private and family life, his home and his correspondence . . .[1]

And,

> Men and women of marriageable age have the right to marry and to found a family, according to the national laws governing the exercise of this right.[2]

A balance must be maintained between respecting individual rights to family relationships, friendships, sexual relationships, marriage, and parenthood, and the duty of society (the state, parents, carers and others) to protect vulnerable adults at risk of abuse or neglect. These two facets (respect for rights and protection from abuse and exploitation) have traditionally been reflected in the differences between the civil and the criminal law, which have taken different approaches in relation to the capacity of vulnerable people to embark on intimate relationships.

Whereas the civil law has provided for the private rights of all citizens to enjoy family contact and personal or sexual relationships, the criminal law has concentrated on providing an effective deterrent aimed at protecting people at risk from abuse, including sexual abuse. This has traditionally led to a more demanding approach to the question of capacity being imposed in the criminal context. However, it is now clear that the approaches to capacity under the two systems are similar, at least as regards the question of consent to sexual intercourse.[3]

The provisions of the criminal law are discussed in **Chapter 12**. In this chapter, by contrast, the focus is on the civil law and on the aim of enabling all people to make their own voluntary decisions wherever possible.

11.2   FAMILY RELATIONSHIPS

For most people it is important to maintain family relationships (which of course vary in degree and intensity) at least with close relatives. In the context of family proceedings where children are minors, there is a general presumption of a right to a relationship between a parent and child, which should be protected so long as this is in the child's best interests. The welfare of the child is always the paramount consideration in such cases.[4] Where there is a disagreement between the parents, the right to a relationship with a child can be enforced through a contact order under the provisions of the Children Act 1989.[5]

Once children reach the age of 18 the right to a relationship with their parents, or with other family members, extends for only so far as the people involved consent to it. There are no means, in legal proceedings or otherwise, of enforcing a relationship between adult family members who have capacity to decide they no longer wish the relationship to continue. Nevertheless, the courts have been asked to intervene in cases where disputes have arisen between family members about contact with adult relatives who lack capacity to make their own decisions, or to resolve disagreements about where such individuals should live. Questions of residence or contact are clearly important in enabling a relationship to continue.

Under the Mental Capacity Act 2005 (the 'MCA'), the Court of Protection has the power to make declarations and make decisions in respect of the personal welfare of those lacking capacity[6] (for further discussion of the role and powers of the Court of Protection see **Appendix C**). However, the Court of Protection cannot make decisions on behalf of a person lacking capacity on any of the following matters:

- consenting to marriage or a civil partnership;
- consenting to have sexual relations;
- consenting to a decree of divorce on the basis of two years' separation;
- consenting to the dissolution of a civil partnership;

- consenting to a child being placed for adoption or the making of an adoption order;
- discharging parental responsibility for a child in matters not relating to the child's property; or
- giving consent under the Human Fertilisation and Embryology Act 1990.[7]

In the unreported case of *Re GC*,[8] Mr Justice Hedley sitting in the High Court set out some guidelines as to when it might be appropriate for the State (and hence the court) to intervene in personal welfare decisions:

(1) The principle governing state intervention under the Mental Capacity Act 2005 is the same as under the Children Act 1989, namely that the state does not interfere in the private family life of an individual unless the continuance of that private family life is clearly inconsistent with the welfare of the person whose best interests the court is required to determine.

(2) The closer the person is to having capacity the more weight his views are to be given.

(3) Contrary to the professional evidence, it was in GC's best interests to return home as an interim measure: this decision was reached having regard to:

    (a) the concept of least intervention,
    (b) GC's consistently-expressed wishes and feelings,
    (c) a finding that a trial at home was necessary and now was the best time, and
    (d) the importance of the emotional, as opposed to physical, component of best interests to very elderly (or young) people.

Whilst it was the intention of Parliament that the Court of Protection would be the judicial forum of last resort for the resolution of personal welfare questions for mentally incapacitated adults, it has become clear that there may still be occasions on which recourse will have to be made to the inherent jurisdiction of the High Court for decision that fall outside of the MCA. Under this jurisdiction, the High Court can exercise on behalf of the Crown powers relating to the person and property of citizens unable to care for themselves.

In a case called *Re SA*,[9] decided in 2005, the High Court decided that the inherent jurisdiction could be exercised to make personal welfare decisions in respect of those adults who do not formally lack capacity within the meaning of the common law (or, now, the MCA), but who are nonetheless seen as vulnerable because of their particular circumstances. Mr Justice Munby held that:[10]

> . . . it would be unwise, and indeed inappropriate, for me even to attempt to define who might fall into this group in relation to whom the court can properly exercise its inherent jurisdiction. I disavow any such intention. It suffices for present purposes to say that, in my judgment, the authorities to which I have referred demonstrate that the inherent jurisdiction can be exercised in relation to a vulnerable adult who, even if not incapacitated by mental disorder or mental illness, is, or is reasonably believed to be, either (i) under constraint or (ii) subject to coercion or undue influence or (iii) for some other reason deprived of the capacity to make the relevant decision, or disabled from making a free choice, or incapacitated or disabled from giving or expressing a real and genuine consent.

If adults do not fall within the definition of lacking capacity in the MCA, but fall within this category of 'vulnerability', then it appears (although no definitive ruling has yet been made) that their cases may still be considered by the High Court in the exercise of its inherent jurisdiction. It appears, however, that the High Court will be reluctant to exercise this jurisdiction where it may result in a disproportionate interference with the rights of the vulnerable adult to make a decision for themselves.[11]

The considerations that will have to be taken into account when determining whether a person is a 'vulnerable' adult are discussed further below.

Capacity to make decisions about family or personal relationships

When the Court of Protection is considering capacity to make decisions about family or personal relationships, it must apply the test set down in the MCA (discussed further in **Chapter 3**).

When the High Court is considering capacity to make such decisions, it does not formally have to follow the test for capacity set down in the MCA, but will rather be following the line of authority culminating in a case called *Re MB (Medical Treatment)*.[12] This case established a two-stage test of capacity to make a decision, in which in order to be deemed competent the person must be able to both:

(a) understand and retain the information relevant to the decision in question, especially as to the likely consequences; and
(b) use that information and weigh it in the balance as part of the process of arriving at a decision.

Whilst the *Re MB* test was formulated in the context of consent to medical treatment, it applies to all questions of personal welfare.[13] It will be obvious that the *Re MB* test is to most intents and purposes identical to that set down in s.3 of the MCA.[14] The only formal difference is that the *Re MB* test does not encompass the position provided for by the MCA where a person may have the ability to make a decision, but is unable to communicate it.[15] It is overwhelmingly likely, however, that were this situation to arise in a case before the High Court, the court would consider the MCA test in addition to other relevant case law, and find that the person in question lacked capacity to make relevant decisions.

In order to determine a person's capacity at common law to make decisions as to family or personal relationships, it is necessary to determine whether the person:

• can understand the information relevant to the decision, including the level of care available, the psychological and emotional benefits, the risk of harm or distress, and the advantages and disadvantages generally of the decision;
• can retain the information necessary in order to make a decision;

- has the ability to use or weigh the information in order to come to a decision; and
- can communicate the decision.

Capacity is issue-specific, so if the question before the court is a multifaceted one (for instance, as to both residence and contact with particular family members), the question of capacity must be approached in a similarly multifaceted way, addressing each question separately. Also, a separate assessment must be made of the person's capacity to conduct the legal proceedings involved, when the test of capacity is the statutory test in the MCA (see **Chapter 8**).

'Vulnerable' adults

The question of whether a person falls within the definition of a 'vulnerable' adult for purposes of engaging the inherent jurisdiction of the High Court is not straightforward. At least one High Court judge has suggested that such people should be considered, in fact, to lack capacity in 'the true sense' (even if they do not lack capacity within the meaning of the MCA).[16]

Until further cases have clarified the question of precisely what is needed to bring someone within the category of vulnerable adult, perhaps the most that can be done is to set out the relevant passages from the judgment of Mr Justice Munby in *Re SA*:[17]

> 77 . . . the authorities to which I have referred demonstrate that the inherent jurisdiction can be exercised in relation to a vulnerable adult who, even if not incapacitated by mental disorder or mental illness, is, or is reasonably believed to be, either (i) under constraint or (ii) subject to coercion or undue influence or (iii) for some other reason deprived of the capacity to make the relevant decision, or disabled from making a free choice, or incapacitated or disabled from giving or expressing a real and genuine consent.
>
> . . .
>
> 82 In the context of the inherent jurisdiction I would treat as a vulnerable adult someone who, whether or not mentally incapacitated, and whether or not suffering from any mental illness or mental disorder, is or may be unable to take care of him or herself, or unable to protect him or herself against significant harm or exploitation, or who is deaf, blind or dumb, or who is substantially handicapped by illness, injury or congenital deformity. This, I emphasise, is not and is not intended to be a definition. It is descriptive, not definitive; indicative rather than prescriptive.

11.3 SEXUAL RELATIONSHIPS

Deciding to enter into a sexual relationship with another individual is a personal decision which does not generally require any formal contract or test of capacity. Men and women can give legal consent to either opposite or same sex relationships at the age of 16.[18] Relationships can be of any duration and of varying degrees of intensity and commitment. Sexual relationships are personal in nature, which means that it is entirely for the individuals involved to decide whether or not to embark upon them. The courts cannot consent to sexual relations on behalf of incapacitated people who are over 16 but society has obligations to ensure that their choice is voluntary.

Capacity to consent to sexual relationships

The courts have in recent years had cause to consider the question of capacity to consent to sexual relationships in a number of cases. The following principles can be drawn from these cases:

- the civil and criminal tests for capacity to consent to sexual intercourse should be essentially the same;[19]
- capacity to consent to sexual intercourse relates to sexual intercourse with a particular partner in a specific situation;[20]
- capacity to consent to sexual intercourse relates to particular sexual activity;[21]
- there are different tests of capacity for consent to sexual intercourse and consent to contact.[22]

Relatives or carers may try to stop a relationship involving people with a learning disability because of concerns about pregnancy, risks of infection, moral objections to the existence of a sexual relationship, or opposition to possible future marriage and parenthood. Doctors may be asked to give a view about the appropriateness of two people embarking on a close relationship and there may be concern about the ability of one or both parties to give valid consent to sexual intercourse. It is important that each party is seen privately and assessed individually before doctors advise on their capacity. Every attempt must be made to provide individuals with the information they require to be able to make a decision as to whether or not to have a sexual relationship. For example, they may need advice about contraception or other risks of intercourse. The following factors, some derived from court decisions,[23] may be relevant to an assessment of an individual's capacity to consent to sexual relations:

- their understanding of the nature and character of sexual intercourse;
- their understanding of the reasonably foreseeable consequences of sexual intercourse (including their knowledge, even if at a basic level) of the risks of pregnancy and sexually transmitted diseases;
- the kind of relationship they have (for example, if there is a power imbalance);
- the pleasure (or otherwise) which they experience in the relationship;
- their ability to choose or refuse intercourse;
- their ability to communicate their choice to their partner.

A lack of capacity to consent formally to sexual relations does not necessarily mean that the relationship should be prevented or discouraged, as long as the individuals appear willing and content for it to continue. If, however, there are signs that either person is being sexually abused or exploited, the matter should be immediately reported to the police so the protection given by the criminal law can be brought into effect (see **Chapter 12**). The matter should also be reported to the relevant authority so that steps can be taken to instigate relevant 'Safeguarding Adult Procedures' and take other appropriate action under the 'No Secrets' guidance issued by the Department of Health.[24]

If, on the other hand, it is felt that the individuals enjoy and benefit from a non-abusive sexual relationship, consideration must be given to promoting their best interests in terms of providing contraception, and protection from infection (see **Chapter 13** on treatment of adults who lack capacity to consent). In some limited cases, it may be appropriate for an application to be made to the Court of Protection to authorise the person's sterilisation if this seems to be in their best interests (see Court of Protection Practice Direction 9E, at **Appendix D**).

It should also be noted that (as discussed above) the Court of Protection is expressly precluded from consenting on behalf of an incapacitated person to entry into sexual relations.[25]

11.4 CAPACITY TO CONSENT TO MARRIAGE OR TO ENTER INTO A CIVIL PARTNERSHIP

The case of *Sheffield City Council* v. *(1) E and (2) S*[26] sets down the test to determine whether a person has capacity under English law to marry or to enter into a civil partnership (in the interests of space, references in this and the following sections are, where relevant, to marriage alone).

In the *E* case, a declaration was sought by a local authority to prevent a young lady 'E' with spina bifida and an alleged mental age of 13 from marrying or associating with S. A preliminary issue arose to whether the appropriate test for E's capacity to marry was:

(a) whether E was capable of understanding the nature of a marriage contract generally; or

(b) whether E had the capacity to understand the implications of marriage to S.

Mr Justice Munby reviewed the authorities before coming to the following conclusions:

- The question is not whether a person has capacity to marry X rather than Y. The relevant question is whether the person has capacity to marry. If the person does, it is not necessary to show that she also has capacity to take care of her own person and property.

- The question of whether a person has capacity to marry is quite distinct from the question of whether the person is wise to marry: either wise to marry at all, or wise to marry X rather than Y, or wise to marry X.
- In relation to a proposed marriage the only question for the court is whether the person has capacity to marry. The court has no jurisdiction to consider whether it is in the person's best interests to marry or to marry X.
- In relation to the question of whether the person has capacity to marry the law remains as it was set out by Singleton LJ in *In the Estate of Park deceased, Park* v. *Park*:[27]

> . . . [was the person] capable of understanding the nature of the contract into which he was entering, or was his mental condition such that he was incapable of understanding it? To ascertain the nature of the contract of marriage a man must be mentally capable of appreciating that it involves the responsibilities normally attaching to marriage. Without that degree of mentality, it cannot be said that he understands the nature of the contract.

- It is not enough that someone appreciates that they are taking part in a marriage ceremony or understands its words. They must understand the nature of the marriage contract. This means that they must be mentally capable of understanding the duties and responsibilities that normally attach to marriage.

There are thus, in essence, two aspects to the inquiry whether someone has capacity to marry:

- Does the person understand the nature of the marriage contract (which is, in essence, a simple one, which does not require a high degree of intelligence to comprehend)?[28]
- Do they understand the duties and responsibilities that normally attach to marriage?

The duties and responsibilities that normally attach to marriage were summarised in the *E* case as follows:

> Marriage, whether civil or religious, is a contract, formally entered into. It confers on the parties the status of husband and wife, the essence of the contract being an agreement between a man and a woman to live together, and to love one another as husband and wife, to the exclusion of all others. It creates a relationship of mutual and reciprocal obligations, typically involving the sharing of a common home and a common domestic life and the right to enjoy each other's society, comfort and assistance.

In addition to the points that arise from the *E* judgment, three further points should be noted:

- Given the nature of marriage, capacity to consent to marriage will normally require the capacity to consent to sexual intercourse.[29]
- The question of capacity arises in a somewhat different context in respect of marriages contracted under Sharia law, where the capacity to consent

110

of the spouses is not relevant, and a marriage can therefore validly be contracted even if one or both would lack capacity under the tests set out above. However, such a marriage may not be recognised as such under the English civil law.[30]

- As set out above (see **11.2**), the Court of Protection is expressly precluded from consenting on behalf of an incapacitated person to marriage or sexual relations.[31]

The effect of mental disorder

Under the Matrimonial Causes Act 1973 a marriage is voidable (that is, it can be annulled at the request of one of the parties) if at the time of marriage either party, although capable of giving valid consent, was suffering (whether continuously or intermittently) from mental disorder of such a kind or to such an extent as to be unfitted to marriage.[32] The mental disorder (now defined under the Mental Health Act 1983 (s.1(2), as amended) as 'any disorder or disability of the mind') may be of the petitioner or the respondent. There is no other way under English law for a marriage to be declared void but by bringing a petition under the 1973 Act.[33]

To succeed in proving that a marriage is voidable on a petition under the 1973 Act, the petitioner must show that the person's mental disorder made them incapable of living in a married state and carrying out the duties and obligations of marriage. Merely being difficult to live with will not make a person unfitted to marriage.[34] This provision of the Act is not strictly a 'capacity test'.

Proceedings must be started within three years of the marriage, although the court may give leave for proceedings to be instituted at a later date. The court may not grant a decree in the case of a voidable marriage if the petitioner, knowing it was open to them to have the marriage avoided, had acted in such a way that the respondent reasonably believed an annulment would not be sought and it would be unjust to grant a decree (for example, in a marriage for companionship only). A doctor asked to give an opinion about such an application should consult with those who know the party who is alleged to be mentally disordered and who have professional experience of the mental disorder.

What objections can be raised to a proposed marriage?

Sometimes a relative or carer of a person whose capacity to consent to marriage may be in doubt is concerned about a proposed marriage. There are a number of ways in which an objection to a pending marriage can be made. A person can:

- dissent from the publication of banns in the case of a church wedding;
- enter a caveat against the granting of a special or common licence;

- enter a caveat with a superintendent registrar or the Registrar General (in the case of register office or other civil weddings).

If a caveat is entered, this puts the registrar or clergyman on notice and creates a requirement to investigate and enquire into the capacity of both parties to marry. The burden of proof of lack of capacity falls on the person seeking to oppose the marriage. The registrar may ask for a doctor's report or a report from a social worker, a psychologist, or other person who can give information about the ability of the parties to understand the contract of marriage. The tests to be applied are those stated above and it is important that a full consultation with all relevant people takes place. Any opinion should be based on a sound knowledge of the person, their way of life and any relevant religious or cultural facts. It is not necessary for the person to appreciate or consider every aspect of a marital relationship.

When one or both parties proposing to marry has a learning disability it may be important to suggest counselling and advice about the practical aspects of marriage including financial, housing and legal matters. Information and advice about sexuality and sexual relations, including contraception, may be useful and should be made available. A judgment about the person's capacity to understand the responsibilities of parenthood may also be relevant here. For example, additional support may be needed to avoid the possibility of future proceedings under the Children Act 1989 resulting in a child being removed from the person's care.

Implications of marriage

As discussed above, the level of understanding required for marriage is less than that required for some other decisions or transactions. Since the status of marriage affects other matters, such as financial affairs and rights to property, subsequent arrangements may need to be made for a person who lacks capacity to manage these affairs (see **Chapter 5**). In particular, marriage revokes any existing will made by either of the parties. If one person lacks testamentary capacity (see **6.2**) an application may need to be made to the Court of Protection for a statutory will to be made on the person's behalf (see **6.8**).[35]

11.5   CAPACITY TO SEPARATE, DIVORCE OR DISSOLVE A CIVIL PARTNERSHIP

There are no reported court decisions concerning the capacity required to separate, divorce or dissolve a civil partnership except *Calvert (Litigation Guardian)* v. *Calvert* in the Ontario Court[36] (such decisions are regarded as persuasive but not binding on UK courts). In this case, Mr and Mrs Calvert married in 1979, having signed a pre-marriage contract which said that any property owned by one of the parties at the date of the agreement would not be a family asset. Mrs Calvert managed a clothes shop and Mr Calvert owned a substantial farm in Ontario. Each of them had a grown-up child from a previous marriage. Nine years later Mr Calvert sold the farm for a small fortune. Despite his enormous wealth, he paid his wife a minimal allowance and begrudged the small gifts she sent to her daughter and grandchildren. In 1993, Mrs Calvert began to show signs of the early stages of Alzheimer's disease. A few months later, however, she made her own arrangements to visit her daughter in Calgary and travelled alone. She never returned to her husband and instructed a lawyer to start divorce proceedings. Mr Calvert contended that his wife did not have capacity to form the intention to separate from him and thus was not entitled to any financial settlement. Relying on *In the Estate of Park, deceased, Park* v. *Park*[37] (see **11.4**) the Ontario Court recognised the varying levels of capacity required to make different decisions and gave separate consideration to the three levels of capacity relevant to that case: capacity to separate, capacity to divorce, and capacity to instruct counsel in connection with the divorce. The judge held as follows:[38]

> Separation is the simplest act requiring the lowest level of understanding. A person has to know with whom he or she does or does not want to live. Divorce, while still simple, requires a bit more understanding. It requires the desire to remain separate and to be no longer married to one's spouse. It is the undoing of the contract of marriage. . . . If marriage is simple, divorce must be equally simple . . . the mental capacity required for divorce is the same as required for entering into a marriage. . . . The capacity to instruct counsel involves the ability to understand financial and legal issues. This puts it significantly higher on the competence hierarchy. . . . While Mrs Calvert may have lacked the ability to instruct counsel, that did not mean she could not make the basic personal decision to separate and divorce.

Chapter 8 provides further details on capacity to litigate and on the appointment of a 'litigation friend' or 'next friend' to act on behalf of people involved in legal proceedings (such as divorce proceedings) who lack capacity to instruct a legal representative. Further advice about capacity to instruct a solicitor is given in **2.1**.

Finally, it should be noted that the Court of Protection is expressly precluded from consenting on behalf of an incapacitated person to either a decree of divorce being granted (or a dissolution order being made in relation to a civil partnership) on the basis of two years' separation.[39]

11.6 CONCLUSION

It is important to remember the rights of people with a disability or illness when considering their ability to make their own decisions. As noted above, the United Nations Declaration of Human Rights states that all adults are of equal value and have a right to the same freedoms. One of these rights for adults is the right to express their sexuality and to participate in family life.

NOTES

1. European Convention on Human Rights, Article 8.
2. Ibid: Article 12.
3. *Local Authority X* v. *MM & Anor* [2007] EWHC 2003 (Fam): paras. 88–9; *X City Council* v. *MB & Ors* [2006] EWHC 168 (Fam), [2006] 2 FLR 968 at para. 84. However, the House of Lords has since cast doubt on some aspects of Mr Justice Munby's approach in these cases in the common law context: *R* v. *C* [2009] UKHL 42, at paras. 24–27 (see also **Chapter 12**).
4. Children Act 1989, s.1.
5. Ibid: s.8.
6. Mental Capacity Act 2005, ss.15 and 16.
7. Ibid: s.27.
8. *Re GC* [2008] EWHC 3402 (Fam) (unreported), paras 14, 26–27 (see **www.wiki-mentalhealth.co.uk**).
9. *Re SA (A Local Authority)* v. *HA & Ors* [2005] EWHC 2942 (Fam).
10. Ibid: para. 77.
11. *Ealing LBC* v. *KS and Ors* [2008] EWHC 636 (Fam) at para. 148.
12. *Re MB (Medical Treatment)* [1997] 2 FLR 426, 437.
13. *Local Authority X* v. *MM & Anor* [2007] EWHC 2003 (Fam): para. 78.
14. In *MM* Mr Justice Munby accepted (at para. 74) the Official Solicitor's submission that there was no relevant distinction between the *Re MB* test and that set down at s.3(1) of the Mental Capacity Act 2005.
15. Mental Capacity Act 2005, s.3(1)(d).
16. Mr Justice Wood at para. 148 of *Ealing LBC* v. *KS & Ors* [2008] EWHC 636 (Fam).
17. *Re SA* [2005] EWHC 2942 (Fam).
18. Sexual Offences (Amendment) Act 2000, s.1.
19. *Local Authority X* v. *MM & Anor* [2007] EWHC 2003 (Fam) at paras. 88–9.
20. *R* v. *C* [2009] UKHL 42 at 27, casting doubt on the earlier decision in MM at paras. 86–7 which itself relied upon *Sheffield City Council* v. *E* [2004] EWHC 2808 (Fam), [2005] Fam 326, at paras. 83–5. The proposition set down in *R* v. *C* has yet to be examined in the context of proceedings before the Court of Protection, but is likely to be shortly after this work is published. Given the unambiguous statement by Baroness Hale to this end in *R* v. *C* the authors consider the Court of Protection is likely to adopt the 'issue specific' test set down in *R* v. *C*.
21. *Local Authority X* v. *(1) MM (2) KM* [2007] EWHC 2003 (Fam) at paras. 86–7, relying on *X City Council* v. *MB, NB and MAB (by his litigation friend the Official Solicitor)* [2006] EWHC 168 (Fam), [2006] 2 FLR 968, at para. 84.
22. *Local Authority X* v. *(1) MM (2) KM* [2007] EWHC 2003 (Fam) at paras. 94–5.
23. *X City Council* v. *MB, NB and MAB* [2006] EWHC 168 (Fam), [2006] 2 FLR 968 at para. 8; *The London Borough of Ealing* v. *KS, LU, MHAS and SR* [2008] EWHC 636 (Fam); and *R* v. *C* [2009] UKHL 42 at paras. 27, 29.
24. Department of Health (2000) *No Secrets: Guidance on developing and implementing multi-agency policies and procedures to protect vulnerable adults from abuse.* Department of Health (see **www.dh.gov.uk**). During 2008–2009, the Government undertook a review of 'Safeguarding Adults' procedures and the *No Secrets* guidance, but has not yet published its response (see **www.wales.gov.uk**). The Welsh Assembly conducted a similar review of the equivalent guidance *In Safe Hands* in Wales.
25. Mental Capacity Act 2005, s.27(1)(b).
26. *Sheffield City Council* v. *(1) E and (2) S* [2004] EWHC 2808 (Fam), [2005] Fam 326.

27. *In the Estate of Park deceased, Park* v. *Park* [1954] P 112 at p 127.
28. *Sheffield City Council* v. *(1) E and (2) S* [2004] EWHC 2808 (Fam), [2005] Fam 326 at para. 141(viii), quoting Sir James Hannen in *Durham* v. *Durham* (1885) 10 PD 80 at p 81.
29. *(1) KC (2) NC* v. *City of Westminster Social and Community Services & Anor* [2008] EWCA Civ 198 at para. 32 per Thorpe LJ: 'physical intimacy is an ordinary consequence of a celebration of a marriage.'
30. *(1) KC (2) NC* v. *City of Westminster Social and Community Services & Anor* [2008] EWCA Civ 198.
31. Mental Capacity Act 2005, s.27(1)(a).
32. Matrimonial Causes Act 1973, ss.11–13.
33. *(1) KC (2) NC* v. *City of Westminster Social and Community Services & Anor* [2008] EWCA Civ 198 at para. 21.
34. *Bennett* v. *Bennett* [1969] 1 WLR 430.
35. *Re Davey (Deceased)* [1980] 3 All ER 342.
36. *Calvert (Litigation Guardian)* v. *Calvert* (1997) 32 OR (3d) 281.
37. *In the Estate of Park deceased, Park* v. *Park* [1954] P 112.
38. *Calvert (Litigation Guardian)* v. *Calvert* (1997) 32 OR (3d) 281: 293f, 294g and 298e–g.
39. Mental Capacity Act 2005, s.27(1)(c)–(d).

CHAPTER 12

Capacity to consent: the criminal law and sexual offences

12.1 INTRODUCTION

This chapter deals with the approach of the criminal law towards sexual behaviour and people who are at risk of abuse because of mental health problems or learning disability. The primary focus of the criminal law is upon non-consensual conduct; however, it is recognised that people with mental health problems or learning disabilities have an equal right to express their sexuality and to form relationships commensurate with their ability to give consent[1] (see **Chapter 11**). The role of the law is to police the line between the legitimate right of all adult persons to engage in sexual relationships and the need to protect vulnerable people from exploitation and abuse.

The law in this area underwent significant changes following the passage of the Sexual Offences Act 2003, which clarified a previously confused and overlapping series of provisions.

12.2 THE SEXUAL OFFENCES ACT 2003

Consent and mental capacity

A person consents to engaging in sexual activity if they agree by choice and have the freedom and capacity to make that choice.[2] There is no definition of capacity in the Sexual Offences Act 2003, but the Court of Appeal has made clear that the common law and criminal tests of capacity to consent to sexual activity should be essentially the same.[3] Reference should therefore also be made to **11.3** where the common law approach is discussed. In addition, the 2003 Act states that a person may lack capacity to consent not just on the common law grounds, but 'for any other reason'.[4] In an appeal to the House of Lords, Baroness Hale of Richmond has held that these words:

> ... are clearly capable of encompassing a wide range of circumstances in which a person's mental disorder may rob them of the ability to make an autonomous choice, even though they may have sufficient understanding of the information relevant to making it.[5]

The 2003 Act made clear that, where the defendant intentionally deceived the victim as to the nature or purpose of the sexual act, or intentionally induced the complainant to consent to it by impersonating someone known personally to the complainant, consent will conclusively be presumed to be absent.[6] A series of situations are also set out in the Act where it will be presumed that no consent exists unless there is evidence to the contrary. These include situations of violence, fear of violence, or unlawful detention, and where the complainant had been asleep or unconscious or unable to communicate whether or not they consented, due to physical disability.[7]

Rape

In respect of those complainants aged 13 above, rape is the intentional penetration with the penis of the vagina, anus or mouth of a complainant without their consent.[8] To be guilty of rape, the perpetrator must lack a reasonable belief that there is consent. There can in any event be no defence of consent where sexual activity is alleged in relation a child aged under 13 years.

The burden of proving the absence of consent lies upon the prosecution. It is important to bear in mind the following general principles, which apply in all cases where rape is alleged and whatever the capacity of the complainant.

- The vital ingredients of the offence are penetration (including partial penetration) and lack of consent.
- The use of force is not required.
- The victim's consent may be vitiated by threat, duress, or inculcation of fear.
- Mere submission does not equate to consent although the dividing line may on occasion be difficult to draw.[9]

Where a complainant is able to give evidence, the jury will accordingly have to decide whether they did in fact consent whatever their difficulties. A particular problem may arise where the complainant is not capable of giving a lucid or coherent account of events. Expert evidence of limited mental age, social functioning or intellectual impairment will not necessarily prove lack of consent apart from in the most extreme cases.

In such cases where it may be difficult to provide conclusive evidence of rape, the prosecution may have to grasp the nettle and seek a conviction for an alternative lesser offence (see below).[10] The consequence may be that on conviction, a perpetrator faces a markedly lower sentence than his behaviour might otherwise justify.

Other sexual offences: general

The previous offence of indecent assault has been replaced by several different offences:

- assault by penetration[11] (with a separate offence relating to child victims[12]);
- sexual assault[13] (or sexual assault on a child under 13[14]); and
- causing a person to engage in sexual activity without consent[15] (or causing or inciting a child under 13 to engage in sexual activity[16]).

The Sexual Offences Act 2003 deals with the question of consent in the same way as consent for rape (see above).

Sexual offences against people with mental disorders or learning disabilities

The Sexual Offences Act 2003 introduced a range of offences specific to victims with a 'mental disorder' or 'learning disability'. The offences are committed by sexual activity with,[17] or in the presence or view of,[18] someone who is unable to refuse because they are suffering from mental disorder or learning disability, or by intentionally causing or inciting such a person to engage in sexual activity.[19] It must be the case that the defendant knows, or could reasonably be expected to know, of the victim's condition and that this is likely to make them unable to refuse. A separate group of sections in the Sexual Offences Act 2003 created offences where the same situations are brought about by inducement, threat or deception.[20]

Where some capacity to consent exists there may still be the potential for exploitation. Even where a person with mental health problems or a learning disability fully understands and consents to a sexual relationship there may be grounds for the criminal law to intervene for public policy reasons should that person be under the professional care of the other person involved.

To provide for such circumstances, the 2003 Act created a final group of offences which can be committed only by 'care workers'.[21] This term is defined to include workers in NHS bodies, independent medical agencies, care homes, community homes, voluntary homes, and children's homes, independent clinics, and independent hospitals, who have had or are likely to have regular face-to-face contact with the victim in the course of their employment.[22] It also includes those who, whether or not in the course of employment, provide care, assistance, or services to the victim in connection with the victim's learning disability or mental disorder, where they have regular face-to-face contact with the victim.

12.3   GIVING EVIDENCE IN COURT

Assisting the vulnerable witness

Even if a person with mental health problems or a learning disability is able to provide a witness statement as to an alleged assault upon them, giving evidence to a court may be more difficult for them than for other witnesses. The legal process can be intimidating or confusing enough to potential witnesses who have full capacity. For someone with learning disabilities or other mental disorder it may be practically impossible. For such a witness the terms used by lawyers and the purpose of specific questions may cause such bewilderment that the ends of justice may be difficult to achieve.

The need to offer effective support and assistance in giving evidence to those who may be particularly vulnerable was addressed in Part II of the Youth Justice and Criminal Evidence Act 1999. A lack of ability to understand and communicate may in due course be met by the making of a 'special measures direction'. This will enable the witness to receive assistance from an intermediary in explaining questions and communicating answers 'so far as is necessary to enable them to be understood by the witness or person in question'.[23]

Witnesses are eligible for this assistance[24] if they suffer from a mental disorder within the meaning of mental health legislation (the Mental Health Act 1983)[25] or otherwise have 'significant impairment of intelligence and social functioning'. The purpose of providing the assistance is to preserve the 'quality' of the witness's evidence in terms of its 'completeness, coherence and accuracy'.[26]

The presence in court of the alleged abuser may provide a powerful disincentive for a witness to give an account of what took place. Legislation now permits the giving of evidence by pre-recorded video tape and cross-examination via a video link, thereby avoiding the need for direct confrontation of complainant and accused.[27]

The absent witness

If a witness is unable to give evidence, consideration may be given to having their witness statement read to the court instead,[28] subject to strict rules. For present purposes, the most relevant rules are:

1. The witness is 'unfit to be a witness' by reason of 'bodily or mental condition'.[29]
2. The witness, through fear, does not give (or continue to give) oral evidence in the proceedings, either at all or in connection with the subject matter of the statement.[30] If an application is made to introduce evidence under this rule, the application will only be granted if it is considered by the trial judge to be in the interests of justice so to do.[31]

Whatever the difficulties, a prosecution may in certain circumstances proceed in the absence of the complainant's evidence provided that 'consent' is not the primary issue. In those circumstances it may be practically impossible to secure a conviction. Where a complainant's consent is not material (as in the offences against people with mental disorders or learning disabilities discussed at **12.2**) then the essential requirement will be evidence to prove that sexual touching or interference took place combined with proof of the condition of the complainant.

12.4 CONCLUSION

The rights of disabled people to make their own decisions, to express their sexuality and to participate as fully as possible in family life remain profoundly important. Whether the criminal law appears to strike the correct balance between the protection of people at risk of abuse on the one hand, and an unduly paternalistic and authoritarian stance upon the other, will doubtless depend upon the circumstances of each individual case.

NOTES

1. The right to private life, of which intimate sexual activity forms a part, is protected by Article 8 of the European Convention on Human Rights.
2. Sexual Offences Act 2003, s.74.
3. *R* v. *C* [2008] EWCA Crim 1155, relying on the observations of Mr Justice Munby in *Local Authority X* v. *(1) MM (2) KM* [2007] EWHC 2003 (Fam): paras. 88–9; *X City Council* v. *MB, NB and MAB (by his litigation friend the Official Solicitor)* [2006] EWHC 168 (Fam), [2006] 2 FLR 968, at para. 84. However, the House of Lords has since cast doubt on some aspects of Munby J's approach in the common law context: *R* v. *C* [2009] UKHL 42, at paras. 24–27. As matters stand it is not entirely clear, therefore, whether the observations of the Court of Appeal in *R* v. C remain good. Once the Court of Protection has had cause to consider this question (as it will do in the near future) the authors consider it likely the Court will conclude that the criminal and common law do indeed march in step in this regard.
4. Sexual Offences Act 2003, s.30(2)(a).
5. *R* v. *C* [2009] UKHL 42, at para. 25.
6. Sexual Offences Act 2003, s.76.
7. Ibid: s.75.
8. Ibid: s.1(1).
9. See *R* v. *Olugboja* [1981] 3 WLR 585: 585–93.
10. For instance an offence under s.30(1) of the Sexual Offences Act 2003, which makes it an offence to undertake sexual activity with a person with a mental disorder impeding capacity to make a choice, or an alternative charge under s.34(1) that agreement was obtained by means of inducement, threat or deception of a person with a mental disorder. The House of Lords has commented that alternative charges would enable the judge to explain the various concepts and relate them to the evidence: *R* v. *C* [2009] UKHL 42, at para. 32.
11. Sexual Offences Act 2003, s.2(1).
12. Ibid: s.6(1).
13. Ibid: s.3(1).
14. Ibid: s.7(1).
15. Ibid: s.4(1).
16. Ibid: s.8(1).
17. Ibid: s.30(1).
18. Ibid: ss.32(1) and 33(1).
19. Ibid: s.31(1).
20. Ibid: ss.34–37.
21. Ibid: ss.38–41.
22. Ibid: s.42.

23. Youth Justice and Criminal Evidence Act 1999, s.29(2).
24. Ibid: s.16(2).
25. Defined as 'any disorder or disability of the mind' in the Mental Health Act 1983, s.1(2), as amended by the Mental Health Act 2007.
26. Youth Justice and Criminal Evidence Act 1999, ss.16(1)(b) and 16(5).
27. Ibid: ss.24 and 27.
28. Criminal Justice Act 2003, s.116(1).
29. Ibid: s.116(2)(b).
30. Ibid: s.116(2)(e).
31. Ibid: s.116(4).

CHAPTER 13

Capacity to consent to and refuse medical treatment and procedures

13.1   Medical procedures
13.2   The need for patient consent
13.3   Capacity to consent to medical procedures
13.4   Care and treatment for adults who lack capacity to consent
13.5   Attorneys and deputies
13.6   Advance statements and decisions
13.7   Confidentiality

13.1   MEDICAL PROCEDURES

This Chapter deals with the capacity of adult patients to consent and refuse consent to medical procedures. 'Adult' in this context means those aged 18 and over, since special considerations apply to young people aged 16-17 (see **3.7**). 'Medical procedures' means examination, diagnostic tests, and medical or nursing interventions (including treatment) aimed at alleviating a medical condition or preventing its deterioration. Therapies designed to rehabilitate patients are also included in this definition. Medical research and innovative treatments are considered in **Chapter 14**.

13.2   THE NEED FOR PATIENT CONSENT

In almost all case where a patient has the capacity to make a decision as to whether they wish to be treated or examined, legally and ethically, their informed consent is required before the treatment or examination can proceed (the main exceptions apply in mental health legislation and in cases of infectious disease). Where a person lacks capacity to consent, the Mental Capacity Act 2005 (the 'MCA') sets out the circumstances when the proposed treatment and any necessary procedures can be carried out in that person's best interests. This Chapter describes those provisions as they apply to decisions about medical procedures (see also **Chapter 3** where key concepts of the MCA are explained).

In general, it is unlawful and unethical to treat a person who is capable of understanding and willing to know, without first explaining the nature of the procedure, its purpose and implications, and obtaining that person's consent.[1] While there is no statute setting out the legal principles relating to consent, case law has established that touching a patient without valid consent may constitute the criminal offence of battery or the tort of trespass and, except in cases where the law permits otherwise (see below), any treatment given to a competent person without their consent will be unlawful.[2]

It is also a fundamental principle of the MCA that 'A person is not to be treated as unable to make a decision unless all practicable steps to help him to do so have been taken without success.'[3] Therefore every effort must be made to explain all relevant information relating to the proposed treatment in terms the patient can understand, offering appropriate support and other aids to communication.

Some people, however, may consent to treatment while choosing not to be given the full details of their diagnosis or treatment. This 'uninformed' consent is nevertheless valid so long as they had the option of receiving more information. People who refuse information must still be provided with some basic information, since without this they cannot make a valid choice to delegate responsibility for treatment decisions to the doctor. The amount of basic information depends upon the individual circumstances, the severity of the condition, and the risks associated with the treatment. Doctors must seek to strike a balance between giving the patient sufficient information for a valid decision, and respecting the patient's wish not to know.

An exception to the requirement for informed consent from competent adults is treatment provided under mental health legislation, which permits, in certain circumstances, the provision of treatment without consent and sometimes contrary to a patient's competent refusal. The detailed treatment provisions of mental health legislation are beyond the scope of this book, but the areas of interface between the Mental Health Act 1983 and the MCA are outlined in **1.3**.

Also, **Chapter 15** discusses important safeguards (known as the deprivation of liberty safeguards (DoLS)) introduced into the MCA in relation to individuals who lack capacity to consent who are being given care and treatment in conditions that amount to their being deprived of their liberty within the meaning of Article 5(1) of the European Convention on Human Rights.

13.3   CAPACITY TO CONSENT TO MEDICAL PROCEDURES

Application of the MCA principles to capacity to consent to or refuse treatment

The assessment of an adult patient's capacity to make a decision about their own healthcare or medical treatment is a matter for the professional judgement of the doctor or healthcare professional proposing the intervention, applying the statutory test of capacity set out in the MCA (see 'the test of capacity' below).

The assessment of capacity relates to the particular healthcare decision at the time the decision needs to be made. The starting point is the presumption that every adult has capacity to make their own healthcare decisions unless there is evidence to the contrary. All practicable steps must be taken to help the person make the decision for themselves, including explaining in a way the patient is most likely to understand, the nature and effects of the proposed treatment, the purpose for which it is needed, the likelihood of success and any alternative forms of treatment. The possible consequences to the patient of receiving, or not receiving, the proposed treatment should also be explained, including any likely side effects. Even where there is a welfare attorney or deputy with authority to make healthcare decisions, every effort should be made to help the patient make the decision for themselves since the patient's capacitous decision takes prioity. If the patient does not accept the doctor's advice, and therefore makes what the doctor considers to be an unwise decision, it should not automatically be assumed that the patient lacks capacity to make that decision (see 'capacity to refuse medical procedures' below).

The test of capacity

The test of capacity of an adult patient to give consent to medical treatment is the test of capacity set out in the MCA.[4] The test in the MCA enshrines, with some modifications, the common law tests established in the judgments of *Re C (Adult: Refusal of Medical Treatment)*[5] and *Re MB (Medical Treatment)*[6] which continue to provide assistance in applying the MCA test of capacity in relation to decisions about medical procedures.

The reasons why capacity is in doubt should be recorded in the medical record, as should details of the assessment process and its findings. The more serious the decision, the more formal the assessment of capacity may need to be. In cases of doubt or in relation to complex or major decisions, it might also be advisable to refer to another professional with experience of assessing mental capacity in relation to the needs of the specific individual, such as a psychiatrist, psychologist, speech and language therapist or social worker. Situations where a professional opinion may be required are set out in the MCA Code of Practice.[7] However, it would be inappropriate and impractical for professional experts to be routinely called upon in situations when assessments using the statutory test of capacity can be carried out by other decision-makers. Responsibility rests with the person intending to make the decision on behalf of the incapacitated adult or to carry out the proposed medical procedure, not with the professional advising about capacity.

Practical aspects of assessment of capacity are discussed in more detail in **Part IV** of this book.

Capacity to refuse medical procedures

Competent adults have a right to refuse medical diagnostic procedures or treatment for reasons which are 'rational, irrational or for no reason'. This principle was established in the case of *Sidaway* v. *Board of Governors of the Bethlem Royal Hospital and Maudsley Hospital*[8] and upheld in subsequent cases. The person's capacity to refuse must be assessed in relation to the specific treatment proposed and the gravity of the decision to be made, applying the statutory test of capacity under the MCA.[9] It is irrelevant whether refusal is contrary to the views of most other people if it is broadly consistent with the individual's own value system. The case law described below relating to refusal of medical treatment before the MCA came into effect will continue to be of assistance in applying the statutory test.

The principle that an adult patient has the right to refuse treatment as long as they have been properly informed of the implications and can make a free choice was affirmed by the Court of Appeal in the case of *Re T (Adult: Refusal of Treatment)*.[10] That case concerned a 20-year-old woman who was injured in a road traffic accident when she was 34 weeks pregnant. She had been brought up as a Jehovah's Witness and on admission to hospital refused a blood transfusion after having spent a period of time alone with her mother. T gave birth to a stillborn child, after which her condition became critical. Her father and boyfriend applied for a court declaration that it would not be unlawful to administer a transfusion without her consent.

The Court of Appeal held that for such a refusal to be valid, doctors had to be satisfied that the patient's capacity to decide had not been diminished by illness, medication, false assumptions or misinformation, or that the patient's will had not been overborne by another's influence. In T's situation, it was held that the effect of her condition, together with misinformation and her mother's influence rendered her refusal of consent ineffective.

What is important about this case, notwithstanding the outcome for the individual patient, is the general affirmation of a patient's absolute right, properly exercised, to refuse medical treatment. Lady Justice Butler Sloss confirmed that:

> A man or woman of full age and sound understanding may choose to reject medical advice and medical or surgical treatment either partially or in its entirety. A decision to refuse medical treatment by a patient capable of making the decision does not have to be sensible, rational or well considered . . .[11]

A doctor's legal duties in relation to a patient's refusal of treatment were discussed in the same case when the Master of the Rolls stated:

> Doctors faced with a refusal of consent have to give very careful and detailed consideration to the patient's capacity to decide at the time when the decision was made. It may not be the simple case of the patient having no capacity because, for example, at that time he had hallucinations. It may be the more difficult case of a

temporarily reduced capacity at the time when his decision was made. What matters is that the doctors should consider whether at that time he had a capacity which was commensurate with the gravity of the decision which he purported to make. The more serious the decision, the greater the capacity required. If the patient had the requisite capacity, they are bound by his decision. If not, they are free to treat him in what they believe to be his best interests.[12]

These principles were applied by the Court of Appeal in *Re MB*, relating to the capacity of a pregnant woman with acute needle phobia to refuse the medical procedures necessary for a Caesarian section (specifically venepuncture). Lady Justice Butler-Sloss concluded:[13]

A competent woman who has the capacity to decide may, for religious reasons, other reasons, for rational or irrational reasons or for no reason at all, choose not to have medical intervention, even though the consequence may be the death or serious handicap of the child she bears, or her own death. . . . Although it might be thought that irrationality sits uneasily with competence to decide, panic, indecisiveness and irrationality in themselves do not as such amount to incompetence, but they may be symptoms or evidence of incompetence. The graver the consequences of the decision, the commensurately greater the level of competence is required to take the decision.

In a subsequent case, *Ms B* v. *An NHS Hospital Trust*, concerning the right of a severely disabled woman to refuse to be kept alive through artificial ventilation, doctors were reminded that:[14]

If there are difficulties in deciding whether the patient has sufficient mental capacity, particularly if the refusal may have grave consequences for the patient, it is most important that those considering the issue should not confuse the question of mental capacity with the nature of the decision made by the patient, however grave the consequences. The view of the patient may reflect a difference in values rather than an absence of competence and the assessment of capacity should be approached with this firmly in mind. The doctors must not allow their emotional reaction to or strong disagreement with the decision of the patient to cloud their judgment in answering the primary question whether the patient has the mental capacity to make the decision. . . . The treating clinicians and the hospital should always have in mind that a seriously physically disabled patient who is mentally competent has the same right to personal autonomy and to make decisions as any other person with mental capacity.

The courts have recommended that, in cases of uncertainty about the capacity of the patient to consent to or refuse treatment, doubt should be resolved as soon as possible by doctors within the hospital or NHS Trust or by other normal medical procedures. Under the MCA, in cases of doubt that cannot be resolved locally, application should be made to the Court of Protection for a declaration as to the patient's capacity to consent to treatment and, if the Court determines that the patient lacks capacity, whether the proposed treatment is in the patient's best interests (see **Appendix C**).

13.4   CARE AND TREATMENT FOR ADULTS WHO LACK CAPACITY TO CONSENT

Best interests

If it has been established that an adult lacks the capacity to consent to a treatment or intervention it is a fundamental principle of the MCA that any act done or decision made for or on behalf of that person, must be done, or made, in his best interests.[15] This requirement has been established for some time at common law.[16] The only exceptions to this principle are where the person has previously made an advance decision refusing medical treatment which is both valid and applicable in the current circumstances (see **13.6**) and in some situations where the incapacitated person is involved in research (see **Chapter 14**).

Given the enormous variety of decisions governed by the MCA, it is understandable that the Act avoids giving a definition of best interests, providing instead a checklist of factors[17] that must always be taken into account (see **3.6**), including when deciding whether a particular medical procedure is in the person's best interests.

A crucial part of any best interests assessment will involve a discussion with those close to the person lacking capacity as they will often have important information about what would be in the person's best interests. The MCA provides a list of those who should be consulted, where it is practical or appropriate to do so, including:

- anyone previously named by the person as someone they wish to be consulted;
- anyone engaged in caring for the person or interested in their welfare; and
- any donee or deputy appointed for the person.[18]

There may be circumstances, such as in an emergency, or for very routine decisions, such as taking a temperature, where consultation might not be possible or appropriate on every occasion when a procedure is carried out. It is important, however, not to take short cuts when making an assessment of best interests. Health professionals involved in making best interests determinations should ensure that a record is kept of the process by which the person's best interests were worked out.

Where decisions need to be made about serious medical treatment (described further below) or where a healthcare decision may involve a decision about where the person should live in the longer-term (such as a placement in a care home or hospital), and there is no one available who fits into the above categories who it is appropriate to consult in an assessment of best interests, an Independent Mental Capacity Advocate (IMCA) must be appointed to represent and support the incapacitated person.[19]

Acts in connection with care and treatment

If an adult patient temporarily or permanently lacks capacity to consent to medical treatment, no other person can consent on the patient's behalf unless they are acting under the authority of a registered health and welfare LPA or under a deputyship authorised by the Court of Protection (see **13.5**). Some forms of medical treatment are lawful, however, even in the absence of the patient's consent or consent given by an attorney or deputy. The legal basis for carrying out a medical procedure in such cases is that:

- the procedures are 'necessary'; and
- in the patient's best interests.

Under the common law, it has been clear that where an adult lacks capacity to make decisions on their own behalf, health interventions will be lawful where there is both a necessity to act, and any action is in the best interests of the incapacitated adult.[20]

The MCA has clarified this aspect of the common law by making provision to allow carers (both informal and paid carers) and health professionals to carry out certain acts in connection with the personal care, healthcare or treatment of a person lacking capacity to consent to those acts.[21] These provisions give legal backing, in the form of protection from liability, for actions which are essential for the personal welfare or healthcare of people lacking capacity to consent to having things done to or for them. Such actions can be performed as if the person concerned had capacity and had given consent, provided that:

- the decision-maker has a reasonable belief that the individual lacks capacity; and
- the act, decision or treatment is in the best interests of the incapacitated person.[22]

In these circumstances, it is not necessary to obtain any formal powers or authority to act. However, anyone involved in the person's care or interested in their welfare including any attorney, should be consulted in determining whether the proposed treatment is in their best interests. This legal protection applies not only to an episode of treatment itself, but also to those ancillary procedures that are necessary, such as conveying a person to hospital. All interventions under these provisions must be in accord with the principles of the MCA (see **Chapter 3**). The MCA also makes clear that anyone acting unreasonably, negligently or not in the person's best interests could forfeit protection from liability.

This protection given to decision-makers to act in connection with care or treatment does not permit them to give a treatment contrary to a person's valid and applicable advance decision to refuse treatment[23] (see **13.6** below). Similarly a decision by an attorney acting under a registered health and welfare LPA or a court appointed deputy (see **13.5**) would also take precedence, so long as they have authority to make the decision in question.

Restraint

The MCA sets out the limits of the protection offered to decision-makers carrying out acts in connection with a person's care or treatment.[24] In particular, it places conditions on the protection offered to healthcare professionals under s.5 of the MCA when they perform an act which 'restrains' a person who lacks capacity.[25] Restraint is defined by the MCA as the use or threat of force to secure the doing of an act which the person resists, or restriction of the person's liberty of movement, whether or not they resist.[26]

As a general rule, any act that is intended to restrain a person lacking capacity will not attract protection from liability, unless the following conditions are met:

- the person using restraint must reasonably believe that it is necessary to do the act in order to prevent harm to the person lacking capacity; and
- the restraint is proportionate to the likelihood of the person suffering harm and to the seriousness of that harm.

In such circumstances, only the minimum necessary force or intervention may be used and for the shortest possible duration. Careful records must be kept of the reasons justifying any use of restraint. The point at which excessive restraint may be construed as depriving a person of their liberty is discussed further in **Chapter 15**.

Serious medical treatment

The MCA provides additional safeguards where 'serious medical treatment' may be required for someone who lacks capacity to consent to it. Serious medical treatment includes the provision, withholding or withdrawal of treatment in circumstances where:

- if a single treatment is proposed, there is a fine balance between the likely benefits and the burdens to the patient and the risks involved; or
- a decision between a choice of treatments is finely balanced; or
- the proposed treatment is likely to have serious consequences for the patient.[27]

Where a serious medical treatment decision is contemplated for a person lacking capacity to consent, and there is no one available to consult as to the person's best interests other than those engaged in providing professional or paid care or treatment for that person, the NHS body responsible for the patient's treatment must ensure that advice is sought from an IMCA.

Before the MCA came into force, the courts had decided that some medical treatment decisions were so serious that each case should be taken to court so that a declaration of lawfulness could be made. This procedure has continued under the MCA. Practice Direction 9E (reproduced at **Appendix D**) issued under the Court of Protection Rules 2007 describes the procedures to be followed and sets out the types of cases which should be brought before the court.[28]

13.5 ATTORNEYS AND DEPUTIES

Lasting Powers of Attorney

One of the innovations introduced by the MCA is the creation of a power of attorney enabling competent adults to nominate another individual or individuals to make health and welfare decisions on their own behalf when they lose the capacity to make those decisions. This power, known as a Lasting Power of Attorney ('LPA'), replaces the Enduring Power of Attorney ('EPA'), which relates only to property and affairs. There are two types of LPA:

- one relating to a person's property and affairs;
- the other for decisions relating to a person's health and welfare.

An LPA relating to health and welfare decisions can only be used when the individual lacks the capacity to make a relevant decision covered by the LPA. This Chapter offers a further explanation of the health and welfare LPA as it affects decisions relating to medical treatment.

Chapter 5 considers the property and affairs LPA and **5.3** also includes further details about capacity to create an LPA and the procedures for creating and registering an LPA, which apply to both property and affairs LPAs and health and welfare LPAs.

Creating and registering a health and welfare LPA

In order to create an LPA an individual must be aged 18 or over and have the necessary mental capacity in accordance with the statutory test of capacity set out in the MCA.[29] An LPA has to be created by completing a form prescribed by regulations[30] and it must state that it applies to health and welfare decisions at such a time as the individual creating the LPA loses the capacity to make those decisions. An LPA must also contain a certificate, signed by an independent person chosen by the donor (either someone who has known the donor for at least two years or a professional), stating that in their opinion, at the time the LPA is created, the donor understands what is involved in making an LPA and has not been put under any undue pressure to do so (see **5.3** for further details). A health and welfare LPA does not give the attorney authority to refuse life-sustaining treatment unless it is explicitly stated on the LPA form. The donor creating the LPA can also set a variety of conditions and limits on the exercise of the powers given to the attorney.

An LPA cannot be used until it has been registered with the Public Guardian. It can be registered before or after the individual loses capacity. An application to register can be made either by the donor, or by the attorney(s) and is intended to be a straightforward process, but the procedures involved can take several weeks. Early registration is therefore advisable to ensure the LPA is valid at the time it needs to be used. Health professionals should check that a health and welfare LPA has been registered before accepting the attorney's authority to make healthcare decisions.

Scope of a health and welfare LPA

Where an individual requires medical treatment, and has been assessed as lacking capacity to consent, an attorney (also called a donee) nominated to act on their behalf under a health and welfare LPA can consent or refuse medical treatment on behalf of the person lacking capacity. An attorney with relevant powers to make health care decisions must be consulted, unless an emergency makes consultation impossible. There are, however, a number of restrictions imposed on the attorney:

- The scope of the attorney's authority to make health and/or welfare decisions must be specified in the LPA. In particular, it is important to check whether the LPA authorises the attorney to make decisions about life-sustaining treatment.
- Any act or decision made under the LPA must be in the incapacitated person's best interests and be in keeping with the other guiding principles of the MCA.
- An attorney cannot consent to treatment if the donor has capacity at the time to make the decision for themselves.
- If the donor has previously made a valid advance decision refusing the specified treatment (see **13.6** below), the advance decision takes priority unless the LPA was made after the advance decision and gives the attorney the right to consent or refuse the proposed treatment.
- While LPAs can relate to treatment for a mental disorder, the attorney's decision can be overridden if the individual is being treated under mental health legislation.

When a health professional has a significant concern relating to decisions taken under the authority of an LPA about serious medical treatment, or believes that an attorney is not acting in the best interests of the person lacking capacity, the case can be referred to the Public Guardian or the Court of Protection for review and adjudication.

Deputies appointed by the Court of Protection

In rare circumstances where on-going healthcare decisions may need to be made on behalf of a person lacking capacity to consent, the Court of Protection may make an order appointing a welfare deputy to make those specific decisions on the person's behalf (see **Appendix C**). The deputy could be a family member or a professional, as decided by the Court. The Court must be satisfied that appointing a deputy is in the person's best interests and the court order will set out the extent of the deputy's powers (which should be as limited in scope and duration as is practicable in the circumstances). The deputy can only make decisions that the person lacks capacity to make, and must always act in the person's best interests. The MCA (s.20(5)) makes clear that a welfare deputy has no power to make decisions about life-sustaining treatment – such matters must be referred to the Court.

13.6 ADVANCE STATEMENTS AND DECISIONS

Adults who are capable of making decisions about their medical treatment can, if properly informed of the implications and consequences, also make anticipatory decisions about their preferences for medical treatment, intending them to apply at a later stage when they lose capacity to make such decisions for themselves. The legal enforceability of one type of anticipatory decision, known as 'an advance decision to refuse medical treatment' has been established by the common law and given statutory authority by the MCA.[31] Other advance statements of wishes and preferences, as opposed to advance refusals of treatment, have a different status in common law[32] and are also now reflected in the MCA.

Advance statements

Advance statements are declarations whereby people with capacity make known their views on what should happen if they lose the capacity to make decisions for themselves. Advance statements can take a variety of forms ranging from general lists of life values and preferences, to specific requests for or refusals of treatment. They can be written or oral. The purpose of an advance statement is to provide a means for people to exercise their autonomy by expressing an opinion in advance about future medical treatments or any other aspect of their life. Individuals who are aware of a terminal illness or a progressive condition which may effect their capacity often seek to discuss with their doctors how they wish to be treated. Advance statements enable a structured discussion and recording of the person's views to take place.

A person is presumed to have capacity to make an advance statement about medical treatment unless it is proven otherwise. The test for capacity to make an advance statement about medical treatment is similar to that for capacity to make a contemporaneous medical decision, that is the statutory test of capacity in the MCA.[33] The treatment options, their implications and alternatives should be broadly understood. Individuals should also be aware that circumstances and medical science may develop in unforeseen ways in the interval before the advance statement becomes operative. Also, if the statement concerns a positive consent or request for certain treatments, the person making the statement should be aware that doctors are not legally bound by such a consent or request.

Doctors cannot be compelled to carry out treatments which are contrary to their clinical judgement or to guidance given by the National Institute for Health and Clinical Excellence. However, under the MCA such wishes and preferences set out in an advance statement are treated as indicative of the person's past wishes and feelings, and in written form as relevant written statements, which must be considered when determining whether any proposed treatment is in the incapacitated person's best interests[34] (see **3.6**). The BMA has published a detailed guidance note on aspects of drafting, storage and implementation of advance statements.[35]

Advance decisions to refuse medical treatment

An advance decision to refuse medical treatment enables adults aged 18 or over to refuse specified medical treatment at a future time when they lack capacity to give or refuse consent to that treatment.[36] An advance decision cannot be used to give effect to an unlawful act, such as euthanasia or assisted suicide or any intervention with the express aim of ending life.[37]

Making an advance decision

Except for decisions relating to life-sustaining treatment (see below), the MCA does not impose any particular formalities concerning the making of advance decisions to refuse treatment. For other types of treatment, both written and oral decisions are acceptable and legally valid, so long as they are supported by appropriate evidence to confirm their existence, validity and applicability (see below). Although there is no prescribed form for making an advance decision, the MCA Code of Practice recommends that it is helpful to include:[38]

- Full details of the person making the advance decision, including date of birth, home address and any distinguishing features (in case healthcare professionals need to identify an unconscious person, for example)
- The name and address of the person's GP and whether they have a copy of the document
- A statement that the document should be used if the person ever lacks capacity to make treatment decisions
- A clear statement of the decision, the treatment to be refused and the circumstances in which the decision will apply
- The date the document was written (or reviewed)
- The person's signature (or the signature of someone the person has asked to sign on their behalf and in their presence)
- The signature of the person witnessing the signature, if there is one (or a statement directing somebody to sign on the person's behalf).

Where an advance decision is made verbally, health professionals should make a record in the patient's notes. This record should include:

- a note that the decision should apply if the person loses capacity to make the decision in the future;
- a note of the decision and the treatment to be refused and the circumstances in which the refusal is to apply;
- details of somebody who was present when the refusal was made.

Advance decision refusing life-sustaining treatment

The MCA imposes additional safeguards in relation to advance decisions refusing life-sustaining treatment.[39] Life-sustaining treatment is defined by the MCA as treatment which a person providing healthcare regards as necessary to sustain life.[40] It is for the doctor to assess whether a treatment is life-sustaining in each particular situation and this will depend not only on the type of treatment, but also on the particular circumstances in which it may be prescribed. An advance decision to refuse life-sustaining treatment must meet the following requirements:[41]

- It must be made in writing. If the person is unable to write, someone must write it down for them.
- The person must sign it in the presence of a witness, or if unable to sign it, the person must direct someone to sign it on their behalf, in their presence and in the presence of a witness.
- The witness must sign it, or acknowledge his signature, in the person's presence.
- The document must include a clear, specific written statement from the person making the advance decision that the advance decision is to apply to the specific treatment even if life is at risk.

The MCA distinguishes between 'treatment' and 'care', so it would seem that 'basic care' is not categorised as treatment and can therefore not be refused in an advance decision (but this is an area which may yet be tested out in court). Basic care includes warmth, shelter, hygiene measures to maintain body cleanliness, and the offer of food and water by mouth. Under s.5 of the MCA this basic and essential care can be carried out in the best interests of the person lacking capacity to consent. However, an advance decision may apply to the refusal of artificial nutrition and hydration (ANH) which has been recognised as medical treatment[42] (as opposed to feeding which is not medically assisted).

Although it is not compulsory, it is advisable that anyone drawing up an advance decision discusses it with a health professional such as a GP. It is generally recognised that one of the difficulties with advance decisions is ensuring that they will apply to the particular circumstances that may arise. Discussion with individuals with experience of the progress of certain diseases can help to ensure greater compatibility between the terms of an advance decision and the circumstances that are likely to arise.

Legal aid is not generally available for making an advance decision, but the Lord Chancellor has authorised public funding for legal help to be made available for people aged 70 or over and for disabled people[43] who are financially eligible and who wish to make an advance decision.[44]

Safeguards relating to advance decisions

The MCA also provides important statutory safeguards concerning the making and implementation of advance decisions to refuse treatment.[45] It must first be shown that an advance decision to refuse medical treatment as provided for by the MCA[46] actually exists. This includes meeting the following requirements:

- The advance decision must be made by a person of 18 years or older with the mental capacity to make it, in accordance with the MCA test of capacity (see above and **Chapter 3**).
- It must specify, in lay terms if necessary, the specific treatment to be refused and the particular circumstances in which the refusal is to apply.

In order for the refusal to be legally effective at the time when it is proposed to carry out or continue treatment, an advance decision to refuse it must also be both valid and applicable to the proposed treatment. A healthcare professional who provides treatment to a patient who has made an advance decision refusing it will not be legally liable unless the advance decision is both valid and applicable to that treatment at the material time.

Validity

Events or circumstances that would make an advance decision invalid are:

- that the person has withdrawn the decision while they still had capacity to do so;
- that, after making the advance decision, the person has created a lasting power of attorney conferring authority on the attorney to give or refuse consent to the treatment specified in the advance decision; or
- that the person has done something which is clearly inconsistent with the advance decision remaining their fixed decision (for example, an advance decision refusing blood products made by a former Jehovah's Witness was held to be invalid after she became betrothed to a Muslim and had indicated she would live by the principles of that faith[47]).

Applicability

An advance decision to refuse treatment is not applicable if:

- the maker still has capacity to give or refuse consent to the treatment in question at the time the treatment is proposed;

- the proposed treatment is not the treatment specified in the advance decision;
- the circumstances are different from those set out in the advance decision; or
- there are reasonable grounds for believing that circumstances have now arisen (such as the development of new treatments or changes in personal circumstances) which were not anticipated by the person when making the advance decision and which would have affected the advance decision had they anticipated them at the time.

How long ago the advance decision was made and whether it has been regularly reviewed and updated to take account of changed circumstances will be key factors in determining its applicability. For example, an advance decision made by a woman who later becomes pregnant may not be applicable during her pregnancy unless the implications for her unborn child have been specifically addressed in the advance decision.

Effect of an advance decision

An advance decision to refuse treatment, which is both valid and applicable to the treatment in question, is as effective as a contemporaneous refusal of a person with capacity to make that decision.[48] Any health professionals who knowingly provide treatment contrary to the terms of a valid and applicable advance decision may be liable to a claim for damages for battery or possibly to criminal liability for assault. However, treatment providers would be protected from liability if they:

- were unaware of the existence of an advance decision; or
- were not satisfied that an advance decision existed which was both valid and applicable to the particular treatment.

In an emergency or where there is doubt about the existence, validity or applicability of an advance decision, doctors can provide treatment that is immediately necessary to stabilise or to prevent a deterioration in the patient until the legality of the advance directive can be established. The MCA Code of Practice gives some further guidance on this subject:[49]

> Healthcare professionals should not delay emergency treatment to look for an advance decision if there is no clear indication that one exists. But if it is clear that a person has made an advance decision that is likely to be relevant, healthcare professionals should assess its validity and applicability as soon as possible. Sometimes the urgency of treatment decisions will make this difficult.

Where there are genuine doubts (i.e. if health professionals are not 'satisfied') about the existence, validity or applicability of the advance decision, treatment can be provided without incurring liability, so long as that treatment is in the person's best interests.

Conversely, health professionals who follow the terms of what they believe to be a valid and applicable advance decision to refuse treatment would not be liable for the consequences of withholding or withdrawing treatment specified in the advance decision, so long as they can demonstrate that their belief was reasonable.[50] Having a 'reasonable belief' requires less certainty than being 'satisfied' that a valid and applicable advance decision exists and can only be based on the information and evidence available at the time.

Where a patient is subject to detention and compulsory treatment under the Mental Health Act 1983, an advance refusal relating to treatment provided for the mental disorder for which compulsory powers have been invoked will not be binding, although the treating professional should take the advance decision into account when deciding whether the proposed treatment is in the person's best interests. In accordance with the MCA principles, they must also consider whether there are any other treatment options available that are less restrictive. An agreed advance treatment plan for mental health conditions can be helpful and would represent a kind of advance statement, although it would not be binding if the person was subject to compulsory powers. However, if the person is being treated on a voluntary basis for a mental disorder, an advance decision refusing specific types of treatment for that disorder should be respected in the same way as any other advance decision, so long as it is valid and applicable to the treatment in question.

If there is disagreement about an advance decision relating, for example, to its validity or applicability, an application can be made to the Court of Protection for clarification. While a decision is being sought from the court, health professionals are entitled to provide any necessary treatment required either to sustain life, or to prevent a serious deterioration in the patient's health, until such time as the court makes a decision.

13.7 CONFIDENTIALITY

All patients have rights to privacy and to control information about themselves. In the case of people with impaired capacity, however, the principle of confidentiality must be balanced with protection of their interests and, in very exceptional cases, the protection of others.

Individual decision-making is always to be encouraged but inevitably carers and other people close to the individual lacking capacity will be involved in helping them to make decisions or, so far as they are permitted to do so in their daily care of the individual, in taking decisions on the person's behalf. Increasing provision of care in the community means that more people have responsibilities in the provision of support for individuals lacking capacity. Nevertheless, unnecessary or widespread disclosure of identifiable personal health information without the individual's valid consent should not be a routine or automatic response.

Patients lacking capacity do not forfeit the right to control disclosure of personal information. They can authorise or prohibit the sharing of information about themselves if they broadly understand the implication of so doing. On the other hand, confidentiality is never absolute and, as with all patients, health professionals may have to consider breaching confidentiality, even in the face of a direct refusal by the patient, if there is a likelihood of foreseeable harm to the patient or others resulting from their refusal.

Disclosure without consent should normally be restricted to the sharing of essential information with those who have a demonstrable need to know it in order to provide proper care and supervision of the individual[51] (see also **2.2**). In exceptional cases, there may be justification for the disclosure of information to other people to whom the incapacitated person may represent a potential health hazard, having first informed the patient of the intention to disclose. An example might be of a mentally incapacitated HIV-infected person embarking upon an intimate relationship. There can be no justification, however, of routine disclosure of a person's HIV-status to people whose contact with the HIV-infected person contains no element of risk of infection.

As yet, there is no statute on the subject of confidentiality. In 2009, the statutory body for doctors, the General Medical Council, revised its guidance on confidentiality to include the following statements:[52]

> When making decisions about whether to disclose information about a patient who lacks capacity, you must:
>
> (a) make the care of the patient your first concern
> (b) respect the patient's dignity and privacy, and
> (c) support and encourage the patient to be involved, as far as they want and are able, in decisions about disclosure of their personal information.
>
> ...
>
> If a patient who lacks capacity asks you not to disclose personal information about their condition or treatment, you should try to persuade them to allow an appropriate person to be involved in the consultation. If they refuse, and you are convinced that it is essential in their best interests, you may disclose relevant information to an appropriate person or authority. In such a case you should tell the patient before disclosing the information and, if appropriate, seek and carefully consider the views of an advocate or carer. You should document in the patient's record your discussions and the reasons for deciding to disclose the information.
>
> You may need to share personal information with a patient's relatives, friends or carers to enable you to assess the patient's best interests. But that does not mean they have a general right of access to the patient's records or to have irrelevant information about, for example, the patient's past healthcare. You should also share relevant personal information with anyone who is authorised to make decisions on behalf of, or who is appointed to support and represent, a mentally incapacitated patient.
>
> If you believe that a patient may be a victim of neglect or physical, sexual or emotional abuse, and that they lack capacity to consent to disclosure, you must give

information promptly to an appropriate responsible person or authority, if you believe that the disclosure is in the patient's best interests or necessary to protect others from a risk of serious harm. If, for any reason, you believe that disclosure of information is not in the best interests of a neglected or abused patient, you should discuss the issues with an experienced colleague. If you decide not to disclose information, you should document in the patient's record your discussions and the reasons for deciding not to disclose. You should be prepared to justify your decision.

The Data Protection Act 1998 (the 'DPA'), which came into force in March 2000 also provides individuals with a number of important rights to ensure that personal information and in particular, sensitive personal information such as health information is processed fairly and lawfully. Processing includes holding, recording, using and disclosing information. The Act applies to all forms of media, including paper and images. The DPA's requirement that all data processing must be 'fair' and 'lawful' means that all patients including those who lack capacity must know when and what information about them is being processed. The processing itself must be lawful: this includes meeting common law confidentiality obligations, which are likely to require patient or nominated proxy consent to be obtained. The DPA also requires organisations that wish to process identifying information to use the minimum of information necessary and to retain it only for as long as it is needed for the purpose for which it was originally collected.

The MCA Code of Practice provides advice on access to information about individuals lacking capacity.[53] The Code states that relevant factors as to whether someone else might be able to see information relating to an individual who lacks capacity include:[54]

- whether the person requesting the information is acting as an agent, such as a court appointed deputy or attorney for the individual;
- whether disclosure is in the best interests of the person who lacks capacity;
- what type of information has been requested.

Further information and guidance on confidentiality and disclosure of health information is available from the BMA[55] and from the Department of Health.[56]

NOTES

1. There are various sources of guidance on consent to medical treatment which are summarised in British Medical Association (2008) *Consent Tool Kit 4th edition*, British Medical Association. Available online at **www.bma.org.uk**. See also Department of Health (2009) Reference Guide to Consent for Examination or Treatment 2nd edition. Department of Health. Available online at **www.dh.gov.uk**.
2. See for example, *In re F (Mental Patient: Sterilisation)* [1990] 2 AC 1; and *Ms B* v. *An NHS Hospital Trust* [2002] EWHC 429 (Fam).
3. Mental Capacity Act 2005, s.1(3).

4. The statutory test of capacity in ss.2 and 3 of the Mental Capacity Act 2005, taking account of the principles in s.1. (See also **Chapter 3**.)
5. *Re C (Adult: Refusal of Medical Treatment)* [1994] 1 All ER 819.
6. *Re MB (Medical Treatment)* [1997] 2 FLR 426.
7. Department of Constitutional Affairs (2007) *Mental Capacity Act 2005 Code of Practice*, TSO, paras. 4.51–4.54 (See **www.publicguardian.gov.uk**).
8. *Sidaway* v. *Board of Govenors of the Bethlem Royal Hospital and Maudsley Hospital* [1985] AC 871.
9. The statutory test of capacity in ss.2 and 3 of the Mental Capacity Act 2005, taking account of the principles in s.1. (See also **Chapter 3**.)
10. *Re T (Adult: Refusal of Treatment)* [1992] 4 All ER 649.
11. Ibid: at 664j.
12. Ibid: at 661h.
13. *Re MB (Medical Treatment)* [1997] EWCA Civ 3093 at 30.
14. *Ms B* v. *An NHS Hospital Trust* [2002] EWHC 429 (Fam) at 100.
15. Mental Capacity Act 2005, s.1(5).
16. *Re F (Mental Patient: Sterilisation)* [1990] 2 AC 1, HL.
17. Mental Capacity Act 2005, s.4(1)–(7).
18. Ibid: s.4(7).
19. Sections 35–41 of the MCA established the Independent Mental Capacity Advocate (IMCA) service, to provide a statutory right to advocacy services for particularly vulnerable people who lack capacity to make certain serious decisions. See **www.dh.gov.uk**.
20. *Re F (Mental Patient: Sterilisation)* [1990] 2 AC 1, HL.
21. Mental Capacity Act 2005, s.5.
22. Ibid: s.5(1).
23. Ibid: s.5(4).
24. Ibid: s.6.
25. Ibid: s.6(1)–(3).
26. Ibid: s.6(4).
27. For the meaning of 'serious medical treatment', see Mental Capacity Act (Independent Mental Capacity Advocates) (General) Regulations 2006, SI 2006/1832, reg.4. A similar definition is used in Court of Protection Practice Direction 9E reproduced in **Appendix D**.
28. Court of Protection Practice Direction 9E Applications relating to serious medical treatment. (Supplements Part 9 of the Court of Protection Rules 2007 (SI 2007/1744)). Paragraphs 5–6.
29. The statutory test of capacity in ss.2 and 3 of the MCA, taking account of the principles in s.1. (See also **Chapter 3**.)
30. Available from the Office of the Public Guardian (**www.publicguardian.gov.uk**). The LPA forms were revised in 2009, and these revised forms prescribed in the Schedule to the Lasting Powers of Attorney, Enduring Powers of Attorney and Public Guardian (Amendment) Regulations 2009 (SI 2009/1884) must be used after 1 October 2009.
31. Mental Capacity Act 2005, ss.24–26.
32. *R (on the application of Burke)* v. *General Medical Council* [2005] All ER (D) 445, [2005] EWCA Civ 1003.
33. The statutory test of capacity in ss.2 and 3 of the MCA, taking account of the principles in s.1. (See also **Chapter 3**.)
34. Mental Capacity Act 2005, s.4(6)(a).
35. British Medical Association (2007) Advance Decisions and Proxy Decision-Making in Medical Treatment and Research, British Medical Association. Available online at **www.bma.org.uk**.

36. Mental Capacity Act 2005, s.24(1).
37. Ibid: s.62.
38. Department of Constitutional Affairs (2007) *Mental Capacity Act 2005 Code of Practice*, TSO. Paragraph 9.19.
39. Mental Capacity Act 2005, ss.25(5)–(6).
40. Ibid: s.4(10).
41. Ibid: ss.25(5)–(6).
42. *Airedale NHS Trust* v. *Bland* [1993] AC 789, [1993] 1 All ER 821.
43. As defined in s.1 of the Disability Discrimination Act 1995.
44. Legal Services Commission (2009) *Legal Services Commission Manual*, TSO. Paragraph 28.2 of Section 28 'Mental Capacity Act 2005' in Volume 3, Funding Code Decision Making Guidance – Other Guidance. Available at **www.legalservices.gov.uk**.
45. Mental Capacity Act 2005, ss.24–25.
46. Ibid: s.24.
47. *HE* v. *A Hospital NHS Trust* [2003] EWHC 1017 (Fam).
48. Mental Capacity Act 2005, s.26(1).
49. Department of Constitutional Affairs (2007) *Mental Capacity Act 2005 Code of Practice*, TSO, para. 9.56.
50. Mental Capacity Act 2005, s.26(3).
51. *R (on the application of A S)* v. *Plymouth City Council and C* [2002] EWCA Civ 388.
52. General Medical Council (2009) *Confidentiality: Guidance for Doctors*, General Medical Council, paras.59–63.
53. Department of Constitutional Affairs (2007) *Mental Capacity Act 2005 Code of Practice*. TSO. Chapter 16.
54. Ibid: para. 16.8.
55. There are various sources of guidance on confidentiality which are summarised in British Medical Association (2008) *Confidentiality and disclosure of health information tool kit*, British Medical Association. Available online at **www.bma.org.uk**.
56. Department of Health (2003) *Confidentiality: NHS Code of Practice*. Department of Health. See **www.dh.gov.uk**.

CHAPTER 14

Capacity to consent to research and innovative treatment

14.1   INTRODUCTION

A person's capacity to consent to research is assessed in the same way as capacity to consent to medical treatment (see **Chapter 13**) according to the statutory test in the Mental Capacity Act 2005 (the 'MCA').[1] This Chapter considers the capacity of adults to agree to participate in research and the safeguards required for the involvement of adults who lack the capacity to consent. The legality of enrolling adults in certain closely regulated forms of research has been established by two recent pieces of legislation:

- clinical trials for pharmaceutical products for human use are regulated by the Medicines of Human Use (Clinical Trials) Regulations;[2] and
- all other forms of research involving incapacitated adults are regulated by the MCA.

14.2   CAPACITY TO CONSENT TO RESEARCH

Consent is a key concept in research. Generally speaking, an individual's ability to give valid consent or refusal to participate in research will depend on that person's ability to understand what the research entails, provided they have been given sufficient information to make an informed decision. The degree of detail required will vary according to the needs of the individual patient and the complexity of the procedures involved. In particular, assessment of risk (an important part of decision-making in all forms of health care) takes on greater significance in this sphere, since research can involve a degree of uncertainty as to the risks involved. Ultimately, where the patient has capacity, it is for the patient to decide whether to participate in research and take the associated risks, having been given the fullest possible information.

An adult is deemed to lack capacity to give a valid consent to research if at the material time that person is unable, because of an impairment of, or disturbance in the functioning of, the mind or brain:

- to understand the information relevant to the decision
- to retain that information
- to use or weigh that information as part of the process of making the decision, or
- to communicate his decision (whether by talking, using sign language or any other means)[3]

For further information about the statutory test of capacity under the MCA, see **Chapter 3**.

14.3   RESEARCH GOVERNANCE: THE ETHICAL FRAMEWORK

Although both the MCA and the Medicines of Human Use (Clinical Trials) Regulations provide different regimes for the regulation of research, there is considerable common ground between them. The World Medical Association's Declaration of Helsinki[4] sets internationally recognised standards for ethical governance of research, which are reflected in both legal instruments. A summary of the basic principles in the Declaration of Helsinki in relation to the involvement of incapacitated adults is given below:

- Incompetent adults should not be included in research which is unlikely to benefit them personally, unless the research is necessary to promote the health of the population represented by the potential research subjects; this research cannot instead be performed on legally competent persons; and it involves only minimal risk and minimal burden to participants.
- Where an adult is incapable of giving consent, the responsible researcher must obtain informed consent from a legally authorised representative.
- Where an incompetent adult is capable of assenting to decisions about participation in research, this assent must be obtained, in addition to the consent of the legally authorised representative. Any dissent by the person should be respected.
- The research must be intended to provide knowledge relating to the condition or conditions that have contributed to the impairment of the individual's incapacity.

14.4   RESEARCH INVOLVING ADULTS WHO LACK CAPACITY

Ideally, all research subjects should give well informed and considered consent to participation but in practice research cannot be limited to people who are able to decide for themselves, since the effect would be to deprive people who lack capacity of proven therapies for the conditions which specifically affect them. The presence of a mental disorder or disability does not itself mean that an individual lacks the capacity to consent. As with all other areas where an individual's capacity may be in doubt, it is important to try and enhance as far as possible their decision-making capacity, and care must be taken in explaining in clear language the procedures and risks involved.

The legal framework

Until recently, the legality of enrolling incapacitated adults in research that could not reasonably be expected to provide a benefit to them was unclear. The coming into force of the Medicines for Human Use (Clinical Trials) Regulations in 2004, followed by the MCA in 2005, has clarified the situation. The aim of regulation is to balance the need to undertake research to ensure that innovative therapies can be developed which will benefit incapacitated individuals, and the need to protect them from potential abuse. Research on anonymised medical information or tissue is not included, but this is regulated either by the Data Protection Act 1998 or the Human Tissue Act 2004.

The Mental Capacity Act 2005

Apart from the exemptions of clinical trials and research on anonymised data, the MCA covers all research that is 'intrusive'.[5] Intrusive research is defined as research that would require the consent of a participant if they had capacity to consent. Although the MCA does not define research, the MCA Code of Practice[6] refers to the definition given by the Department of Health and National Assembly for Wales:[7]

> The attempt to derive generalisable new knowledge by addressing clearly defined questions with systematic and rigorous methods.

Under the MCA, research cannot include incapacitated adults unless it has first received the authorisation of an 'appropriate body':[8]

- In England, the 'appropriate body' must be a research ethics committee recognised by the Secretary of State.
- In Wales, the 'appropriate body' must be a research ethics committee recognised by the Welsh Assembly Government.

Further information about research ethics committees can be obtained from the NHS National Research Ethics Service.[9]

A research ethics committee can only approve a research project that involves a person who lacks the capacity to consent to involvement if the following requirements of MCA are met:[10]

1. The research must be connected to an impairing condition affecting the person or its treatment
2. There must be reasonable grounds for believing that research of comparable effectiveness cannot be carried out if the project has to be confined to, or only relate to, people who have capacity to consent to taking part.
3. The research must:

    (a) have the potential to benefit the person without imposing a burden that is disproportionate to the benefit, or

    (b) be intended to provide knowledge about the causes of the impairing condition, its treatment or about the care of people affected by the same or a similar condition.

Where research meets the requirement of 3(b) but not 3(a), the MCA imposes a number of additional requirements, specifically that there must be reasonable grounds for believing that:[11]

- the risk to the research subject is likely to be negligible;
- that anything done to, or in relation to, the research subject will not interfere with the person's privacy or freedom of action in a significant way;
- that anything done to, or in relation to, the research subject will not be unduly invasive or restrictive.

The kinds of research that are envisaged in this category might include research that focuses exclusively on medical records or on human tissue that has been collected for other purposes. It could also include observational research or discussion or interviews with carers about the kinds of services provided to the incapacitated person. It could also include taking samples, such as blood samples, for research purposes.

An appropriate body may not approve a research project involving the participation of a person lacking capacity until reasonable arrangements are in place for ensuring the safeguards in the MCA will be met.[12]

The MCA imposes a number of conditions that must be met to ensure the incapacitated person's interests are protected.[13] First, the researcher must make reasonable efforts to identify an individual (who is not acting in a professional capacity), who has been involved in the research subject's care or is interested in their welfare, and is prepared to act as a 'consultee'. This will ordinarily be a family member or someone close to the person. It could also be someone acting under an LPA or a court appointed deputy. If the researcher cannot identify a suitable person to act as a consultee, then the researcher must nominate someone independent of the research project, in accordance with the guidance jointly issued by the Secretary of State and the Welsh Ministers.[14] This is likely to be a professional such as a GP or a specialist providing care to the individual.

The researcher must provide the consultee with information about the project and ask for the consultee's opinion of:[15]

- whether the incapacitated person should take part in the research; and
- what the incapacitated person's wishes and feelings would be likely to be, if they had capacity to decide whether to take part in the project.

If at any time the consultee advises that the incapacitated person would not want to be involved, or to continue to be involved, in the research then the researcher must ensure that the incapacitated person is withdrawn from the research project. The individual may continue to receive any treatment they received as part of the research if the researcher has reasonable grounds for believing there would be a significant risk to the person's health if that treatment is withdrawn.

The MCA also provides additional safeguards in an emergency when urgent treatment is required in circumstances when it is not possible to carry out the necessary consultations.[16] The need for such procedures should be anticipated and set out in the research proposal.

Even where a consultee has agreed that an incapacitated person can take part in a research project, the MCA imposes a number of additional safeguards once the research has started. These are given below:[17]

(a) Nothing may be done to, or in relation to, the person who lacks capacity in the course of the research:
   (i) to which the person appears to object (except if what is being done is intended to protect that person from harm or to reduce or prevent pain or discomfort), or
   (ii) which would be contrary to any valid and applicable advance decision refusing relevant treatment or contrary to any other statement of wishes or preferences previously made by the person and not subsequently withdrawn.

(b) The interests of the research subject must be assumed to outweigh the interests of medical science and society.

(c) If the person lacking capacity indicates in any way that they wish to be withdrawn from the research, or if the researcher has reasonable grounds to believe that the requirements for approval[18] of the research are no longer met, the incapacitated adult must be removed from the research without delay.

(d) If the person lacking capacity is withdrawn for either reason in (c) above, he may continue to receive any treatment that he was receiving as part of the research if the researcher believes on reasonable grounds that withdrawal from that treatment would pose a significant risk to the person's health.

Loss of capacity during a research project

Transitional regulations have been drawn up under the powers of the MCA to make provisions for the protection of adults who initially consented to enrolment in a research project but have subsequently lost capacity while the research project is under way.[19] These transitional regulations apply to research projects started before 1 October 2007, where the research subject consented before 31 March 2008 to take part in the project. The regulations also only apply to tissue and data collected before the person lost capacity.

They do not cover any further interventions, such as collecting blood or tissue, that would require consent from a person with capacity, after the individual has lost capacity. Such interventions would need to be compliant with the general research provisions in the MCA. Where the transitional regulations do apply, the research involving incapacitated adults can only continue if the project has procedures in place to deal with individuals who lose capacity. These procedures must have been approved by a research ethics committee. As with all other research undertaken under the MCA, the researcher must also seek out or nominate a consultee, respect any advance decisions or past wishes where these are known, and ensure that the interests of the individual are put before those of science or society.

Medicines for Human Use (Clinical Trials) Regulations 2004

These regulations govern clinical trials in relation to medicinal products for human use. They govern research involving both those who have capacity to consent and those who do not. They also extend to research involving children. In addition to the principles set out under the clinical governance section above, the Medicines for Human Use (Clinical Trials) Regulations set out a number of principles that must apply to all clinical trials involving human participants, and a number of these are set out below:[20]

- Before the trial is initiated, foreseeable risks and inconveniences must have been weighed against the anticipated benefit for the individual trial subject and other present and future patients. A trial should be initiated and continued only if the anticipated benefits justify the risks.
- The rights, safety and well-being of the trial subjects shall prevail over the interests of science and society.
- Clinical trials shall be scientifically sound and guided by ethical principles in all their aspects.
- A trial shall be initiated only if an ethics committee and the licensing authority comes to the conclusion that the anticipated therapeutic and public health benefits justify the risks and may be continued only if compliance with this requirement is permanently monitored.

If a person lacking capacity is to participate in a clinical trial covered by these regulations, the consent of that person's 'legal representative' must first be given. The regulations define a legal representative[21] as either:

- a person close to the patient who is suitable to act as their legal representative and willing and able to do so; or
- (if there is no one available who is close to the patient) the doctor primarily responsible for the provision of treatment to them; or
- a person nominated by the relevant healthcare provider.

Clinical trials for medicinal products in emergency situations

On 12 December 2006 amendments to the Medicines for Human Use (Clinical Trials) Regulations came into force.[22] The amended regulations permit unconscious patients in emergency situations to be enrolled in clinical trials without prior consent, provided the research has been approved by an appropriate research ethics committee. The regulations also amend the mental capacity legislation in Scotland[23] to the same effect. Where the clinical trials do not relate to medicinal products, the research would be regulated by the MCA.

14.5   INNOVATIVE TREATMENT

Although the MCA covers the involvement of incapacitated adults in research, it does not make specific mention of innovative treatments. These are often an extension of usual treatments but they may expose the patient to a greater degree of risk than established procedures. An experienced surgeon, for example, may modify a particular surgical procedure for an individual patient if a superior outcome might be expected from the modification. Efforts should be made to inform patients, so far as they are able to understand, how and why the proposed treatment differs from the usual measures and the known or likely risks attached. They should also be given any relevant information about the success rate of the treating clinician.

Innovative treatments are usually a standard feature of medical practice and the fact that useful information may be gained in the process is seen as largely incidental, rather than part of medical research. However, any test by 'trial and error' obviously leaves patients in a vulnerable situation unless carefully monitored and will require high standards of informed consent. If carried out on someone lacking capacity to consent, any such intervention must be governed by the underlying principles of the MCA, including the requirement that it must be in the incapacitated person's best interests (see **Chapter 3**). Great care must be taken as exposing incapacitated patients to innovative therapies is likely to give rise to legal and ethical uncertainty. Where a doctor proposes a procedure which diverges substantially from accepted practice, involving an unknown or increased risk, it would be advisable to obtain in advance both expert scrutiny and legal advice as to the ethics and legality of the procedure. In some circumstances, it may be necessary to apply to a court for authorisation to carry out the procedure.

The search for effective treatment of Creutzfeldt Jakob Disease (CJD) provides an example of the need for court intervention. In December 2002, a court was asked to decide whether it would be lawful to provide treatment that had not been tested on human beings to two young patients who were thought to be suffering from variant CJD. Both patients, JS aged 18 and JA aged 16, lacked the capacity to make treatment decisions but their parents argued that it would be in their best interests to have the new therapy. The treatment had only been tested in a Japanese research project on rodents and dogs, but was soon to be given to Japanese patients with iatrogenic CJD. Although not expected to provide a cure, it was hoped that the treatment could improve patients' lives. The judge said that although the patients would not recover, the concept of 'benefit' to a patient suffering from variant CJD would encompass:[24]

> . . . an improvement from the present state of illness, or a continuation of the existing state of illness without deterioration for a longer period than might otherwise have occurred, or the prolongation of life for a longer period than might otherwise have occurred.

Given the possibility of some benefit being derived and the lack of any other alternative, it was held that this treatment would be in the best interests of both JS and JA and so could lawfully be provided.[25] Although this decision was made before the MCA came into force, it is likely that the Court of Protection would reach a similar decision, given that the innovative treatment was deemed to be in the overall best interests of the person lacking capacity to consent.

NOTES

1. The statutory test of capacity in ss.2 and 3 of the Mental Capacity Act 2005, taking account of the principles in s.1. (See also **Chapter 3**.)
2. Medicines for Human Use (Clinical Trials) Regulations 2004 (SI 2004/1031).
3. Mental Capacity Act 2005, s.3.
4. World Medical Association (1964) *Declaration of Helsinki*, World Medical Association (as subsequently amended: see **www.wma.net**).
5. Mental Capacity Act 2005, ss.30–34.
6. Department of Constitutional Affairs (2007) *Mental Capacity Act 2005 Code of Practice*, TSO, para. 11.2.
7. Department of Health (2005) *Research governance framework for health and social care* 2nd edition, Department of Health.
8. Mental Capacity Act 2005, s.30(1).
9. See **www.nres.npsa.nhs.uk**.
10. Mental Capacity Act 2005, ss.31(2)–(5).
11. Ibid: s.31(6).
12. Ibid: ss.32 and 33.
13. Ibid: s.32.
14. Department of Health and Welsh Assembly Government (February 2008) *Guidance on nominating a consultee for research involving adults who lack capacity to consent*, Department of Health.
15. Mental Capacity Act 2005, s.32(4).
16. Ibid: s.39(9).
17. Ibid: s.33.
18. The requirements are set out in s.31(2) to (7) of the Mental Capacity Act 2005.
19. Mental Capacity Act 2005 (Loss of Capacity During Research) (England) Regulations 2007 (SI 2007/679) and the Mental Capacity Act 2005 (Loss of Capacity During Research) (Wales) Regulations 2007 (SI 2007/837).
20. Medicines for Human Use (Clinical Trials) Regulations 2004 (SI 2004/1031), Sched. 1, Part 2, as amended by Medicines for Human Use (Clinical Trials) (Amendment) Regulations 2006 (SI 2006/1928), para. 27.

21. Ibid: Part 1, para. 2.
22. Medicines for Human Use (Clinical Trials) (Amendment) Regulations 2006 (SI 2006/1928).
23. Adults with Incapacity (Scotland) Act 2000.
24. *Simms* v. *Simms, PA* v. *JA (Also known as: A v. A, JS v. An NHS Trust)* [2003] 1 All ER 669, [2002] EWHC 2734 (Fam) at para. 57.
25. Ibid: para. 73.

CHAPTER 15

Capacity and the deprivation of liberty

15.1 INTRODUCTION

It might appear odd to have a chapter dedicated to the assessment of capacity to consent to arrangements which may mean that someone is deprived of liberty, but the question of such consent arises regularly in respect of people accommodated in care homes, nursing homes and in hospitals where they may be compliant but appear unable to consent to remaining there. Depending on the circumstances under which they are accommodated, difficult questions may arise as to whether they are deprived of their liberty within the meaning of Article 5 of the European Convention on Human Rights (ECHR). If they are deprived of their liberty and if this is not authorised[1] the deprivation of liberty may be unlawful under Article 5.

15.2 DEPRIVATION OF LIBERTY

The leading case concerning the meaning of deprivation of liberty in the context of people with a mental disorder is the *Bournewood* case.[2] The claimant, HL, was autistic with profound learning disabilities, and had no ability to consent to his admission to hospital. He was, however, admitted to hospital and kept there as an inpatient for treatment. He had restricted contact with his carers, and was kept sedated and under continuous supervision by nursing staff. Those responsible for his care indicated that, if he tried to leave, he would be prevented from doing so and he would only then be assessed with a view to detaining him under the Mental Health Act 1983. The European Court of Human Rights found that:

. . . in order to determine whether there has been a deprivation of liberty, the starting point must be the specific situation of the individual concerned and account must be taken of a whole range of factors arising in a particular case such as the type, duration, effects and manner of implementation of the measure in question. The distinction between a deprivation of, and restriction upon, liberty is merely one of degree or intensity and not one of nature or substance . . . the Court considers the key factor in the present case to be that the health care professionals treating and managing the applicant exercised complete and effective control over his care and movements . . . strict control over his assessment, treatment, contacts, and, notably, movement and residence . . . the concrete situation was the applicant was under continuous supervision and control and was not free to leave . . . it is not determinative whether the ward was 'locked' or 'lockable'.[3]

The unanimous decision of the European Court of Human Rights was as follows:

1. Mr HL had been deprived of his liberty contrary to Article 5(1) of the European Convention on Human Rights;
2. that detention was arbitrary and not in accordance with a procedure prescribed by law; and
3. the procedures available to Mr HL to challenge his detention did not comply with the requirements of Article 5(4) as there was no procedure under which the lawfulness of his detention could be reviewed and decided speedily by a court.

The Government accepted that changes in the law were required to ensure compliance with the ECHR. After a delay of a number of years, a new statutory regime has now been implemented to provide safeguards (described below) for those falling into the so-called 'Bournewood gap'. The Deprivation of Liberty Safeguards Code of Practice (the 'DoLS Code of Practice')[4] published to accompany the new regime provides some useful assistance with the question of whether a person is deprived of their liberty. Echoing the *Bournewood* decision, the DoLS Code of Practice provides that the difference between deprivation of liberty and restriction upon liberty is one of degree or intensity, and that it may be helpful to envisage a scale, which moves from 'restraint' or 'restriction' to 'deprivation of liberty'. Where an individual is on the scale will depend on the concrete circumstances of the individual and may change over time. The DoLS Code of Practice also sets out the following list of factors relevant to identifying whether steps taken in the person's care and treatment involve more than restraint and amount to a deprivation of liberty:[5]

- Restraint is used, including sedation, to admit a person to an institution where that person is resisting admission.
- Staff exercise complete and effective control over the care and movement of a person for a significant period.
- Staff exercise control over assessments, treatment, contacts and residence.
- A decision has been taken by the institution that the person will not be released into the care of others, or permitted to live elsewhere, unless the staff in the institution consider it appropriate.

- A request by carers for a person to be discharged to their care is refused.
- The person is unable to maintain social contacts because of restrictions placed on their access to other people.
- The person loses autonomy because they are under continuous supervision and control.

Finally, it should be noted that the MCA provides protection from liability for professionals and carers who carry out acts in connection with the care or treatment of a person lacking capacity to consent (see **Chapter 13**), including where restraint may be used to protect the person from harm, so long as certain conditions are met[6] (the definition of 'restraint' and the circumstances when it may be used are described at **13.4**). However, restraint is different in law to deprivation of liberty,[7] and the MCA itself does not set out where the dividing line is to be drawn, leading back to the questions set out above.

15.3 AUTHORISING A DEPRIVATION OF LIBERTY

As of 1 April 2009, it is possible for the deprivation of liberty of a person lacking capacity to consent to their care and treatment to be authorised under the MCA in one of three ways:

- by the Court of Protection exercising its powers to make personal welfare decisions under MCA;[8]
- in accordance with the authorisation scheme known as the DoLS set out in MCA[9] (see below);
- where it is necessary in order to give life-sustaining treatment or do any 'vital act'[10] while a decision is sought from the court.

If continues to be possible to authorise deprivation of liberty where a person falls under the provisions of the Mental Health Act 1983 and meets the criteria for detention under that Act, as well as under the inherent jurisdiction of the high court.

Space precludes a full discussion of the DoLS, but in very broad terms the authorisation scheme provides a regime whereby a PCT[11] or local authority (known as the 'supervisory body') can authorise the deprivation of liberty of an adult in a hospital or care home respectively, subject to the satisfaction of certain requirements (see below). Once authorisation has been granted, a representative is appointed for the person deprived of their liberty and a regular review process is carried out. Either the person being deprived of their liberty (if able to do so) or their representative may request a review at any time and both have the right to apply to the Court of Protection to challenge the authorisation or seek to vary it.[12]

15.4   CAPACITY AND THE DEPRIVATION OF LIBERTY

Personal welfare orders of the Court of Protection

If the question as to whether a person is being, or should be deprived of their liberty arises in the context of an application to the Court of Protection for a personal welfare order,[13] then the Court will need to be satisfied that the person lacks capacity to consent to the care and treatment provided for them, applying the test of capacity set down in MCA.[14] The Court must then decide whether it is in the person's best interests to be accommodated and cared for in conditions which amount to a deprivation of their liberty, after considering whether any less restrictive alternative might meet the person's needs.

Deprivation of liberty safeguards

If the question of deprivation of liberty arises in any other context, an application for authorisation must be made under the DoLS procedures, when additional considerations arise. The supervisory body must arrange for assessments to be carried out to determine whether the following six qualifying requirements are met:[15]

1.   Age – The person must be aged 18 or over.
2.   Mental health – The person must be suffering from mental disorder within the meaning of the Mental Health Act 1983 (as amended) which is 'any disorder or disability of the mind', including for these purposes, a learning disability, whether or not associated with abnormally aggressive or seriously irresponsible conduct. This test is distinct from, and narrower than, the broad 'diagnostic' element of the MCA test of capacity (see **Chapter 3**). The assessment must be carried out by a doctor approved under s.12 of the Mental Health Act 1983 or who has special experience in the diagnosis and treatment of mental disorder.[16]
3.   Mental capacity – The person must lack capacity to decide whether or not they should be accommodated in the particular hospital or care home for the purpose of being given the care or treatment concerned.[17] This must be in accordance with the statutory test of capacity in the MCA.[18] This assessment may be carried out by anyone qualified to be either a mental health assessor or a best interests assessor.
4.   Best interests – It must be in the person's best interests to be detained in the hospital or care home and the deprivation of liberty must be necessary to prevent harm to the person and must be a proportionate response to the likelihood and seriousness of that harm. The assessor must apply the best interests checklist in the MCA[19] having consulted with all relevant people (see **3.6**). If there is no one available or appropriate to consult who is not paid to provide care, an Independent

Mental Capacity Advocate (IMCA) must be appointed to support and represent the person during the assessment process. The best interests assessor may be an approved mental health professional; a social worker registered with the General Social Care Council; a first level nurse; an occupational therapist; or a chartered psychologist who has undergone specialist training.[20]

5. Eligibility – A person is ineligible if already subject, or could be subject, to compulsory powers under the Mental Health Act 1983.[21]

6. 'No refusals' – There must be no valid and applicable advance decision made previously by the detained person refusing the treatment in question (see **Chapter 13**), nor a valid refusal by a deputy or donee of a health and welfare LPA acting within the scope of their authority.

It is the responsibility of the supervisory body to appoint appropriate assessors. Regulations specify who can carry out assessments, the professional skills, training and competences required and the time frame within which the assessments must be completed.[22] The mental health and best interests assessments must be carried out by different assessors. All assessors must be independent from decisions about providing or commissioning care for the person concerned. Anyone carrying out assessments (other than the age assessment) must have undergone specific training. In addition, the DoLS Code of Practice[23] provides that the supervisory body should take account of the need for understanding and practical experience of the nature of the person's particular condition and its impact on decision-making. It also suggests that:

> . . . supervisory bodies may wish to consider using an eligible assessor who already knows the relevant person to undertake this assessment, if they think it would be of benefit. This will primarily arise if somebody involved in the person's care is considered best placed to carry out a reliable assessment, using their knowledge of the person over a period of time. It may also help in reducing any distress that might be caused to the person if they were assessed by somebody they did not know.[24]

NOTES

1. It may be authorised under the Mental Health Act 1983, by the Court of Protection or under the authorisation regime provided for by the Mental Capacity Act 2005.
2. *HL v. United Kingdom* Case No. 45508/99, [2004] 40 EHRR 761 81 BMLR 131.
3. Ibid: para. 89–93.
4. Ministry of Justice (2008) *Mental Capacity Act 2005: Deprivation of Liberty Safeguards. Code of Practice to supplement the main Mental Capacity Act 2005 Code of Practice*, TSO. Also available online at **www.dh.gov.uk**.
5. Ibid: para. 2.5.
6. Mental Capacity Act 2005, ss.5 and 6. The conditions are described in more detail in **Chapter 13**.
7. There is a wealth of case law on this point, some described in chapter 2 of the DoLS Code of Practice. See in particular, *JE v. DE and Surrey County Council*

[2006] EWHC 3459 (Fam) and *Salford City Council* v. *GJ & Ors* [2008] EWHC 1097. In *JE* v. *DE*, Mr Justice Munby suggested that primacy should be given to the question of whether the person is 'free to leave' (see paras.77, 114-115) but the DoLS code suggests the multi-factorial approach is adopted.

8. Mental Capacity Act 2005, s.16(2).
9. Ibid: Sched. A1.
10. Ibid: s.4B, where a vital act is defined as 'any act which the person doing it reasonably believes to be necessary to prevent a serious deterioration in P's condition'.
11. Alternatively, in Wales, the National Assembly for Wales.
12. Mental Capacity Act 2005, s.21A.
13. An order under s.16(2) of the Mental Capacity Act 2005.
14. The statutory test of capacity in ss.2 and 3 of the Mental Capacity Act 2005, taking account of the principles in s.1. (See also **Chapter 3**.)
15. Mental Capacity Act 2005, Sched. A1, para. 10.
16. Mental Capacity (Deprivation of Liberty: Standard Authorisations, Assessments and Ordinary Residence) Regulations 2008 (SI 2008/1858), reg. 4.
17. Mental Capacity Act 2005, Sched. A1, para. 15.
18. The statutory test of capacity in ss.2 and 3 of the Mental Capacity Act 2005, taking account of the principles in s.1. (See also **Chapter 3**.) This is expressly provided for in Ministry of Justice (2008) *Mental Capacity Act 2005: Deprivation of Liberty Safeguards. Code of Practice to supplement the main Mental Capacity Act 2005 Code of Practice,* TSO, para. 4.30.
19. Mental Capacity Act 2005, s.4.
20. Mental Capacity (Deprivation of Liberty: Standard Authorisations, Assessments and Ordinary Residence) Regulations 2008 (SI 2008/1858), reg. 5.
21. Schedule 1A of the Mental Capacity Act 2005 sets out detailed provisions for determining whether or not a person meets the eligibility requirement. See also *W Primary Care Trust* v. *TB and others* [2009] EWHC 1737 (Fam).
22. Mental Capacity (Deprivation of Liberty: Standard Authorisations, Assessments and Ordinary Residence) Regulations 2008 (SI 2008/1858).
23. Ministry of Justice (2008) *Mental Capacity Act 2005: Deprivation of Liberty Safeguards. Code of Practice to supplement the main Mental Capacity Act 2005 Code of Practice,* TSO.
24. Ibid: para. 4.32.

PART IV

Practical aspects of the assessment of capacity

CHAPTER 16

Practical guidelines for doctors

16.1   INTRODUCTION

Doctors have great powers to benefit their patients by providing them with effective treatments. Doctors may also be able to help safeguard patients from exploitation and abuse or facilitate pursuit of patients' best interests, by identifying medical conditions which may cause them to lack capacity to protect themselves or make autonomous choices. However, they also risk doing harm to patients if their treatments are unsuccessful or if their assessments of capacity result in patients being deprived of the right to make their own decisions. In all their work, doctors have to balance the risks of doing harm against the possible advantages of intervention, including in clinical assessment of capacity.

Capacity is a legal concept and the tests which are applied to determine whether a person has capacity to make specific decisions are laid out in the Mental Capacity Act 2005 (the 'MCA') and for some decisions, by the common law.[1] Ultimately, where there is disagreement or doubt about a person's capacity, the matter can be decided by the Court of Protection (see **Appendix C**). In practice, however, doctors frequently give opinions about capacity or make such decisions for themselves which are accepted without further legal checks or intervention. For example, a doctor may be required to:

- make an assessment of a patient's capacity to consent prior to giving or prescribing medical treatment;
- provide a medical 'certificate' or opinion at a solicitor's request as to a person's particular capacity to do something unrelated to medical treatment (such as making a will);
- witness or otherwise certify a legal document signed by a patient;
- give an opinion as to a particular capacity which is relevant to other legal proceedings.

One matter on which a doctor's opinion is frequently sought concerns whether an older person is able to continue to live in their own home or whether a move to sheltered housing or a care home is advisable. The doctor's assessment in such cases will cover the person's physical and mental abilities relating to personal care and welfare as well as their capacity to make the decision, applying the statutory test in the MCA.[2] The various assessments should be based on information provided by the individual concerned, family members and carers, as well as other relevant factors. Refusal to leave their own home, even when this is considered by others to be contrary to their best interests, is not in itself evidence of incapacity and the decision should be respected, unless lack of capacity is otherwise demonstrated.

Irrespective of whether doctors are assessing the capacity to consent to medical treatment or a capacity which is in a different area, unrelated to medical treatment, they should make careful reference to criteria laid out in the MCA (see **Chapter 3**). Where assessments are carried out at the request of a solicitor or other legal professional, doctors should insist that the lawyer is explicit about the particular questions to be answered. Doctors must also ensure that any legal jargon is properly explained by the lawyer and that they are given all the necessary information to be able to complete the assessment. For example, if a doctor is asked to assess a person's capacity to make a will, they will need details of the extent of the person's assets and members of the person's family and any other people who may have a claim on the testator's estate (see **Chapter 6** and **Appendix H**).

Doctors should then assess clinically whether the person's abilities are adequate to satisfy the relevant legal criteria. It is important for doctors to recognise that there may also be non-medical evidence relevant to a person's capacity, which may sometimes contradict their own medical view. This emphasises that the doctor's role is to give an opinion, rather than to be the sole arbiter as to capacity.[3] Indeed, any medical opinion about capacity is open to legal challenge, either by the person whose capacity is being assessed or by some other interested party and, ultimately, the doctor can be called to give evidence in court. Doctors are therefore advised to keep careful records of the steps taken in assessing capacity. The Court of Protection is the final arbiter where there is doubt as to whether an individual lacks capacity.

16.2　DEFINING CAPACITY

Decision-making capacity refers to the everyday ability that individuals possess to make decisions or to take actions that influence their life, from simple decisions about what to have for breakfast, to far-reaching decisions about investments or serious medical treatment. In a legal context, capacity refers to a person's ability to do something, including making a decision, which may have legal consequences for the person themselves or for other people (see **Chapter 1**). Capacity is therefore pivotal in balancing the right to autonomy in decision-making and the right to protection from harm.

The starting point in any assessment of capacity is the presumption that a person has capacity until the contrary is proven[4] (see **Chapter 3**). This means that lack of cooperation or apathy with respect to an assessment of capacity should not lead to a conclusion that the person lacks capacity. For example, an eccentric recluse does not lose legal autonomy simply because of non-cooperation with an assessment (see **2.4** on refusal to be assessed).

An assessment of capacity is based on a judgement about the mental processes a person must be able to go through in order to arrive at a decision, not the outcome or the decision itself. The question 'would a rational person decide as this person has decided?' is not directly relevant to the question of capacity. Individuals who have mental capacity may make decisions which are apparently irrational or unwise – and the law allows them to do so.[5]

Under the MCA, a person lacks capacity if, at the time the decision in question needs to be made, there is a reasonable belief that the person is unable to make or communicate the decision because of an 'impairment of, or a disturbance in the functioning of, the mind or brain.'[6] There is therefore a two-stage test of capacity:

- Is there an impairment of, or disturbance in the functioning of, the person's mind or brain? If so,
- Is the impairment or disturbance sufficient to cause the person to be unable to make that particular decision at the time it needs to be made?

Stage 1 – The 'diagnostic threshold'

The first stage in a clinical assessment of capacity (sometimes referred to as the 'diagnostic threshold') involves defining the presence of some 'medical condition'. Although a specific medical diagnosis is not required, medical symptoms or signs must be present in order for a doctor to have any role in determining capacity. Indeed, if there is no indication of any impairment or disturbance, the person should be presumed to have capacity and their ability to make decisions should not be questioned. The assessment of capacity must focus on the specific decision that needs to be made at the specified time the decision is required. It does not matter therefore if the condition is temporary, or that the person retains the capacity to make other decisions, or if the person's capacity fluctuates. The inability to make a decision, however, must be a result of an impairment of, or disturbance in the functioning of, the person's mind or brain. This could relate to 'a range of problems, such as psychiatric illness, learning disability, dementia, brain damage or even a toxic confusional state, as long as it has the necessary effect on the functioning of the mind or brain, causing the person to be unable to make the decision'.[7] The important point is that the impairment or disturbance causes the individual to be unable to make the decision in question (see stage 2 below). Clearly, however, if the impairment is temporary and the decision can realistically be put off until such a time as the person is likely to regain capacity, then it should be deferred.

Stage 2 – Inability to make a decision

The second stage in assessing capacity is to determine whether the impairment or disturbance is sufficient to render the person unable to make the decision in question. The MCA sets out the test for assessing whether a person is unable to make a decision for themselves. This is a 'functional' test, focusing on the personal ability of the individual concerned to make a particular decision at a particular time and the processes followed by the person in arriving at the decision. A person is unable to make a decision if that person is unable:[8]

(a) to understand the information relevant to the decision,
(b) to retain that information,
(c) to use or weigh that information as part of the process of making the decision, or
(d) to communicate his decision (whether by talking, using sign language or any other means).

Where the impairment or disturbance stems from a diagnosable medical condition, it is not the diagnosis itself which implies capacity or incapacity but rather its impact on the individual's mental processes affecting their ability to understand, retain and use information in order to make a choice. Similarly, the ability to make different decisions can be variously affected by a particular medical disability. For example, a diagnosis of schizophrenia does not determine whether or not a person lacks a particular capacity. A person with schizophrenia may have the capacity to accept or refuse some medical treatments but not others, depending upon the extent or nature of their illness.[9] More generally, a person may have the capacity to carry out one type of legal act, such as marrying, whilst not having the capacity to carry out another, such as making a will.[10]

A person's capacity will largely be determined by their mental state. However, there may also be some physical conditions, such as severe pain or fatigue, which do not directly affect mental functioning but which can sometimes interfere with capacity. Poor eyesight, deafness and problems with speech and language may be relevant to whether a person's wishes can be ascertained and to how information relevant to the decision is given to them.

As it is a principle of the MCA that a person is 'not to be treated as unable to make a decision unless all practicable steps to help him do so have been taken without success',[11] every effort must be made to overcome such problems with perception and communication (see also chapter 3 of the Code of Practice reproduced at **Appendix B**).

Where it is not clear that a person has capacity to make a decision, doctors must balance the need to protect the person from harm against respecting their autonomy. The assessment they make could be criticised or challenged and should therefore be carefully documented and their findings recorded.

16.3   THE DOCTOR'S ROLE

Although assessing any particular capacity does not require detailed legal knowledge, the doctor must understand in broad terms the relevant legal tests. The doctor's role is to supply information on which an assessment of the person's capacity can be based. They need to describe the consequences of medical conditions which may compromise an individual's ability to pass a legal test. If there is no medical diagnosis or medically describable symptoms or signs, there can be no medical evidence relevant to determining capacity. For example, to say that a person 'makes poor judgements' is not a medical opinion but a lay observation and one which is heavily subjective. This emphasises the importance of the doctor first of all determining that it is appropriate to give a medical opinion about capacity.

Although a doctor may be asked to give an opinion about capacity, this opinion is not necessarily the deciding factor since evidence from other people and other sources may also need to be taken into account.[12] Also, some tests of capacity make explicit or implicit reference to social functioning rather than to medical disabilities per se (see for example **Chapter 11** on personal relationships) and a doctor is no more expert in assessing social functioning than anyone else.

Where the relevant legal capacity is the capacity to consent to a specific medical treatment, doctors should take particular care and have regard to the professional and other guidance available[13] (see also **Chapter 13**). The doctor may be in a situation where the doctor's opinion of what is the best or most appropriate form of treatment conflicts with what the patient wants. It is tempting, but ethically and legally wrong, for the doctor to underestimate the capacity of a patient in order to achieve what they believe to be in that person's best interests. In so doing, the doctor deprives the patient of autonomy and would be acting unlawfully.

Professional ethics

There are two distinct contexts in which doctors examine people. The most common is the therapeutic context aimed at ensuring that patients receive appropriate care and treatment. Patient consent can be explicit or implied. For example, permission to disclose information essential for the provision of care to other health professionals involved in the episode of treatment is usually implied. Nevertheless, the BMA maintains[14] that it is good practice to inform patients about the scope of disclosure within the therapeutic context, since care is increasingly provided by multidisciplinary teams and information may be spread more widely than patients anticipate (see **2.2** and **13.7** on confidentiality).

The second situation is where doctors act as independent examiners in order to provide a report for purposes other than medical treatment, for example for use in legal proceedings. When a doctor is carrying out this second type of assessment, it cannot be assumed that the person has given their consent to examination and to disclosure of information. It is therefore essential that the doctor's role and the purpose of the exercise are explained to the person at the outset. Where an adult lacks the capacity to consent to examination and subsequent disclosure, the MCA contains specific powers, such as LPAs, that permit certain forms of delegated decision-making. Where these powers are not available (for example, because no one is nominated to act as an attorney), decisions have to be made based upon an assessment of the incapacitated adult's best interests (see **Chapter 3**).

Particular care may be required when assessment for a report to third parties is carried out by the patient's own doctor and takes place within the context of a continuing therapeutic relationship. In such cases, the doctor must explain how the examination differs from the usual doctor–patient encounter and obtain explicit consent from the patient. Patients must also be told who will have access to the information gained and whether other material from their past records will be needed. The patient's consent to such disclosure should be recorded.

If an individual appears competent and refuses to cooperate with the assessment, the doctor must note that fact in conjunction with the other evidence available (see also **2.4** on the refusal to be assessed). If it appears likely that the person lacks capacity to consent to assessment or to disclosure, the doctor should take a decision whether or not to proceed with the assessment based on a judgement of the person's best interests. Such judgement necessarily includes, amongst all other relevant considerations, that appropriate weight be given to the ascertainable past and current wishes of that individual (see **Chapter 3**).

Which doctor should assess the person?

The choice of doctor to make an assessment of capacity will depend on the particular requirements of the assessment and the medical condition of the person being assessed. Many people can be assessed by their GP, and indeed in some cases, a close, long-term acquaintance with the person being assessed may be an asset, particularly if that person is more relaxed with a familiar doctor. However on some occasions, the GP's personal knowledge of a patient, and perhaps also of the patient's family, may make an objective assessment more difficult. Alternatively, the patient may attend a practice where they see different GPs, so no single doctor may have detailed knowledge of the patient. If the nature or complexity of the person's medical disorder or disabilities suggests that a hospital specialist would be more appropriate then it will usually be important for that doctor to obtain information from the person's GP, and take this into account in making their own assessment of the patient's capacity. Other members of the multidisciplinary team, particularly nurses, clinical psychologists, speech and language therapists and occupational therapists may also have specific skills to assist the doctor in assessing capacity.

Whoever carries out the assessment should make efforts to create the most congenial environment to optimise the conditions for assessing the person's capacity at their highest level of functioning (see **2.3** and **16.7**).

16.4   A SYSTEMATIC APPROACH TO ASSESSING CAPACITY

Background information

Once sure of the relevant legal test, the assessing doctor should become familiar with any background information about the person likely to be relevant to that particular test. The amount of information required will be determined by the complexity of the decision to be taken. For example, if the assessment relates to the capacity to make a will, the assessing doctor will need to have some idea about the extent and complexity of the person's estate and whether the person understands the claims of those who may have a call on the estate when deciding about disposal of their assets (see **Chapter 6**). The doctor must therefore have some knowledge of the number and nature of the potential claims on the individual. Although the medical assessment should be carried out with regard to the relevant legal criteria, there must be a clear distinction between the description of the disabilities and the interpretation of how they affect legal capacity. Therefore the doctor should first define the diagnosis and the medical disabilities and then assess how these affect the person's ability to make the decision or decisions in question.

Medical records and reports

Prior to undertaking the assessment, if possible the doctor should have access to relevant past medical and psychiatric records. An understanding of the progression of the person's illness or condition will be relevant to prognosis, to any likely response to treatment, and thus to future potential capacity. Assessment of the permanence or transience of disabilities may be crucially important in offering a view about achievable capacity. Also, the medical records may give a picture of those disabilities in general terms which differs from the impression that the doctor gains at an individual assessment. It is important for the doctor to make an assessment on the basis of current evidence from various information sources, including examination of the person concerned, rather than relying entirely on past evaluations.

The doctor should also take full account of relevant information from other disciplines. An assessment by a clinical psychologist may already be available, or could be sought, and this may assist in giving a detailed, validated and systematic assessment of cognitive functioning. An occupational therapist might be consulted when information about activities of daily living is of importance. Also, a report from a social worker, a nurse or a care worker may be helpful, for example where the person is living in a care home.

Information from others

Information from friends, relatives or carers is often important in the assessment of capacity and may reveal the person's known previous patterns of behaviour, values and goals. Such information may indicate whether their current behaviour and thinking reflects an abnormal mental state. However, great care must be taken when gaining information from third parties, particularly if they have an interest in the outcome of the assessment of capacity. Aspects of a person's current thinking may derive not from a disability but from their personality, or from a particular cultural or ethnic background, and this will need to be considered carefully before any assessment of capacity is made. It may even be necessary for the doctor to seek advice from others on such cultural issues, or to suggest that the patient be examined by a doctor of a cultural or ethnic background similar to that of the person being assessed.[15]

Medical diagnosis

Where the person suffers from a mental disorder, it is good practice to express the diagnosis in terms of one of the accepted international classifications of mental disorders, the World Health Organization International Classification of Diseases (WHO ICD 10), or the American Psychiatric Association, Diagnostic and Statistical Manual (DSM IV). This will ensure greater diagnostic consistency between doctors and minimise diagnostic confusion.

16.5   THE MENTAL STATE IN RELATION TO CAPACITY

Examination of the mental state is fundamental to the assessment of capacity. Although particular diagnoses may tend to be associated with particular mental state disabilities which can affect capacity, what matters are the disabilities themselves. It is only through detailed assessment of specific aspects of mental functioning that capacity can be properly assessed.

Mental state examination

The doctor should consider the patient's mental functioning under the following headings when making an assessment of mental state, indicating the relevance of any findings to the specific test of capacity. It is also important to document any medical or psychometric tests or other assessment tools used in the process (see **16.8** below for information about assessment tools).[16]

Appearance and behaviour

A patient may be so agitated or overactive in their behaviour that it may be impossible to impart relevant information to them. Otherwise, appearance and behaviour may suggest a mood disorder or cognitive impairment which might be relevant to the person's capacity.

Speech

The rate, quantity, form or flow of speech may be such as to interfere with communication, as well as reflecting abnormality of thought processes. For example, a depressed patient may be so lacking in speech that they are unable to communicate effectively; or the speech of a person with bi-polar effective disorder may be rapid with quickly changing subjects ('flight of ideas') so that communication is severely impaired. Similarly, the thought disorder of a patient with schizophrenia (moving between topics without apparent logical connections) may make communication very difficult or even impossible. Damage to the language areas of the brain following a stroke may also make direct verbal communication impossible.

Mood

Mood may be very important in determining capacity. A depressed patient with delusions of poverty may make decisions relevant to their affairs on an entirely erroneous basis. Similarly, the grandiose approach of a patient with bi-polar effective disorder may lead to rash financial or other decisions. Lability of mood, common after stroke, may render a patient unable to make consistent decisions. Anxiety may also have some effect on the assessed level of capacity.

Thought

Abnormalities of thought may have a profound effect upon decision-making. Delusions which are strongly held, and which relate specifically to the decision at hand, may substantially distort a person's ability to make the decision. For example, a delusional belief that a close relative is plotting against them might affect capacity to make a will. Similarly, a delusional belief that doctors have magical powers to cure may render the patient incapable of consenting to medical treatment. Thought abnormalities falling short of delusions, such as extreme preoccupation or obsessional thoughts, can also interfere with capacity but are less likely to do so. Overvalued ideas falling short of delusions, such as occur in anorexia nervosa, present particular difficulties in relation to the capacity of such patients to consent to treatment or to accept or refuse food.

Perception

Illusions (misinterpretation of the nature of real objects) are rarely significant enough to inhibit capacity. Hallucinations, however, may well be of direct relevance to decision-making. They are often congruent with, or reinforce, delusions and so the two should be considered together. Auditory hallucinations instructing the patient may have two distinct effects. First, by their content and authority they may directly interfere with the patient's ability to think about relevant issues as well as decision-making ability. Second, hallucinations may be so incessant that they distract the person from thinking about the decision at all.

Cognition

Defects in cognitive functioning can have profound significance for capacity. Decision-making and all tests of legal capacity require not only consciousness but some continuity of consciousness and of recollection. Attention (the ability to focus on the matter in hand) and concentration (the ability to sustain attention) are necessary for effective thought and for capacity. Patients who are highly distracted, whether by other mental events such as hallucinations or because of delirium, may lack capacity. Most psychiatrists use the Mini-Mental State Examination[17] as a convenient way of assessing different domains of cognitive function. If this test reveals areas of impairment it may be helpful to make a more detailed appraisal of the affected cognitive abilities.

Orientation

Awareness of time, place and person might be seen as relevant only to set the context for decisions rather than being directly relevant to capacity. However, disorientation is usually a marker of brain dysfunction, for instance in delirium or dementia, and in these conditions capacity is commonly impaired.

Memory

Problems with long-term memory may not necessarily reduce capacity. However a person who cannot remember their relatives or the extent of financial assets could be significantly impaired in decision-making ability. A person with a severe short-term memory deficit (an inability to recall information given a few minutes earlier) which may occur as a result of chronic alcoholism, a stroke, or Alzheimer's disease, is likely to lack capacity for some, but not necessarily all, decisions.

Intellectual functioning

Low IQ level (for example, as a result of learning disability) may reduce capacity for certain decisions, although it may be possible to use aids to communication, such as pictures or videos to enhance understanding. Care should be taken not to presume incapacity just because the person has a learning disability, however severe. There should be careful investigation of the person's abilities specifically in relation to the decision in question. Acquired brain damage, whether from trauma or from disease processes affecting the brain, may also affect cognitive functioning and, therefore, capacity. However, where only certain aspects of intellectual functioning are significantly impaired it is important to be very specific in distinguishing which functions, or combination of functions, are necessary for the legal capacity which the person must have. Standardised psychometric tests may be of help in assessing the severity of cognitive impairment. Many simple tests of cognitive functioning assess only orientation and memory, but it is important also to assess other areas of mental functioning, such as calculation, reasoning, visuo-spatial functioning and sequencing. An occupational therapist or clinical psychologist may be able to help in these areas.

Insight

People can lack insight into one aspect of their lives and retain it for others. For example, lack of insight as to the presence of illness might not deprive a person of the capacity to make decisions about treatment of the illness if the person has insight into the need for such treatment. Furthermore, insight may not be completely absent. The person with reduced insight may have specific awareness of their condition so as to have the capacity necessary for decisions about treatment. Of course, lack of insight into mental illness may not inhibit the person's capacity to decide about something else in their life. No report should read 'has insight' or 'has no insight' as either statement is valueless if left unqualified.

16.6 PERSONALITY DISORDERS

By contrast with mental illness or organic brain syndromes, personality disorders present particular problems in relation to assessment of capacity. Such patients have disorders which affect many areas of mental and social functioning, as well as behaviour. They often experience profound mood disturbances and are frequently impulsive. Their thought processes are unusual, but they are not deluded. It is the manner in which such persons weigh information in the balance which is generally affected, not their ability to think or to understand the information.[18] Assessment of capacity in such patients is therefore extremely difficult since there are no clear-cut abnormalities in the mental state such as dementia, hallucinations or delusions and yet the doctor will often perceive that they are not making decisions in the way that an ordinary person would (see **16.8** on the use of assessment tools to aid such assessments). There should be no automatic assumption that this necessarily indicates lack of capacity.

16.7 THE DUTY TO 'ENHANCE' MENTAL CAPACITY

Doctors will be aware both that medical disabilities can fluctuate and that there are many factors other than a person's medical disorder which may adversely influence capacity. It is the duty of the assessing doctor, reinforced by one of the guiding principles of the MCA,[19] to optimise the conditions and to provide appropriate kinds of support that allow the person's capacity to be assessed at their highest level of functioning in relation to the decision in question.

Some pointers are suggested in **2.3** 'Creating the right environment for assessing capacity' and a further elaboration on the relevant pointers for doctors is set out below:

- Any treatable medical condition which affects capacity should, as far as possible, be treated before a final assessment is made.
- Incapacity may be temporary, albeit for a prolonged period. For example, the mental capacity of an older patient with delirium caused by infection may continue to improve for some time after the infection has been eradicated. If a person's condition is likely to improve, the assessment of capacity should, if possible, be delayed. The effect of drugs, particularly hypnotics and tranquillisers should be considered carefully. If there is a treatable physical disorder present, assessment should, if possible, be delayed until the patient is as well and as comfortable as possible.
- Some conditions, such as dementia with Lewy bodies, may give rise to fluctuating capacity. Thus, although a person with dementia may lack capacity at the time of one assessment, the result may be different if a second assessment is undertaken during a lucid interval. In cases of fluctuating capacity the medical report should detail the level of capacity during periods of maximal and minimal ability.
- Some mental health problems may be untreatable and yet their impact can be minimised. For example, the capacity of a person with a short-term

memory deficit to make a particular decision may be improved if trained in suitable techniques by an occupational therapist or psychologist. If the assessing doctor believes that capacity could be improved by such assistance then this should be stated in any opinion.

- Some physical conditions which do not directly affect the mental state can appear to interfere with capacity. For example, disabilities of communication will not impair the ability to understand relevant information or make a choice, but they may prevent the person's wishes being made known. Many communication difficulties which result from physical disabilities can be helped. There should, therefore, be careful assessment of speech, language functioning, hearing and (if appropriate) sight. Any disabilities discovered should, as far as possible (and if time allows), be corrected before any conclusion is reached about capacity. The MCA makes it clear, however, that where an individual lacks the ability 'to communicate his decision (whether by talking, using sign language or any other means)'[20] that person is deemed to lack capacity in relation to the matter.

- Care should be taken to choose the best location and time for the assessment. For someone who is on the borderline of having capacity, added anxiety may tip them into apparent incapacity. It may be appropriate to assess the person in their own home if it is thought that an interview at either a hospital or a GP's surgery would adversely affect the result. A relative or carer may be able to indicate the most suitable location and time for the assessment.

- The way in which someone is approached and dealt with generally can have a significant impact upon apparent capacity and the doctor should be sensitive to this.

- Educating the person being assessed as to the factors relevant to the proposed decision may enhance capacity. Indeed, the assessing doctor should always establish what the person understands about the decision they are being asked to undertake. It is important for the doctor to re-explain and, if necessary, write down those aspects of the decision which have not been fully grasped. The person being assessed should be allowed sufficient time to become familiar with concepts relevant to the decision. For example, people with learning disabilities may acquire the capacity to consent to a blood test after receiving appropriate information in an accessible manner.[21]

- The capacity of some people may be enhanced by the presence of a friend, relative or other person at the interview. Alternatively, the presence of a third party may increase the anxiety and thus reduce the person's capacity. The person being assessed should be asked specifically whether they would feel more comfortable with another person present. A professional advocate may be able to ensure that the person's views have been adequately represented.

- Depression is common amongst disabled people but is often not recognised. Its presence may profoundly affect capacity and yet it may be amenable to treatment. Making a diagnosis of depression in the presence of other disabilities affecting mental functioning can be particularly difficult, especially in patients with dementia. The opinion of a psychiatrist may be necessary in such cases. The low self-esteem of many patients whose capacity may be in question means that they are at particular risk of 'going along with' suggestions regardless of their own private views. The assessing doctor should be aware of this and structure the interview so as to avoid the use of leading questions.

16.8 ASSESSMENT TOOLS

To assist practitioners involved in assessing capacity, and to enhance the reliability and validity of assessments, several assessment tools have been developed and are likely to be used increasingly. One example, the FACE Mental Capacity Assessment was specifically designed for health and care practitioners applying the MCA test of capacity in situations where there is no need for detailed clinical assessment.[22] Where specific clinical assessment is needed, assessment tools are not a substitute but merely an aid to be used within such assessment.

The most commonly used tool in clinical assessments of capacity, the MacArthur Competence Assessment Tool for Treatment (MacCAT-T),[23] structures the assessment around four elements of capacity to consent to treatment, which roughly correspond to the elements in the MCA test. Three of the four elements are highly 'cognitive', and the levels of reliability and validity are highest in respect of these components, for example when assessing patients with acute or chronic brain conditions or those with functional (not organic) psychoses. The fourth element, referred to as the 'appreciation' test, assesses whether the person is able not just to receive and retain treatment information, and to manipulate it, but whether they can appreciate its relevance to them and their situation. Such assessment is more 'subjective' and open to variation of opinion, for example when assessing a person who is cognitively relatively intact but who may be 'distorting' the relevance to their situation. Similar concerns apply to the element of the MCA test of capacity concerning the ability to 'weigh' relevant information, which refers not only to 'manipulating' the information but also to the way in which that exercise is carried out.

16.9 RETROSPECTIVE ASSESSMENT

On occasions a doctor may be asked to advise whether a person had the capacity at some time in the past to make a decision which they made. Examples might be the capacity to make a will (see **Chapter 6**) where the person has subsequently died and the will is contested or capacity to enter into a contract (see **Chapter 9**) where the validity of the contract is subsequently challenged. Any such retrospective assessment will have to be based upon medical notes made at the time, as well as on other non-medical information which may help to suggest the nature of the person's mental functioning at the time, and whether they may have been susceptible to the exertion of undue influence or pressure. Clearly the doctor will have to indicate that the assessment was retrospective and may therefore be unreliable.

16.10 GENERAL GUIDANCE

Assessment of capacity is not a function which can usually be carried out in only a few minutes. Aside from situations where the patient is comatose, or otherwise so severely disabled that incapacity is obvious, assessment will usually take a substantial period of time, even if only a single area of capacity is to be explored. This is required both because of the need to be thorough and comprehensive and because of the legal importance which attaches to the assessment. The doctor should never be constrained in making an assessment by time or resources. Each assessment of capacity must be an assessment of an individual in their own circumstances. No assumptions should be made about capacity just on the basis of the person's known diagnosis or their age or appearance.[24] What matters is how the medical condition affects that particular person's own ability to make the decision in question, not the diagnosed medical condition itself.

It is worth emphasising again that the doctor must guard against allowing a personal view of what is in the person's best interest to influence an assessment of capacity. It may be disconcerting for the doctor to determine that the patient has capacity when the doctor believes that allowing the patient to make the decision will be against their long-term interests. However, the doctor must not consider the implications for the person of being allowed to make the decision except to the extent that this is relevant in deciding whether the person has the capacity to do so.

NOTES

1. See **Chapter 3** for the MCA test of capacity. Relevant common law texts are described in **Part III**.
2. The statutory test of capacity in ss.2 and 3 of the Mental Capacity Act 2005, taking account of the principles in s.1. (See also **Chapter 3**.)
3. *Richmond* v. *Richmond* (1914) 111 LT 273. In a Canadian case, *Re Price* [1964] 2 DLR 592, at 595 it was stated that a judgement as to capacity 'is a practical question which may be answered by a layman of good sense with as much authority as by a doctor'.
4. Mental Capacity Act 2005, s.1(2).
5. Ibid: s.1(4).

6. Ibid: s.2(1).
7. Explanatory Notes to the Mental Capacity Act 2005, para. 22.
8. Mental Capacity Act 2005, s.3(1).
9. *Re C (Adult: Refusal of Treatment)* [1994] 1 FLR 31, [1994] 1 All ER 819.
10. *In the Estate of Park, Park* v. *Park* [1954] P 112.
11. Mental Capacity Act 2005, s.1(3).
12. For example, in *Masterman-Lister* v. *Brutton & Co.* [2002] EWCA Civ 1889 the court gave detailed consideration to diaries, letters and computer documents. In *Saulle* v. *Nouvet* [2007] EWHC 2902 (QB) the court considered witness statements and oral evidence from family members as well as home videos.
13. There are various sources of guidance on consent to medical treatment which are summarised in British Medical Association (2008) *Consent Tool Kit* 4th edition, British Medical Association. See also Department of Health (2009) *Reference Guide to Consent for Examination or Treatment* 2nd edition, Department of Health.
14. British Medical Association (2008) *Confidentiality and disclosure of health information tool kit*, British Medical Association. Card 2, para. 4.
15. See for example Fernando S and Keating F (2008) *Mental Health in a Multi-Ethnic Society: A Multidisciplinary Handbook* 2nd edition, Routledge; and Sewell H (2009) *Working with Ethnicity, Race and Culture in Mental Health: A Handbook for Practitioners*, Jessica Kingsley.
16. See for example Folstein M F, Folstein S E, McHugh P R (1975) ' "Mini-mental state": a practical method for grading the cognitive state of patients for the clinician'. *Journal of Psychiatric Research*. 1975, 12(3): 189–198; and Grisso T and Appelbaum P S (1998) *Assessing Competence to Consent to Treatment: A Guide for Physicians and Other Health Professionals,* Oxford University Press; and Janofsky J S, McCarthy R J, Folstein M F (1992) 'The Hopkins competency assessment test.' *Hospital and Community Psychiatry*, 1992, 43: 132–136.
17. Folstein et al (1975), *op cit*.
18. *R* v. *Collins and Ashworth Hospital Authority ex p Brady* (2001) 58 BMLR 173. In this case, it was held that severe personality disorder alone could be sufficient to have 'eschewed the weighing of information and the balancing of risks and needs to such an extent that . . . his decisions on food refusal and force feeding had been incapacitated.'
19. Mental Capacity Act 2005, s.1(3).
20. Ibid: s.3(1)(d).
21. Wong J G, Clare I C H, Gunn M J, Holland A J (1999) 'Capacity to make health care decisions: its importance in clinical practice', *Psychological Medicine* 1999, 29: 437–446
22. The FACE Mental Capacity Assessment has been adopted by some NHS Trusts and Local Authorities (see **www.face.eu.com**).
23. The MacArthor Competence Assessment Tool for Treatment (MacCAT-T) was developed in the USA to assess capacity to consent to medical treatment (see **www.macauthur.virginiaedu/treatment**). See also Grisso T and Appelboum P.S. (1998) *Assessing Competence to Consent to Treatment: A Guide for Physicians and Other Health Professionals*, Oxford University Press.
24. Mental Capacity Act 2005, s.2(3).

CHAPTER 17

Practical guidelines for lawyers

17.1 Introduction
17.2 Who should assess the person?
17.3 Psychiatric diagnoses
17.4 Medical assessment of mental conditions
17.5 General guidance

17.1 INTRODUCTION

In cases where a client's mental capacity is in doubt, it is often desirable, or a matter of good practice, for lawyers to obtain a medical or other expert opinion. This is particularly important where the capacity in question relates to complex or serious decisions. Indeed, in some circumstances the courts have strongly advised obtaining medical evidence about a person's capacity (see the 'golden rule' in **4.5** and **6.5**). A summary of points for the lawyer obtaining a medical opinion is given below:

- Lawyers should ensure they understand which kind of doctor to ask to give an expert opinion about any particular legal capacity (see **17.2** below).
- Explain in detail which particular areas of capacity the lawyer wishes the doctor to report on, as individuals may retain capacity to make decisions in some areas of functioning and not in others.[1] For example, they might be able to understand the issues involved in making a Lasting Power of Attorney ('LPA') appointing an attorney to deal with their finances, but lack the capacity to make specific financial decisions for themselves.
- Clarify for the doctor the relevant legal tests of capacity as described in **Part III**. Where the Mental Capacity Act (the 'MCA') applies, it would be helpful to include an explanation of the statutory test of capacity and other relevant aspects of the MCA.[2] Where the particular test of capacity has been established in case law, it may sometimes be appropriate to send to the medical practitioner the actual text of the relevant judgment.
- In all cases, it is important that any summary of the law is understandable to someone who is not a lawyer, and in a form which would be acceptable

to the courts. Unless such detailed information is given, doctors are likely to refer to medical textbooks to find out what is required, and medical texts cannot be relied upon in a legal context.

- Where a specific form must be used, such as Form COP3 for Court of Protection proceedings (see **Appendix G**) or the Official Solicitor's Certificate of Capacity (see **Appendix F**) where the Official Solicitor is requested to act as litigation friend, a copy of the relevant form and accompanying guidance should be provided for the doctor.

- Describe to the doctor the client's circumstances where these are relevant to the person's capacity to make the decision in question. For example, if testamentary capacity is to be assessed it will be necessary for the doctor to be given some independent information about the extent of the testator's assets and those who may have a call on the estate, and perhaps a draft of the proposed will (see **Chapter 6**). This is particularly relevant where the doctor is asked to witness the will in accordance with the so-called 'golden rule'.[3]

- In any situation where doctors or nurses are asked to witness documents, it is important to emphasise to them that they are expected to use their professional skills in assessing and confirming the patient's competence to sign, and not merely acting as lay witnesses (see **4.5**).

It is often helpful for there to be a discussion between lawyer and doctor prior to the doctor's consideration of the case, both to clarify the legal questions and to establish what documentary information is available which the doctor should see. It is also helpful for lawyers to have some knowledge of the basic principles which underlie medical assessment in order both to evaluate the opinion and to be sure of understanding its legal implications. A summary is set out in **17.4** below and further details are given in **Chapter 16**. When deciding which particular doctor to approach to request a medical assessment, lawyers must be sensitive to issues of language and culture for their clients, and also, in some cases, to whether the client has a preference for seeing a male or female doctor.

As a matter of good practice, lawyers who visit clients in hospitals or care homes, and doctors who visit to carry out assessments should notify the ward or home, preferably in writing, in advance of their expected visit and then introduce themselves to the duty manager to ascertain that the client is well enough to receive a professional visit. Where someone has already been appointed under a registered LPA to act as an attorney on behalf of the individual, or a nearest relative is involved where the person is detained under mental health legislation, it might also be appropriate to consult them as part of the assessment of the person's capacity, depending on the particular circumstances. While a client's access to his legal adviser should not be hindered, lawyers need to be sensitive to the client's condition and medical needs and arrange an appropriate time to visit. When visiting clients at home it is advisable that all professionals carry or display their official identity badges.

The remainder of this Chapter offers basic information about different specialties and medical personnel, and about the nature of psychiatric assessment and diagnosis.

17.2   WHO SHOULD ASSESS THE PERSON?

A doctor can offer an expert opinion when the person being assessed suffers (or appears to suffer) from a diagnosable medical condition. Occasionally, the lawyer may request an opinion from the doctor clarifying that the client does not suffer from a medical or psychiatric condition. Lawyers should be wary of any assessment which appears to be 'medical' but which has nothing to do with medical disabilities. Under the MCA,[4] a person can only be assessed as lacking capacity to make a particular decision if they have 'an impairment of, or disturbance in the functioning of, the mind or brain' which is the cause of their being unable to make the decision in question and this is an aspect that doctors will usually be asked to comment on. Although the distinction is not an absolute one, an impairment or disturbance can arise from either 'physical' or 'psychiatric' conditions. Most doctors should be able to take a psychiatric history and to conduct a basic mental state examination, in order to define straightforward abnormalities, irrespective of their diagnostic cause. Where the person's capacity is uncertain and their disabilities make the interpretation of legal tests of capacity complex, it may be appropriate to seek a specialist opinion.

Specialist knowledge

Hospital medicine is divided into specialities and specialist knowledge may be required to assess how a particular illness or condition may affect the person's ability to make particular decisions. Some people may require assessment by a psychiatrist. A psychiatrist is a medical practitioner who is trained to assess and treat disorders which may present with mental symptoms. Such symptoms can arise from 'physical' (brain or body affecting brain) or 'functional' abnormality. For example, a patient complaining of 'hearing voices' might have schizophrenia (a functional disorder, see **17.3** below) or dementia (an organic condition). If there is any possibility that the condition may be organically caused, it is important that a primary diagnosis is first made by a medical practitioner (by contrast with a clinical psychologist). Medical practitioners also have a significant role to play in assessing whether and to what extent symptoms, such as 'voices' or delusionary beliefs, may impact on a patient's decision-making capacity. A female patient, for example, who believes mistakenly that an abdominal swelling is a sign of pregnancy rather than an ovarian cyst may well lack the capacity to make relevant treatment decisions.

Where the diagnosis is clearly established as 'organic' it may sometimes be appropriate for the patient's condition to be treated, and their capacity to be assessed by a non-psychiatric specialist (for example a neurologist). If there is a reasonable belief that the impairment affecting the individual's capacity is likely to respond to treatment, and the decision can be deferred until capacity improves, then it should be deferred. It is important to choose a specialist who has extensive clinical experience of the particular disorder and is familiar with caring for patients with that condition, rather than having detailed research knowledge. Hence, a consultant in old-age psychiatry may be a better 'expert' on Alzheimer's disease than for example, a research neurologist. Since assessments of capacity have a practical purpose, they should be based on a practical knowledge of the condition and of its manifestations, management and prognosis.

Many patients can be appropriately assessed by their GP. A close, long-term acquaintance between the doctor and the patient may be a major asset in creating the best environment to maximise the patient's capacity (see **2.3**). However, it is important to emphasise that a GP's close and personal knowledge of a patient, even concern and affection, must not be allowed to interfere with an objective assessment of the patient's actual mental disabilities and capacity to make the decision in question. It is also desirable for the GP and a hospital specialist, if one is involved, to consult with one another in determining their individual views of the patient's capacity. This offers the advantage of combining expertise in the effects and management of a complicated condition with close acquaintance with the patient.

Examples of relevant specialist opinions, in relation to particular diagnoses, might be as follows:

- Consultant general psychiatrist (schizophrenia, severe depressive illness, mania, paranoid psychosis, personality disorder).
- Consultant in old-age psychiatry, formerly known as psycho-geriatrician (Alzheimer's disease or other dementias, mental illness in older people).
- Consultant psychiatrist in learning disability (learning disability, formerly known as mental handicap).
- Consultant general psychiatrist or consultant general physician with a special interest in eating disorders (anorexia nervosa and other eating disorders).
- Consultant neurologist or consultant neuropsychiatrist (head injury, epilepsy, multiple sclerosis, Huntington's disease).
- Consultant neurologist or consultant neurosurgeon (brain tumour).
- Consultant in addiction psychiatry (drug and alcohol addiction).

Other disciplines

Any medical opinion should take full account of relevant information from other disciplines. An assessment by a clinical psychologist may already be available, or could be sought, and this may assist in giving a detailed, validated and systematic assessment of cognitive functioning.[5] An occupational therapist has special skills in assessing disabilities which may interfere with activities in everyday tasks. A report from a nurse or a social worker may be helpful where information about daily activities or social functioning is of importance. What is important is not the diagnosis per se, but the specific disabilities and how they may affect the person's ability to make particular decisions.

Medico-legal expertise

In a complex medico-legal case it may be helpful for the lawyer to choose a doctor with particular experience in medico-legal work. Experience of sifting through large volumes of medical and other information, plus knowledge of some of the potential complexities of the interface between medicine and law can greatly assist a clear presentation of the medical issues into a legal context. However, it is important that experts are chosen primarily for their medical knowledge and not simply because they 'do a lot of court work'. Medical knowledge plus medico-legal experience is often a helpful combination.

17.3 PSYCHIATRIC DIAGNOSES

Categories of diagnoses

The field of psychiatric diagnosis is complex and evolving, and what follows is a very brief introductory outline. Psychiatric disorders are sometimes conveniently subdivided into organic and functional disorders.

Organic conditions

Organic conditions arise from brain disorders or from some general malfunction of the body such as the endocrine or hormone system. Brain disorders can be further subdivided into:

- acute (for example, an acute confusional state from urinary retention or from a toxic infective cause); and
- chronic (for example, dementia).

Chronic brain disorders can also be categorised as congenital disorders (for example some forms of learning disability) or acquired disorders (for example from a head injury).

Functional disorders

Functional disorders may be divided into the following categories:

- mental illness (which involves a change in the person's mental state away from their usual, normal state and can either be temporary or permanent). Mental illness can be further subdivided into:

  - 'psychotic' illness (such as schizophrenia, hypomania and psychotic depression, which involve a lack of insight and are accompanied by delusions or hallucinations); and
  - mental illnesses that are not characterised by delusions and are often accompanied by requests for treatment. These include mild to moderate depression, anxiety disorders and obsessive-compulsive disorders.

  Some neurotic disorders may share aspects of psychosis. Anorexia nervosa, for example, presents with a particular mix of features where there are no hallucinations and strictly no delusions, but where there is substantial distortion of body perception and profoundly distorted forms of thinking in relation to specific areas of food and body weight. Alcohol and drug induced states can also be important here as they can induce temporary or more enduring psychotic states, and can obviously have a significant impact on capacity.

- personality disorder (which has been described as '. . . deeply ingrained and enduring behaviour patterns, manifesting as inflexible responses to a broad range of personal and social situations. They represent extreme or significant deviations from the way in which the average individual in a given culture perceives, thinks, feels and, particularly, relates to others').[6] Personality disorders are further subdivided into:

  - Specific personality disorders ('severe disturbances in the personality and behavioural tendencies of the individual; not directly resulting from disease, damage, or other insult to the brain, or from another psychiatric disorder').[7]
  - Mixed and other personality disorders ('disorders that are often troublesome but do not demonstrate the specific pattern of symptoms that characterize specific personality disorders . . . as a result they are often more difficult to diagnose').[8]
  - Enduring personality changes ('disorders of adult personality and behaviour that have developed in persons with no previous personality disorder following exposure to catastrophic or excessive prolonged stress, or following a severe psychiatric illness').[9]

In the understanding of mental disorders which may affect a person's capacity to make specific decisions, diagnostic categories can be thought of as existing in a hierarchy:

Organic disorders

▼

Functional psychoses

▼

Non-delusional mental illness and behavioural disorders

It is important to note that a patient may satisfy the diagnostic criteria for more than one diagnosis. This is diagnostically acceptable but it must be remembered that, in certain circumstances, disorders in any position of the hierarchy can have a serious impact on decision-making capacity. For example, pervasive personality disorder, anorexia, or a needle phobia can have a profound impact on an individual's ability to make a specific decision at a specific time.

Specific diagnoses

Aside from broad diagnostic categories, specific psychiatric diagnoses are made on the basis of particular clusters of symptoms and signs. Although there is a tendency for these clusters to overlap, which can give rise to diagnostic disputes, proper concentration on specific symptoms and signs will mean that this overlap is usually relatively unimportant. The MCA makes it clear however that a specific diagnosis or condition should not itself be used to determine lack of capacity.[10] It is the impact of any disorder on the individual's ability to make a specific decision at the time the decision needs to be made that must be assessed.

There are two accepted systems for classifying mental disorders:

- the World Health Organization's International Classification of Disease (ICD);[11] and
- the American Psychiatric Association's Diagnostic and Statistical Manual of Mental Disorders revised 4th edition (DSM-IV-TR).[12]

It is common practice to use diagnostic codes, which add further clarity and consistency (for example the ICD 10 code F43.1 and DSM IV code 309.81 both relate to post-traumatic stress disorder).

17.4 MEDICAL ASSESSMENT OF MENTAL CONDITIONS

Although capacity may be influenced by physical conditions it is crucially important for any assessing doctor to take a full psychiatric history and to carry out a mental state examination, as well as a general medical assessment of the person. In psychiatry, as in all medicine, 'symptoms' are what the patient tells you and 'signs' are the doctor's objective observation of the patient. Although some signs are clearly objective (for instance, a depressed patient may be dishevelled when their appearance is usually kempt) many signs involve a medical interpretation of the patient's symptom complaints. For example, is it the case that a patient's complaint about 'voices' really amounts to auditory hallucinations? Is a strange belief held with such conviction that it amounts to a delusion? This can introduce a degree of ambiguity which is less common in other branches of medicine.

However, it is not the case that psychiatric assessments are inherently personal to the individual doctor or inherently ambiguous. High levels of diagnostic reliability should be expected. Doctors must also take into account cultural and ethnic values and their impact on beliefs and behaviour. In some African and Asian cultures, for example, belief in witchcraft is widespread, affecting the way in which decisions are made but unrelated to the person's mental capacity.

Psychiatric assessment includes assessment for both organic and functional conditions. Hence the assessment should always include at least a brief physical assessment and, when indicated by the history or by physical observation, more detailed physical examination and investigation. The following describes briefly the process of psychiatric assessment.

History

History of presenting complaint

A description by the patient of their main symptoms and their duration is important. Acute onset of severe symptoms can, for example, imply an organic origin. The doctor will pursue symptoms, through asking specific direct questions aimed at elucidating the symptoms and specifically considering the possible differential diagnosis. Where the assessment is in relation to the patient's capacity, it may also be appropriate to pursue certain relevant symptoms in detail and to ask questions specifically relevant to the particular decision or test of capacity concerned.

Background history

This includes a brief description of the patient's personal history, family history, psychosexual history (including where relevant, obstetric and gynaecological history), social history and any previous forensic history.

Pre-morbid personality

A description by the patient, or more appropriately by a relative or others, of the patient's usual personality (that is, when the patient is not mentally or otherwise ill). This is important as a baseline against which the patient's current symptoms and presentation at interview can be assessed.

Previous medical history

This will detail all non-psychiatric conditions and treatments, including reference to any drugs that the patient is currently taking. The history may give clues as to a physical cause of apparently psychiatric symptoms.

Previous psychiatric history

This can be of relevance to current mental state assessment. A history of previous disorder may give clues about the origins of present symptoms or signs.

Drugs and alcohol history

This may be of great relevance to the determination of the differential diagnosis of mental disorder, since drugs or chronic alcohol abuse can cause psychiatric presentations.

Information from others

This is important because patients may misrepresent symptoms by either hiding them or exaggerating them, or they may describe their usual personality in a way which is heavily influenced by their current illness. Depressed patients may for example describe themselves as being 'useless' and 'incapable at work' whereas the reverse is the case. In assessing a person for some legal capacity, however, it is important to bear in mind that a relative or other person providing the information may have a vested interest, either social or financial, in the doctor's assessment of the person's capacity and care must be taken to allow for this possibility. Information from a number of people may be essential to sift out truth from bias, but always bearing in mind the patient's right to confidentiality (see **2.2** and **13.7**).

Mental state examination

This is an objective assessment of the patient's mental functioning. The purpose of such an examination is to define specific abnormalities and disabilities and to establish a diagnosis. It is only through detailed assessment of specific aspects of mental functioning that capacity can properly be assessed. The following features will be relevant in any assessment carried out by a doctor:

- appearance and behaviour;
- speech;
- mood;

- thought;
- perception;
- cognition;
- orientation;
- memory;
- intelligence;
- insight.

An explanation of the process of the mental state examination is set out in **16.5**.

Physical examination

Psychiatric assessment may properly include a brief physical assessment. In some cases, where indicated by the person's medical history or by physical observation, a more detailed physical examination and investigation may be required. It is important to remember that an apparent psychiatric presentation can be reflective of an organic neurological disorder and that some patients can present neurologically and yet have a primary psychiatric condition, hysterical symptoms being an obvious example. The neurology of higher cortical functions (such as memory, orientation, concentration, language) and psychiatry are often intricately intertwined, as evidenced in conditions such as dementia, which is both 'psychiatric' and 'neurological'. Many functional psychiatric conditions, such as schizophrenia, have demonstrable organic aspects and are also probably partially determined by genetic predisposition, obstetric complications, childhood infections, and perhaps other conditions affecting the brain.

Medical records

It is important for the assessing doctor to have access to all relevant medical and psychiatric records. These give an historical picture of a known current disorder, as well as giving diagnostic clues to what might be a so far undiagnosed disorder. In assessing capacity an historical view may be of particular importance, especially in relation both to the likely response to treatment and to prognosis, since these may affect future capacity. Assessment of the likely duration of disabilities may be crucially important in offering a view about capacity. These issues are especially important in cases where the decision or the legal process relating to it can be delayed. Wherever possible, priority should be given to enabling people to regain capacity and hence to retake control over their own lives.

17.5   GENERAL GUIDANCE

The giving of effective instructions by lawyers to doctors, and the provision of reliable and focussed assessments of capacity by doctors for lawyers and for the courts, depend upon each profession understanding the very different methods and ways of thinking of the other. Lawyers must be capable of giving clear questions for doctors to answer, and doctors must understand that they are providing medical information that may be used for an entirely non-medical, that is, legal, purpose. What is crucial is that each understands not only the boundaries of their own role, but also the methods and models of the other in order to negotiate the interface between the two disciplines.

NOTES

1. *In the Estate of Park, Park* v. *Park* [1954] P 112; *Masterman-Lister* v. *Brutton & Co and Jewell & Home Counties Dairies* [2002] EWCA Civ 1889, CA.
2. The statutory test of capacity in ss.2 and 3 of the Mental Capacity Act 2005, taking account of the principles in s.1. (See also **Chapter 3**.)
3. *Kenward* v. *Adams* (1975) *The Times*, 29 November 1975. The 'golden rule' about when medical evidence should be obtained is discussed in detail in **4.5** and **6.5**.
4. Mental Capacity Act 2005, s.2(1).
5. See British Psychological Society's Assessment of Capacity Guidelines Group (2006) *Assessment of Capacity in Adults: Interim Guidance for Psychologists*, British Psychological Society.
6. See 'Disorders of adult personality and behaviour (F60-F69)' in World Health Organization (1992–1994) *International Classification of Diseases 10th edition (ICD-10, 2007 update)*, World Health Organization.
7. Ibid: definition of 'specific personality disorders' at F60.
8. Ibid: definition of 'mixed and other personality disorders' at F61.
9. Ibid: definition of 'enduring personality changes, not attributable to brain damage and disease' at F62.
10. Mental Capacity Act 2005, s.2(1)–(3).
11. World Health Organization (1992–1994) *International Classification of Diseases 10th edition (ICD-10, 2007 update)*, World Health Organization. See **www.who.int/classifications/icd/en**.
12. American Psychiatric Association (1994, revised 2000) *Diagnostic and Statistical Manual of Mental Disorders* 4th edition (DSM-IV-TR). American Psychiatric Association. See **www.psychiatry.org**.

APPENDIX A

Mental Capacity Act 2005, ss.1–6 (as amended by Mental Health Act 2007)

PART 1
PERSONS WHO LACK CAPACITY

The principles

1 The principles

    (1)   The following principles apply for the purposes of this Act.

    (2)   A person must be assumed to have capacity unless it is established that he lacks capacity.

    (3)   A person is not to be treated as unable to make a decision unless all practicable steps to help him to do so have been taken without success.

    (4)   A person is not to be treated as unable to make a decision merely because he makes an unwise decision.

    (5)   An act done, or decision made, under this Act for or on behalf of a person who lacks capacity must be done, or made, in his best interests.

    (6)   Before the act is done, or the decision is made, regard must be had to whether the purpose for which it is needed can be as effectively achieved in a way that is less restrictive of the person's rights and freedom of action.

Preliminary

2 People who lack capacity

    (1)   For the purposes of this Act, a person lacks capacity in relation to a matter if at the material time he is unable to make a decision for himself in relation to the matter because of an impairment of, or a disturbance in the functioning of, the mind or brain.

    (2)   It does not matter whether the impairment or disturbance is permanent or temporary.

    (3)   A lack of capacity cannot be established merely by reference to–

        (a)   a person's age or appearance, or

        (b)   a condition of his, or an aspect of his behaviour, which might lead others to make unjustified assumptions about his capacity.

    (4)   In proceedings under this Act or any other enactment, any question whether a person lacks capacity within the meaning of this Act must be decided on the balance of probabilities.

    (5)   No power which a person ('D') may exercise under this Act–

        (a)   in relation to a person who lacks capacity, or

        (b)   where D reasonably thinks that a person lacks capacity, is exercisable in relation to a person under 16.

(6) Subsection (5) is subject to section 18(3).

3 Inability to make decisions

(1) For the purposes of section 2, a person is unable to make a decision for himself if he is unable–

   (a) to understand the information relevant to the decision,

   (b) to retain that information,

   (c) to use or weigh that information as part of the process of making the decision, or

   (d) to communicate his decision (whether by talking, using sign language or any other means).

(2) A person is not to be regarded as unable to understand the information relevant to a decision if he is able to understand an explanation of it given to him in a way that is appropriate to his circumstances (using simple language, visual aids or any other means).

(3) The fact that a person is able to retain the information relevant to a decision for a short period only does not prevent him from being regarded as able to make the decision.

(4) The information relevant to a decision includes information about the reasonably foreseeable consequences of–

   (a) deciding one way or another, or

   (b) failing to make the decision.

4 Best interests

(1) In determining for the purposes of this Act what is in a person's best interests, the person making the determination must not make it merely on the basis of–

   (a) the person's age or appearance, or

   (b) a condition of his, or an aspect of his behaviour, which might lead others to make unjustified assumptions about what might be in his best interests.

(2) The person making the determination must consider all the relevant circumstances and, in particular, take the following steps.

(3) He must consider–

   (a) whether it is likely that the person will at some time have capacity in relation to the matter in question, and

   (b) if it appears likely that he will, when that is likely to be.

(4) He must, so far as reasonably practicable, permit and encourage the person to participate, or to improve his ability to participate, as fully as possible in any act done for him and any decision affecting him.

(5) Where the determination relates to life-sustaining treatment he must not, in considering whether the treatment is in the best interests of the person concerned, be motivated by a desire to bring about his death.

(6) He must consider, so far as is reasonably ascertainable–

   (a) the person's past and present wishes and feelings (and, in particular, any relevant written statement made by him when he had capacity),

    (b)   the beliefs and values that would be likely to influence his decision if he had capacity, and

    (c)   the other factors that he would be likely to consider if he were able to do so.

(7)   He must take into account, if it is practicable and appropriate to consult them, the views of–

    (a)   anyone named by the person as someone to be consulted on the matter in question or on matters of that kind,

    (b)   anyone engaged in caring for the person or interested in his welfare,

    (c)   any donee of a lasting power of attorney granted by the person, and

    (d)   any deputy appointed for the person by the court,

as to what would be in the person's best interests and, in particular, as to the matters mentioned in subsection (6).

(8)   The duties imposed by subsections (1) to (7) also apply in relation to the exercise of any powers which–

    (a)   are exercisable under a lasting power of attorney, or

    (b)   are exercisable by a person under this Act where he reasonably believes that another person lacks capacity.

(9)   In the case of an act done, or a decision made, by a person other than the court, there is sufficient compliance with this section if (having complied with the requirements of subsections (1) to (7)) he reasonably believes that what he does or decides is in the best interests of the person concerned.

(10) 'Life-sustaining treatment' means treatment which in the view of a person providing health care for the person concerned is necessary to sustain life.

(11) 'Relevant circumstances' are those–

    (a)   of which the person making the determination is aware, and

    (b)   which it would be reasonable to regard as relevant.

4A   Restriction on deprivation of liberty

(1)   This Act does not authorise any person ('D') to deprive any other person ('P') of his liberty.

(2)   But that is subject to–

    (a)   the following provisions of this section, and

    (b)   section 4B.

(3)   D may deprive P of his liberty if, by doing so, D is giving effect to a relevant decision of the court.

(4)   A relevant decision of the court is a decision made by an order under section 16(2)(a) in relation to a matter concerning P's personal welfare.

(5)   D may deprive P of his liberty if the deprivation is authorised by Schedule A1 (hospital and care home residents: deprivation of liberty).

4B   Deprivation of liberty necessary for life-sustaining treatment etc

(1)   If the following conditions are met, D is authorised to deprive P of his liberty while a decision as respects any relevant issue is sought from the court.

(2)   The first condition is that there is a question about whether D is authorised to deprive P of his liberty under section 4A.

(3) The second condition is that the deprivation of liberty–

    (a) is wholly or partly for the purpose of–

        (i) giving P life-sustaining treatment, or
        (ii) doing any vital act, or

    (b) consists wholly or partly of–

        (i) giving P life-sustaining treatment, or
        (ii) doing any vital act.

(4) The third condition is that the deprivation of liberty is necessary in order to–

    (a) give the life-sustaining treatment, or
    (b) do the vital act.

(5) A vital act is any act which the person doing it reasonably believes to be necessary to prevent a serious deterioration in P's condition.

5 Acts in connection with care or treatment

(1) If a person ('D') does an act in connection with the care or treatment of another person ('P'), the act is one to which this section applies if–

    (a) before doing the act, D takes reasonable steps to establish whether P lacks capacity in relation to the matter in question, and
    (b) when doing the act, D reasonably believes–

        (i) that P lacks capacity in relation to the matter, and
        (ii) that it will be in P's best interests for the act to be done.

(2) D does not incur any liability in relation to the act that he would not have incurred if P–

    (a) had had capacity to consent in relation to the matter, and
    (b) had consented to D's doing the act.

(3) Nothing in this section excludes a person's civil liability for loss or damage, or his criminal liability, resulting from his negligence in doing the act.

(4) Nothing in this section affects the operation of sections 24 to 26 (advance decisions to refuse treatment).

6 Section 5 acts: limitations

(1) If D does an act that is intended to restrain P, it is not an act to which section 5 applies unless two further conditions are satisfied.

(2) The first condition is that D reasonably believes that it is necessary to do the act in order to prevent harm to P.

(3) The second is that the act is a proportionate response to–

    (a) the likelihood of P's suffering harm, and
    (b) the seriousness of that harm.

(4) For the purposes of this section D restrains P if he–

    (a) uses, or threatens to use, force to secure the doing of an act which P resists, or
    (b) restricts P's liberty of movement, whether or not P resists.

(5)   . . .

(6)   Section 5 does not authorise a person to do an act which conflicts with a decision made, within the scope of his authority and in accordance with this Part, by–

(a)   a donee of a lasting power of attorney granted by P, or

(b)   a deputy appointed for P by the court.

(7)   But nothing in subsection (6) stops a person–

(a)   providing life-sustaining treatment, or

(b)   doing any act which he reasonably believes to be necessary to prevent a serious deterioration in P's condition,

while a decision as respects any relevant issue is sought from the court.

Mental Capacity Act 2005: Code of Practice, Chapters 2–4

2 WHAT ARE THE STATUTORY PRINCIPLES AND HOW SHOULD THEY BE APPLIED?

Section 1 of the Act sets out the five 'statutory principles' – the values that underpin the legal requirements in the Act. The Act is intended to be enabling and supportive of people who lack capacity, not restricting or controlling of their lives. It aims to protect people who lack capacity to make particular decisions, but also to maximise their ability to make decisions, or to participate in decision-making, as far as they are able to do so.

The five statutory principles are:

1. A person must be assumed to have capacity unless it is established that they lack capacity.
2. A person is not to be treated as unable to make a decision unless all practicable steps to help him to do so have been taken without success.
3. A person is not to be treated as unable to make a decision merely because he makes an unwise decision.
4. An act done, or decision made, under this Act for or on behalf of a person who lacks capacity must be done, or made, in his best interests.
5. Before the act is done, or the decision is made, regard must be had to whether the purpose for which it is needed can be as effectively achieved in a way that is less restrictive of the person's rights and freedom of action.

This chapter provides guidance on how people should interpret and apply the statutory principles when using the Act. Following the principles and applying them to the Act's framework for decision-making will help to ensure not only that appropriate action is taken in individual cases, but also to point the way to solutions in difficult or uncertain situations.

In this chapter, as throughout the Code, a person's capacity (or lack of capacity) refers specifically to their capacity to make a particular decision at the time it needs to be made.

Quick summary

- Every adult has the right to make their own decisions if they have the capacity to do so. Family carers and healthcare or social care staff must assume that a person has the capacity to make decisions, unless it can be established that the person does not have capacity.
- People should receive support to help them make their own decisions. Before concluding that individuals lack capacity to make a particular decision, it is important to take all possible steps to try to help them reach a decision themselves.

- People have the right to make decisions that others might think are unwise. A person who makes a decision that others think is unwise should not automatically be labelled as lacking the capacity to make a decision.
- Any act done for, or any decision made on behalf of, someone who lacks capacity must be in their best interests.
- Any act done for, or any decision made on behalf of, someone who lacks capacity should be an option that is less restrictive of their basic rights and freedoms – as long as it is still in their best interests.

What is the role of the statutory principles?

2.1   The statutory principles aim to:

- protect people who lack capacity and
- help them take part, as much as possible, in decisions that affect them.

They aim to assist and support people who may lack capacity to make particular decisions, not to restrict or control their lives.

2.2   The statutory principles apply to any act done or decision made under the Act. When followed and applied to the Act's decision-making framework, they will help people take appropriate action in individual cases. They will also help people find solutions in difficult or uncertain situations.

How should the statutory principles be applied?

Principle 1: 'A person must be assumed to have capacity unless it is established that he lacks capacity.' (section 1(2))

2.3   This principle states that every adult has the right to make their own decisions – unless there is proof that they lack the capacity to make a particular decision when it needs to be made. This has been a fundamental principle of the common law for many years and it is now set out in the Act.

2.4   It is important to balance people's right to make a decision with their right to safety and protection when they can't make decisions to protect themselves. But the starting assumption must always be that an individual has the capacity, until there is proof that they do not. Chapter 4 explains the Act's definition of 'lack of capacity' and the processes involved in assessing capacity.

Scenario: Assessing a person's capacity to make decisions

When planning for her retirement, Mrs Arnold made and registered a Lasting Power of Attorney (LPA) – a legal process that would allow her son to manage her property and financial affairs if she ever lacked capacity to manage them herself. She has now been diagnosed with dementia, and her son is worried that she is becoming confused about money.

Her son must assume that his mother has capacity to manage her affairs. Then he must consider each of Mrs Arnold's financial decisions as she makes them, giving her any help and support she needs to make these decisions herself.

Mrs Arnold's son goes shopping with her, and he sees she is quite capable of finding goods and making sure she gets the correct change. But when she needs to make decisions about her investments, Mrs Arnold gets confused – even though she has made such decisions in the past. She still doesn't understand after her son explains the different options.

Her son concludes that she has capacity to deal with everyday financial matters but not more difficult affairs at this time. Therefore, he is able to use the LPA for the difficult financial decisions his mother can't make. But Mrs Arnold can continue to deal with her other affairs for as long as she has capacity to do so.

2.5 Some people may need help to be able to make a decision or to communicate their decision. However, this does not necessarily mean that they cannot make that decision – unless there is proof that they do lack capacity to do so. Anyone who believes that a person lacks capacity should be able to prove their case. Chapter 4 explains the standard of proof required.

Principle 2: 'A person is not to be treated as unable to make a decision unless all practicable steps to help him to do so have been taken without success.' (section 1(3))

2.6 It is important to do everything practical (the Act uses the term 'practicable') to help a person make a decision for themselves before concluding that they lack capacity to do so. People with an illness or disability affecting their ability to make a decision should receive support to help them make as many decisions as they can. This principle aims to stop people being automatically labelled as lacking capacity to make particular decisions. Because it encourages individuals to play as big a role as possible in decision-making, it also helps prevent unnecessary interventions in their lives.

2.7 The kind of support people might need to help them make a decision varies. It depends on personal circumstances, the kind of decision that has to be made and the time available to make the decision. It might include:

- using a different form of communication (for example, non-verbal communication)
- providing information in a more accessible form (for example, photographs, drawings, or tapes)
- treating a medical condition which may be affecting the person's capacity or
- having a structured programme to improve a person's capacity to make particular decisions (for example, helping a person with learning disabilities to learn new skills).

Chapter 3 gives more information on ways to help people make decisions for themselves.

Scenario: Taking steps to help people make decisions for themselves

Mr Jackson is brought into hospital following a traffic accident. He is conscious but in shock. He cannot speak and is clearly in distress, making noises and gestures.

From his behaviour, hospital staff conclude that Mr Jackson currently lacks the capacity to make decisions about treatment for his injuries, and they give him urgent treatment. They hope that after he has recovered from the shock they can use an advocate to help explain things to him.

However, one of the nurses thinks she recognises some of his gestures as sign language, and tries signing to him. Mr Jackson immediately becomes calmer, and the doctors realise that he can communicate in sign language. He can also answer some written questions about his injuries.

The hospital brings in a qualified sign language interpreter and concludes that Mr Jackson has the capacity to make decisions about any further treatment.

2.8   Anyone supporting a person who may lack capacity should not use excessive persuasion or 'undue pressure'.[1] This might include behaving in a manner which is overbearing or dominating, or seeking to influence the person's decision, and could push a person into making a decision they might not otherwise have made. However, it is important to provide appropriate advice and information.

Scenario: Giving appropriate advice and support

Sara, a young woman with severe depression, is getting treatment from mental health services. Her psychiatrist determines that she has capacity to make decisions about treatment, if she gets advice and support.

Her mother is trying to persuade Sara to agree to electro-convulsive therapy (ECT), which helped her mother when she had clinical depression in the past. However, a friend has told Sara that ECT is 'barbaric'.

The psychiatrist provides factual information about the different types of treatment available and explains their advantages and disadvantages. She also describes how different people experience different reactions or side effects. Sara is then able to consider what treatment is right for her, based on factual information rather than the personal opinions of her mother and friend.

2.9   In some situations treatment cannot be delayed while a person gets support to make a decision. This can happen in emergency situations or when an urgent decision is required (for example, immediate medical treatment). In these situations, the only practical and appropriate steps might be to keep a person informed of what is happening and why.

Principle 3: 'A person is not to be treated as unable to make a decision merely because he makes an unwise decision.' (section 1(4))

2.10   Everybody has their own values, beliefs, preferences and attitudes. A person should not be assumed to lack the capacity to make a decision just because other people think their decision is unwise. This applies even if family members, friends or healthcare or social care staff are unhappy with a decision.

Scenario: Allowing people to make decisions that others think are unwise

Mr Garvey is a 40-year-old man with a history of mental health problems. He sees a Community Psychiatric Nurse (CPN) regularly. Mr Garvey decides to spend £2,000 of his savings on a camper van to travel around Scotland for six months. His CPN is concerned that it will be difficult to give Mr Garvey continuous support and treatment while travelling, and that his mental health might deteriorate as a result.

However, having talked it through with his CPN, it is clear that Mr Garvey is fully aware of these concerns and has the capacity to make this particular decision. He has decided he would like to have a break and thinks this will be good for him.

Just because, in the CPN's opinion, continuity of care might be a wiser option, it should not be assumed that Mr Garvey lacks the capacity to make this decision for himself.

2.11 There may be cause for concern if somebody:

- repeatedly makes unwise decisions that put them at significant risk of harm or exploitation or
- makes a particular unwise decision that is obviously irrational or out of character.

These things do not necessarily mean that somebody lacks capacity. But there might be need for further investigation, taking into account the person's past decisions and choices. For example, have they developed a medical condition or disorder that is affecting their capacity to make particular decisions? Are they easily influenced by undue pressure? Or do they need more information to help them understand the consequences of the decision they are making?

Scenario: Decisions that cause concern

Cyril, an elderly man with early signs of dementia, spends nearly £300 on fresh fish from a door-to-door salesman. He has always been fond of fish and has previously bought small amounts in this way. Before his dementia, Cyril was always very careful with his money and would never have spent so much on fish in one go.

This decision alone may not automatically mean Cyril now lacks capacity to manage all aspects of his property and affairs. But his daughter makes further enquiries and discovers Cyril has overpaid his cleaner on several occasions – something he has never done in the past. He has also made payments from his savings that he cannot account for.

His daughter decides it is time to use the registered Lasting Power of Attorney her father made in the past. This gives her the authority to manage Cyril's property and affairs whenever he lacks the capacity to manage them himself. She takes control of Cyril's chequebook to protect him from possible exploitation, but she can still ensure he has enough money to spend on his everyday needs.

Principle 4: 'An act done, or decision made, under this Act for or on behalf of a person who lacks capacity must be done, or made, in his best interests.' (section 1(5))

2.12 The principle of acting or making a decision in the best interests of a person who lacks capacity to make the decision in question is a well-established principle in the common law.[2] This principle is now set out in the Act, so that a person's best interests must be the basis for all decisions made and actions carried out on their behalf in situations where they lack capacity to make those particular decisions for themselves. The only exceptions to this are around research (see chapter 11) and advance decisions to refuse treatment (see chapter 9) where other safeguards apply.

2.13 It is impossible to give a single description of what 'best interests' are, because they depend on individual circumstances. However, section 4 of the Act sets out a checklist of steps to follow in order to determine what is in the best interests of a person who lacks capacity to make the decision in question each time someone acts or makes a decision on that person's behalf. See chapter 5 for detailed guidance and examples.

Principle 5: 'Before the act is done, or the decision is made, regard must be had to whether the purpose for which it is needed can be as effectively achieved in a way that is less restrictive of the person's rights and freedom of action.' (section 1(6))

2.14 Before somebody makes a decision or acts on behalf of a person who lacks capacity to make that decision or consent to the act, they must always question if they can do something else that would interfere less with the person's basic rights and freedoms. This is called finding the 'less restrictive alternative'. It includes considering whether there is a need to act or make a decision at all.

2.15 Where there is more than one option, it is important to explore ways that would be less restrictive or allow the most freedom for a person who lacks capacity to make the decision in question. However, the final decision must always allow the original purpose of the decision or act to be achieved.

2.16 Any decision or action must still be in the best interests of the person who lacks capacity. So sometimes it may be necessary to choose an option that is not the least restrictive alternative if that option is in the person's best interests. In practice, the process of choosing a less restrictive option and deciding what is in the person's best interests will be combined. But both principles must be applied each time a decision or action may be taken on behalf of a person who lacks capacity to make the relevant decision.

Scenario: Finding a less restrictive option

Sunil, a young man with severe learning disabilities, also has a very severe and unpredictable form of epilepsy that is associated with drop attacks. These can result in serious injury. A neurologist has advised that, to limit the harm that might come from these attacks, Sunil should either be under constant close observation, or wear a protective helmet.

After assessment, it is decided that Sunil lacks capacity to decide on the most appropriate course of action for himself. But through his actions and behaviour, Sunil makes it clear he doesn't like to be too closely observed – even though he likes having company.

The staff of the home where he lives consider various options, such as providing a special room for him with soft furnishings, finding ways to keep him under close observation or getting him to wear a helmet. In discussion with Sunil's parents, they agree that the option that is in his best interests, and is less restrictive, will be the helmet – as it will enable him to go out, and prevent further harm.

---

3 HOW SHOULD PEOPLE BE HELPED TO MAKE THEIR OWN DECISIONS?

Before deciding that someone lacks capacity to make a particular decision, it is important to take all practical and appropriate steps to enable them to make that decision themselves (statutory principle 2, see chapter 2). In addition, as section 3(2) of the Act underlines, these steps (such as helping individuals to communicate) must be taken in a way which reflects the person's individual circumstances and meets their particular needs. This chapter provides practical guidance on how to support people to make decisions for themselves, or play as big a role as possible in decision-making.

In this chapter, as throughout the Code, a person's capacity (or lack of capacity) refers specifically to their capacity to make a particular decision at the time it needs to be made.

Quick summary

To help someone make a decision for themselves, check the following points:

Providing relevant information

- Does the person have all the relevant information they need to make a particular decision?
- If they have a choice, have they been given information on all the alternatives?

Communicating in an appropriate way

- Could information be explained or presented in a way that is easier for the person to understand (for example, by using simple language or visual aids)?
- Have different methods of communication been explored if required, including non-verbal communication?
- Could anyone else help with communication (for example, a family member, support worker, interpreter, speech and language therapist or advocate)?

Making the person feel at ease

- Are there particular times of day when the person's understanding is better?
- Are there particular locations where they may feel more at ease?
- Could the decision be put off to see whether the person can make the decision at a later time when circumstances are right for them?

Supporting the person

- Can anyone else help or support the person to make choices or express a view?

How can someone be helped to make a decision?

3.1   There are several ways in which people can be helped and supported to enable them to make a decision for themselves. These will vary depending on the decision to be made, the timescale for making the decision and the individual circumstances of the person making it.

3.2   The Act applies to a wide range of people with different conditions that may affect their capacity to make particular decisions. So, the appropriate steps to take will depend on:

- a person's individual circumstances (for example, somebody with learning difficulties may need a different approach to somebody with dementia)
- the decision the person has to make and
- the length of time they have to make it.

3.3   Significant, one-off decisions (such as moving house) will require different considerations from day-to-day decisions about a person's care and welfare. However, the same general processes should apply to each decision.

3.4   In most cases, only some of the steps described in this chapter will be relevant or appropriate, and the list included here is not exhaustive. It is up to the people (whether family carers, paid carers, healthcare staff or anyone else) caring for or supporting an individual to consider what is possible and appropriate in individual cases. In all cases it is extremely important to find the most effective way of communicating with the person concerned. Good communication is essential for explaining relevant information in an appropriate way and for ensuring that the steps being taken meet an individual's needs.

3.5   Providing appropriate help with decision-making should form part of care planning processes for people receiving health or social care services. Examples include:

- Person Centred Planning for people with learning disabilities
- the Care Programme Approach for people with mental disorders
- the Single Assessment Process for older people in England, and
- the Unified Assessment Process in Wales.

What happens in emergency situations?

3.6   Clearly, in emergency medical situations (for example, where a person collapses with a heart attack or for some unknown reason and is brought unconscious into a hospital), urgent decisions will have to be made and immediate action taken in the person's best interests. In these situations, it may not be practical or appropriate to delay the treatment while trying to help the person make their own decisions, or to consult with any known attorneys or deputies. However, even in emergency situations, healthcare staff should try to communicate with the person and keep them informed of what is happening.

What information should be provided to people and how should it be provided?

3.7   Providing relevant information is essential in all decision-making. For example, to make a choice about what they want for breakfast, people need to know what food is available. If the decision concerns medical treatment, the doctor must explain the purpose and effect of the course of treatment and the likely consequences of accepting or refusing treatment.

3.8   All practical and appropriate steps must be taken to help people to make a decision for themselves. Information must be tailored to an individual's needs and abilities. It must also be in the easiest and most appropriate form of communication for the person concerned.

What information is relevant?

3.9   The Act cannot state exactly what information will be relevant in each case. Anyone helping someone to make a decision for themselves should therefore follow these steps.

- Take time to explain anything that might help the person make a decision. It is important that they have access to all the information they need to make an informed decision.
- Try not to give more detail than the person needs – this might confuse them. In some cases, a simple, broad explanation will be enough. But it must not miss out important information.
- What are the risks and benefits? Describe any foreseeable consequences of making the decision, and of not making any decision at all.
- Explain the effects the decision might have on the person and those close to them – including the people involved in their care.
- If they have a choice, give them the same information in a balanced way for all the options.
- For some types of decisions, it may be important to give access to advice from elsewhere. This may be independent or specialist advice (for example, from a medical practitioner or a financial or legal adviser). But it might simply be advice from trusted friends or relatives.

Communication – general guidance

3.10 To help someone make a decision for themselves, all possible and appropriate means of communication should be tried.

- Ask people who know the person well about the best form of communication (try speaking to family members, carers, day centre staff or support workers). They may also know somebody the person can communicate with easily, or the time when it is best to communicate with them.
- Use simple language. Where appropriate, use pictures, objects or illustrations to demonstrate ideas.
- Speak at the right volume and speed, with appropriate words and sentence structure. It may be helpful to pause to check understanding or show that a choice is available.
- Break down difficult information into smaller points that are easy to understand. Allow the person time to consider and understand each point before continuing.
- It may be necessary to repeat information or go back over a point several times.
- Is help available from people the person trusts (relatives, friends, GP, social worker, religious or community leaders)? If so, make sure the person's right to confidentiality is respected.
- Be aware of cultural, ethnic or religious factors that shape a person's way of thinking, behaviour or communication. For example, in some cultures it is important to involve the community in decision-making. Some religious beliefs (for example, those of Jehovah's Witnesses or Christian Scientists) may influence the person's approach to medical treatment and information about treatment decisions.
- If necessary, consider using a professional language interpreter. Even if a person communicated in English or Welsh in the past, they may have lost some verbal skills (for example, because of dementia). They may now prefer to communicate in their first language. It is often more appropriate to use a professional interpreter rather than to use family members.
- If using pictures to help communication, make sure they are relevant and the person can understand them easily. For example, a red bus may represent a form of transport to one person but a day trip to another.
- Would an advocate (someone who can support and represent the person) improve communication in the current situation? (See chapters 10 and 15 for more information about advocates.)

Scenario: Providing relevant information

Mrs Thomas has Alzheimer's disease and lives in a care home. She enjoys taking part in the activities provided at the home. Today there is a choice between going to a flower show, attending her usual pottery class or watching a DVD. Although she has the capacity to choose, having to decide is making her anxious.

The care assistant carefully explains the different options. She tells Mrs Thomas about the DVD she could watch, but Mrs Thomas doesn't like the sound of it. The care assistant shows her a leaflet about the flower show. She explains the plans for the day, where the show is being held and how long it will take to get there in the mini-van. She has to repeat this information several times, as Mrs Thomas keeps asking whether they will be back in time for supper. She also tells Mrs Thomas that one of her friends is going on the trip.

At first, Mrs Thomas is reluctant to disturb her usual routine. But the care assistant reassures her she will not lose her place at pottery if she misses a class. With this information, Mrs Thomas can therefore choose whether or not to go on the day trip.

Helping people with specific communication or cognitive problems

3.11 Where people have specific communication or cognitive problems, the following steps can help:

- Find out how the person is used to communicating. Do they use picture boards or Makaton (signs and symbols for people with communication or learning difficulties)? Or do they have a way of communicating that is only known to those close to them?
- If the person has hearing difficulties, use their preferred method of communication (for example, visual aids, written messages or sign language). Where possible, use a qualified interpreter.
- Are mechanical devices such as voice synthesisers, keyboards or other computer equipment available to help?
- If the person does not use verbal communication skills, allow more time to learn how to communicate effectively.
- For people who use non-verbal methods of communication, their behaviour (in particular, changes in behaviour) can provide indications of their feelings.
- Some people may prefer to use non-verbal means of communication and can communicate most effectively in written form using computers or other communication technologies. This is particularly true for those with autistic spectrum disorders.
- For people with specific communication difficulties, consider other types of professional help (for example, a speech and language therapist or an expert in clinical neuropsychology).

Scenario: Helping people with specific communication difficulties

David is a deafblind man with learning disabilities who has no formal communication. He lives in a specialist home. He begins to bang his head against the wall and repeats this behaviour throughout the day. He has not done this before.

The staff in the home are worried and discuss ways to reduce the risk of injury. They come up with a range of possible interventions, aimed at engaging him with activities and keeping him away from objects that could injure him. They assess these as less restrictive ways to ensure he is safe. But David lacks the capacity to make a decision about which would be the best option.

The staff call in a specialist in challenging behaviour, who says that David's behaviour is communicative. After investigating this further, staff discover he is in pain because of tooth decay. They consult a dentist about how to resolve this, and the dentist decides it is in David's best interests to get treatment for the tooth decay. After treatment, David's head-banging stops.

What steps should be taken to put a person at ease?

3.12 To help put someone at ease and so improve their ability to make a decision, careful consideration should be given to both location and timing.

Location

3.13 In terms of location, consider the following:

- Where possible, choose a location where the person feels most at ease. For example, people are usually more comfortable in their own home than at a doctor's surgery.

200

- Would the person find it easier to make their decision in a relevant location? For example, could you help them decide about medical treatment by taking them to hospital to see what is involved?
- Choose a quiet location where the discussion can't be easily interrupted.
- Try to eliminate any background noise or distractions (for example, the television or radio, or people talking).
- Choose a location where the person's privacy and dignity can be properly respected.

Timing

3.14 In terms of timing, consider the following:

- Try to choose the time of day when the person is most alert – some people are better in the mornings, others are more lively in the afternoon or early evening. It may be necessary to try several times before a decision can be made.
- If the person's capacity is likely to improve in the foreseeable future, wait until it has done so – if practical and appropriate. For example, this might be the case after treatment for depression or a psychotic episode. Obviously, this may not be practical and appropriate if the decision is urgent.
- Some medication could affect a person's capacity (for example, medication which causes drowsiness or affects memory). Can the decision be delayed until side effects have subsided?
- Take one decision at a time – be careful to avoid making the person tired or confused.
- Don't rush – allow the person time to think things over or ask for clarification, where that is possible and appropriate.
- Avoid or challenge time limits that are unnecessary if the decision is not urgent. Delaying the decision may enable further steps to be taken to assist people to make the decision for themselves.

Scenario: Getting the location and timing right

Luke, a young man, was seriously injured in a road traffic accident and suffered permanent brain damage. He has been in hospital several months, and has made good progress, but he gets very frustrated at his inability to concentrate or do things for himself.

Luke now needs surgical treatment on his leg. During the early morning ward round, the surgeon tries to explain what is involved in the operation. She asks Luke to sign a consent form, but he gets angry and says he doesn't want to talk about it.

His key nurse knows that Luke becomes more alert and capable later in the day. After lunch, she asks him if he would like to discuss the operation again. She also knows that he responds better one-to-one than in a group. So she takes Luke into a private room and repeats the information that the surgeon gave him earlier. He understands why the treatment is needed, what is involved and the likely consequences. Therefore, Luke has the capacity to make a decision about the operation.

Support from other people

3.15 In some circumstances, individuals will be more comfortable making decisions when someone else is there to support them.

- Might the person benefit from having another person present? Sometimes having a relative or friend nearby can provide helpful support and reduce anxiety. However, some people might find this intrusive, and it could increase their anxiety or affect their ability to make a free choice. Find ways of getting the person's views on this, for example, by watching their behaviour towards other people.

- Always respect a person's right to confidentiality.

Scenario: Getting help from other people

Jane has a learning disability. She expresses herself using some words, facial expressions and body language. She has lived in her current community home all her life, but now needs to move to a new group home. She finds it difficult to discuss abstract ideas or things she hasn't experienced. Staff conclude that she lacks the capacity to decide for herself which new group home she should move to.

The staff involve an advocate to help Jane express her views. Jane's advocate spends time with her in different environments. The advocate uses pictures, symbols and Makaton to find out the things that are important to Jane, and speaks to people who know Jane to find out what they think she likes. She then supports Jane to show their work to her care manager, and checks that the new homes suggested for her are able to meet Jane's needs and preferences.

When the care manager has found some suitable places, Jane's advocate visits the homes with Jane. They take photos of the houses to help her distinguish between them. The advocate then uses the photos to help Jane work out which home she prefers. Jane's own feelings can now play an important part in deciding what is in her best interests – and so in the final decision about where she will live.

What other ways are there to enable decision-making?

3.16 There are other ways to help someone make a decision for themselves.

- Many people find it helpful to talk things over with people they trust – or people who have been in a similar situation or faced similar dilemmas. For example, people with learning difficulties may benefit from the help of a designated support worker or being part of a support network.
- If someone is very distressed (for example, following a death of someone close) or where there are long-standing problems that affect someone's ability to understand an issue, it may be possible to delay a decision so that the person can have psychological therapy, if needed.
- Some organisations have produced materials to help people who need support to make decisions and for those who support them. Some of this material is designed to help people with specific conditions, such as Alzheimer's disease or profound learning disability.
- It may be important to provide access to technology. For example, some people who appear not to communicate well verbally can do so very well using computers.

Scenario: Making the most of technology

Ms Patel has an autistic spectrum disorder. Her family and care staff find it difficult to communicate with her. She refuses to make eye contact, and gets very upset and angry when her carers try to encourage her to speak.

One member of staff notices that Ms Patel is interested in the computer equipment. He shows her how to use the keyboard, and they are able to have a conversation using the computer. An IT specialist works with her to make sure she can make the most of her computing skills to communicate her feelings and decisions.

4 HOW DOES THE ACT DEFINE A PERSON'S CAPACITY TO MAKE A DECISION AND HOW SHOULD CAPACITY BE ASSESSED?

This chapter explains what the Act means by 'capacity' and 'lack of capacity'. It provides guidance on how to assess whether someone has the capacity to make a decision, and suggests when professionals should be involved in the assessment.

In this chapter, as throughout the Code, a person's capacity (or lack of capacity) refers specifically to their capacity to make a particular decision at the time it needs to be made.

Quick summary

This checklist is a summary of points to consider when assessing a person's capacity to make a specific decision. Readers should also refer to the more detailed guidance in this chapter and chapters 2 and 3.

Presuming someone has capacity

* The starting assumption must always be that a person has the capacity to make a decision, unless it can be established that they lack capacity.

Understanding what is meant by capacity and lack of capacity

* A person's capacity must be assessed specifically in terms of their capacity to make a particular decision at the time it needs to be made.

Treating everyone equally

* A person's capacity must not be judged simply on the basis of their age, appearance, condition or an aspect of their behaviour.

Supporting the person to make the decision for themselves

* It is important to take all possible steps to try to help people make a decision for themselves (see chapter 2, principle 2, and chapter 3).

Assessing capacity

Anyone assessing someone's capacity to make a decision for themselves should use the two-stage test of capacity.

* Does the person have an impairment of the mind or brain, or is there some sort of disturbance affecting the way their mind or brain works? (It doesn't matter whether the impairment or disturbance is temporary or permanent.)
* If so, does that impairment or disturbance mean that the person is unable to make the decision in question at the time it needs to be made?

Assessing ability to make a decision

- Does the person have a general understanding of what decision they need to make and why they need to make it?
- Does the person have a general understanding of the likely consequences of making, or not making, this decision?
- Is the person able to understand, retain, use and weigh up the information relevant to this decision?
- Can the person communicate their decision (by talking, using sign language or any other means)? Would the services of a professional (such as a speech and language therapist) be helpful?

Assessing capacity to make more complex or serious decisions

- Is there a need for a more thorough assessment (perhaps by involving a doctor or other professional expert)?

What is mental capacity?

4.1   Mental capacity is the ability to make a decision.

- This includes the ability to make a decision that affects daily life – such as when to get up, what to wear or whether to go to the doctor when feeling ill – as well as more serious or significant decisions.
- It also refers to a person's ability to make a decision that may have legal consequences – for them or others. Examples include agreeing to have medical treatment, buying goods or making a will.

4.2   The starting point must always be to assume that a person has the capacity to make a specific decision (see chapter 2, principle 1). Some people may need help to be able to make or communicate a decision (see chapter 3). But this does not necessarily mean that they lack capacity to do so. What matters is their ability to carry out the processes involved in making the decision – and not the outcome.

What does the Act mean by 'lack of capacity'?

4.3   Section 2(1) of the Act states:

'For the purposes of this Act, a person lacks capacity in relation to a matter if at the material time he is unable to make a decision for himself in relation to the matter because of an impairment of, or a disturbance in the functioning of, the mind or brain.'

This means that a person lacks capacity if:

- they have an impairment or disturbance (for example, a disability, condition or trauma) that affects the way their mind or brain works, and
- the impairment or disturbance means that they are unable to make a specific decision at the time it needs to be made.

4.4   An assessment of a person's capacity must be based on their ability to make a specific decision at the time it needs to be made, and not their ability to make decisions in general. Section 3 of the Act defines what it means to be unable to make a decision (this is explained in paragraph 4.14 below).

4.5 Section 2(2) states that the impairment or disturbance does not have to be permanent. A person can lack capacity to make a decision at the time it needs to be made even if:

- the loss of capacity is partial
- the loss of capacity is temporary
- their capacity changes over time.

A person may also lack capacity to make a decision about one issue but not about others.

4.6 The Act generally applies to people who are aged 16 or older. Chapter 12 explains how the Act affects children and young people – in particular those aged 16 and 17 years.

What safeguards does the Act provide around assessing someone's capacity?

4.7 An assessment that a person lacks capacity to make a decision must never be based simply on:

- their age
- their appearance
- assumptions about their condition, or
- any aspect of their behaviour. (section 2(3))

4.8 The Act deliberately uses the word 'appearance', because it covers all aspects of the way people look. So for example, it includes the physical characteristics of certain conditions (for example, scars, features linked to Down's syndrome or muscle spasms caused by cerebral palsy) as well as aspects of appearance like skin colour, tattoos and body piercings, or the way people dress (including religious dress).

4.9 The word 'condition' is also wide-ranging. It includes physical disabilities, learning difficulties and disabilities, illness related to age, and temporary conditions (for example, drunkenness or unconsciousness). Aspects of behaviour might include extrovert (for example, shouting or gesticulating) and withdrawn behaviour (for example, talking to yourself or avoiding eye contact).

Scenario: Treating everybody equally

Tom, a man with cerebral palsy, has slurred speech. Sometimes he also falls over for no obvious reason.

One day Tom falls in the supermarket. Staff call an ambulance, even though he says he is fine. They think he may need treatment after his fall.

When the ambulance comes, the ambulance crew know they must not make assumptions about Tom's capacity to decide about treatment, based simply on his condition and the effects of his disability. They talk to him and find that he is capable of making healthcare decisions for himself.

What proof of lack of capacity does the Act require?

4.10 Anybody who claims that an individual lacks capacity should be able to provide proof. They need to be able to show, on the balance of probabilities, that the individual lacks capacity to make a particular decision, at the time it needs to be made (section 2(4)). This means being able to show that it is more likely than not that the person lacks capacity to make the decision in question.

What is the test of capacity?

To help determine if a person lacks capacity to make particular decisions, the Act sets out a two-stage test of capacity.

Stage 1: Does the person have an impairment of, or a disturbance in the functioning of, their mind or brain?

4.11 Stage 1 requires proof that the person has an impairment of the mind or brain, or some sort of or disturbance that affects the way their mind or brain works. If a person does not have such an impairment or disturbance of the mind or brain, they will not lack capacity under the Act.

4.12 Examples of an impairment or disturbance in the functioning of the mind or brain may include the following:

- conditions associated with some forms of mental illness
- dementia
- significant learning disabilities
- the long-term effects of brain damage
- physical or medical conditions that cause confusion, drowsiness or loss of consciousness
- delirium
- concussion following a head injury, and
- the symptoms of alcohol or drug use.

Scenario: Assessing whether an impairment or disturbance is affecting someone's ability to make a decision

Mrs Collins is 82 and has had a stroke. This has weakened the left-hand side of her body. She is living in a house that has been the family home for years. Her son wants her to sell her house and live with him.

Mrs Collins likes the idea, but her daughter does not. She thinks her mother will lose independence and her condition will get worse. She talks to her mother's consultant to get information that will help stop the sale. But he says that although Mrs Collins is anxious about the physical effects the stroke has had on her body, it has not caused any mental impairment or affected her brain, so she still has capacity to make her own decision about selling her house.

Stage 2: Does the impairment or disturbance mean that the person is unable to make a specific decision when they need to?

4.13 For a person to lack capacity to make a decision, the Act says their impairment or disturbance must affect their ability to make the specific decision when they need to. But first people must be given all practical and appropriate support to help them make the decision for themselves (see chapter 2, principle 2). Stage 2 can only apply if all practical and appropriate support to help the person make the decision has failed. See chapter 3 for guidance on ways of helping people to make their own decisions.

What does the Act mean by 'inability to make a decision'?

4.14 A person is unable to make a decision if they cannot:

1. understand information about the decision to be made (the Act calls this 'relevant information')
2. retain that information in their mind
3. use or weigh that information as part of the decision-making process, or
4. communicate their decision (by talking, using sign language or any other means). See section 3(1).

4.15 These four points are explained in more detail below. The first three should be applied together. If a person cannot do any of these three things, they will be treated as unable to make the decision. The fourth only applies in situations where people cannot communicate their decision in any way.

Understanding information about the decision to be made

4.16 It is important not to assess someone's understanding before they have been given relevant information about a decision. Every effort must be made to provide information in a way that is most appropriate to help the person to understand. Quick or inadequate explanations are not acceptable unless the situation is urgent (see chapter 3 for some practical steps). Relevant information includes:

- the nature of the decision
- the reason why the decision is needed, and
- the likely effects of deciding one way or another, or making no decision at all.

4.17 Section 3(2) outlines the need to present information in a way that is appropriate to meet the individual's needs and circumstances. It also stresses the importance of explaining information using the most effective form of communication for that person (such as simple language, sign language, visual representations, computer support or any other means).

4.18 For example:

- a person with a learning disability may need somebody to read information to them. They might also need illustrations to help them to understand what is happening. Or they might stop the reader to ask what things mean. It might also be helpful for them to discuss information with an advocate.
- a person with anxiety or depression may find it difficult to reach a decision about treatment in a group meeting with professionals. They may prefer to read the relevant documents in private. This way they can come to a conclusion alone, and ask for help if necessary.
- someone who has a brain injury might need to be given information several times. It will be necessary to check that the person understands the information. If they have difficulty understanding, it might be useful to present information in a different way (for example, different forms of words, pictures or diagrams). Written information, audiotapes, videos and posters can help people remember important facts.

4.19 Relevant information must include what the likely consequences of a decision would be (the possible effects of deciding one way or another) – and also the likely consequences of making no decision at all (section 3(4)). In some cases, it may be enough to give a broad explanation using simple language. But a person might need more detailed information or access to advice, depending on the decision that needs Act define a person's capacity to be made. If a decision could have serious or grave consequences, it is even more important that a person understands the information decision and how relevant to that decision.

Scenario: Providing relevant information in an appropriate format

Mr Leslie has learning disabilities and has developed an irregular heartbeat. He has been prescribed medication for this, but is anxious about having regular blood tests to check his medication levels. His doctor gives him a leaflet to explain:

- the reason for the tests
- what a blood test involves
- the risks in having or not having the tests, and
- that he has the right to decide whether or not to have the test.

The leaflet uses simple language and photographs to explain these things. Mr Leslie's carer helps him read the leaflet over the next few days, and checks that he understands it.

Mr Leslie goes back to tell the doctor that, even though he is scared of needles, he will agree to the blood tests so that he can get the right medication. He is able to pick out the equipment needed to do the blood test. So the doctor concludes that Mr Leslie can understand, retain and use the relevant information and therefore has the capacity to make the decision to have the test.

Retaining information

4.20 The person must be able to hold the information in their mind long enough to use it to make an effective decision. But section 3(3) states that people who can only retain information for a short while must not automatically be assumed to lack the capacity to decide – it depends on what is necessary for the decision in question. Items such as notebooks, photographs, posters, videos and voice recorders can help people record and retain information.

Scenario: Assessing a person's ability to retain information

Walter, an elderly man, is diagnosed with dementia and has problems remembering things in the short term. He can't always remember his great-grandchildren's names, but he recognises them when they come to visit. He can also pick them out on photographs.

Walter would like to buy premium bonds (a type of financial investment) for each of his great-grandchildren. He asks his solicitor to make the arrangements. After assessing his capacity to make financial decisions, the solicitor is satisfied that Walter has capacity to make this decision, despite his short-term memory problems.

Using or weighing information as part of the decision-making process

4.21 For someone to have capacity, they must have the ability to weigh up information and use it to arrive at a decision. Sometimes people can understand information but an impairment or disturbance stops them using it. In other cases, the impairment or disturbance leads to a person making a specific decision without understanding or using the information they have been given.[3]

4.22 For example, a person with the eating disorder anorexia nervosa may understand information about the consequences of not eating. But their compulsion not to eat might be too strong for them to ignore. Some people who have serious brain damage might make impulsive decisions regardless of information they have been given or their understanding of it.

Inability to communicate a decision in any way

4.23 Sometimes there is no way for a person to communicate. This will apply to very few people, but it does include:

- people who are unconscious or in a coma, or
- those with the very rare condition sometimes known as 'locked-in syndrome', who are conscious but cannot speak or move at all.

If a person cannot communicate their decision in any way at all, the Act says they should be treated as if they are unable to make that decision.

4.24 Before deciding that someone falls into this category, it is important to make all practical and appropriate efforts to help them communicate. This might call for the involvement of speech and language therapists, specialists in non-verbal communication or other professionals. Chapter 3 gives advice for communicating with people who have specific disabilities or cognitive problems.

4.25 Communication by simple muscle movements can show that somebody can communicate and may have capacity to make a decision.[4] For example, a person might blink an eye or squeeze a hand to say 'yes' or 'no'. In these cases, assessment must use the first three points listed in paragraph 4.14, which are explained in more depth in paragraphs 4.16–4.22.

What other issues might affect capacity?

People with fluctuating or temporary capacity

4.26 Some people have fluctuating capacity – they have a problem or condition that gets worse occasionally and affects their ability to make decisions. For example, someone who has manic depression may have a temporary manic phase which causes them to lack capacity to make financial decisions, leading them to get into debt even though at other times they are perfectly able to manage their money. A person with a psychotic illness may have delusions that affect their capacity to make decisions at certain times but disappear at others. Temporary factors may also affect someone's ability to make decisions. Examples include acute illness, severe pain, the effect of medication, or distress after a death or shock. More guidance on how to support someone with fluctuating or temporary capacity to make a decision can be found in chapter 3, particularly paragraphs 3.12–3.16. More information about factors that may indicate that a person may regain or develop capacity in the future can be found at paragraph 5.28.

4.27 As in any other situation, an assessment must only examine a person's capacity to make a particular decision when it needs to be made. It may be possible to put off the decision until the person has the capacity to make it (see also guidance on best interests in chapter 5).

Ongoing conditions that may affect capacity

4.28 Generally, capacity assessments should be related to a specific decision. But there may be people with an ongoing condition that affects their ability to make certain decisions or that may affect other decisions in their life. One decision on its own may make sense, but may give cause for concern when considered alongside others.

4.29 Again, it is important to review capacity from time to time, as people can improve their decision-making capabilities. In particular, someone with an ongoing condition may become able to make some, if not all, decisions. Some people (for example, people with learning disabilities) will learn new skills throughout their life, improving their capacity to make certain decisions. So assessments should be reviewed from time to time. Capacity should always be reviewed:

- whenever a care plan is being developed or reviewed
- at other relevant stages of the care planning process, and
- as particular decisions need to be made.

4.30 It is important to acknowledge the difference between:
- unwise decisions, which a person has the right to make (chapter 2, principle 3), and
- decisions based on a lack of understanding of risks or inability to weigh up the information about a decision.

Information about decisions the person has made based on a lack of understanding of risks or inability to weigh up the information can form part of a capacity assessment – particularly if someone repeatedly makes decisions that put them at risk or result in harm to them or someone else.

Scenario: Ongoing conditions

Paul had an accident at work and suffered severe head injuries. He was awarded compensation to pay for care he will need throughout his life as a result of his head injury. An application was made to the Court of Protection to consider how the award of compensation should be managed, including whether to appoint a deputy to manage Paul's financial affairs. Paul objected as he believed he could manage his life and should be able to spend his money however he liked.

He wrote a list of what he intended to spend his money on. This included fully-staffed luxury properties and holiday villas, cars with chauffeurs, jewellery and various other items for himself and his family. But spending money on all these luxury items would not leave enough money to cover the costs of his care in future years.

The court judged that Paul had capacity to make day-to-day financial decisions, but he did not understand why he had received compensation and what the money was supposed to be used for. Nor did he understand how buying luxuries now could affect his future care. The court therefore decided Paul lacked capacity to manage large amounts of money and appointed a deputy to make ongoing financial decisions relating to his care. But it gave him access to enough funds to cover everyday needs and occasional treats.

What other legal tests of capacity are there?

4.31 The Act makes clear that the definition of 'lack of capacity' and the two-stage test for capacity set out in the Act are 'for the purposes of this Act'. This means that the definition and test are to be used in situations covered by this Act. Schedule 6 of the Act also amends existing laws to ensure that the definition and test are used in other areas of law not covered directly by this Act.
For example, Schedule 6, paragraph 20 allows a person to be disqualified from jury service if they lack the capacity (using this Act's definition) to carry out a juror's tasks.

4.32 There are several tests of capacity that have been produced following judgments in court cases (known as common law tests).[5] These cover:

- capacity to make a will[6]
- capacity to make a gift[7]
- capacity to enter into a contract[8]
- capacity to litigate (take part in legal cases),[9] and
- capacity to enter into marriage.[10]

4.33 The Act's new definition of capacity is in line with the existing common law tests, and the Act does not replace them. When cases come before the court on the above issues, judges can adopt the new definition if they think it is appropriate. The Act will apply to all other cases relating to financial, healthcare or welfare decisions.

When should capacity be assessed?

4.34 Assessing capacity correctly is vitally important to everyone affected by the Act. Someone who is assessed as lacking capacity may be denied their right to make a specific decision – particularly if others think that the decision would not be in their best interests or could cause harm. Also, if a person lacks capacity to make specific decisions, that person might make decisions they do not really understand. Again, this could cause harm or put the person at risk. So it is important to carry out an assessment when a person's capacity is in doubt. It is also important that the person who does an assessment can justify their conclusions. Many organisations will provide specific professional guidance for members of their profession.[11]

4.35 There are a number of reasons why people may question a person's capacity to make a specific decision:

- the person's behaviour or circumstances cause doubt as to whether they have the capacity to make a decision
- somebody else says they are concerned about the person's capacity, or
- the person has previously been diagnosed with an impairment or disturbance that affects the way their mind or brain works (see paragraphs 4.11–4.12 above), and it has already been shown they lack capacity to make other decisions in their life.

4.36 The starting assumption must be that the person has the capacity to make the specific decision. If, however, anyone thinks a person lacks capacity, it is important to then ask the following questions:

- Does the person have all the relevant information they need to make the decision?
- If they are making a decision that involves choosing between alternatives, do they have information on all the different options?
- Would the person have a better understanding if information was explained or presented in another way?
- Are there times of day when the person's understanding is better?
- Are there locations where they may feel more at ease?
- Can the decision be put off until the circumstances are different and the person concerned may be able to make the decision?
- Can anyone else help the person to make choices or express a view (for example, a family member or carer, an advocate or someone to help with communication)?

4.37 Chapter 3 describes ways to deal with these questions and suggest steps which may help people make their own decisions. If all practical and appropriate steps fail, an assessment will then be needed of the person's capacity to make the decision that now needs to be made.

Who should assess capacity?

4.38 The person who assesses an individual's capacity to make a decision will usually be the person who is directly concerned with the individual at the time the decision needs to be made. This means that different people will be involved in assessing someone's capacity to make different decisions at different times.

For most day-to-day decisions, this will be the person caring for them at the time a decision must be made. For example, a care worker might need to assess if the person can agree to being bathed. Then a district nurse might assess if the person can consent to have a dressing changed.

4.39 For acts of care or treatment (see chapter 6), the assessor must have a 'reasonable belief' that the person lacks capacity to agree to the action or decision to be taken (see paragraphs 4.44–4.45 for a description of reasonable belief).

4.40 If a doctor or healthcare professional proposes treatment or an examination, they must assess the person's capacity to consent. In settings such as a hospital, this can involve the multi-disciplinary team (a team of people from different professional backgrounds who share responsibility for a patient). But ultimately, it is up to the professional responsible for the person's treatment to make sure that capacity has been assessed.

4.41 For a legal transaction (for example, making a will), a solicitor or legal practitioner must assess the client's capacity to instruct them. They must assess whether the client has the capacity to satisfy any relevant legal test. In cases of doubt, they should get an opinion from a doctor or other professional expert.

4.42 More complex decisions are likely to need more formal assessments (see paragraph 4.54 below). A professional opinion on the person's capacity might be necessary. This could be, for example, from a psychiatrist, psychologist, a speech and language therapist, occupational therapist or social worker. But the final decision about a person's capacity must be made by the person intending to make the decision or carry out the action on behalf of the person who lacks capacity – not the professional, who is there to advise.

4.43 Any assessor should have the skills and ability to communicate effectively with the person (see chapter 3). If necessary, they should get professional help to communicate with the person.

Scenario: Getting help with assessing capacity

Ms Dodd suffered brain damage in a road accident and is unable to speak. At first, her family thought she was not able to make decisions. But they soon discovered that she could choose by pointing at things, such as the clothes she wants to wear or the food she prefers. Her behaviour also indicates that she enjoys attending a day centre, but she refuses to go swimming. Her carers have assessed her as having capacity to make these decisions.

Ms Dodd needs hospital treatment but she gets distressed when away from home. Her mother feels that Ms Dodd is refusing treatment by her behaviour, but her father thinks she lacks capacity to say no to treatment that could improve her condition.

The clinician who is proposing the treatment will have to assess Ms Dodd's capacity to consent. He gets help from a member of staff at the day centre who knows Ms Dodd's communication well and also discusses things with her parents. Over several meetings the clinician explains the treatment options to Ms Dodd with the help of the staff member. The final decision about Ms Dodd's capacity rests with the clinician, but he will need to use information from the staff member and others who know Ms Dodd well to make this assessment.

What is 'reasonable belief' of lack of capacity?

4.44 Carers (whether family carers or other carers) and care workers do not have to be experts in assessing capacity. But to have protection from liability when providing care or treatment (see chapter 6), they must have a 'reasonable belief' that the person they care for lacks capacity to make relevant decisions about their care or treatment (section 5(1)). To have this reasonable belief, they must have taken 'reasonable' steps to establish that that the person lacks capacity to make a decision or consent to an act at the time the decision or consent is needed. They must also establish that the act or decision is in the person's best interests (see chapter 5).

They do not usually need to follow formal processes, such as involving a professional to make an assessment. However, if somebody challenges their assessment (see paragraph 4.63 below), they must be able to describe the steps they have taken. They must also have objective reasons for believing the person lacks capacity to make the decision in question.

4.45 The steps that are accepted as 'reasonable' will depend on individual circumstances and the urgency of the decision. Professionals, who are qualified in their particular field, are normally expected to undertake a fuller assessment, reflecting their higher degree of knowledge and experience, than family members or other carers who have no formal qualifications. See paragraph 4.36 for a list of points to consider when assessing someone's capacity. The following may also be helpful:

- Start by assuming the person has capacity to make the specific decision. Is there anything to prove otherwise?
- Does the person have a previous diagnosis of disability or mental disorder? Does that condition now affect their capacity to make this decision? If there has been no previous diagnosis, it may be best to get a medical opinion.
- Make every effort to communicate with the person to explain what is happening.
- Make every effort to try to help the person make the decision in question.
- See if there is a way to explain or present information about the decision in a way that makes it easier to understand. If the person has a choice, do they have information about all the options?
- Can the decision be delayed to take time to help the person make the decision, or to give the person time to regain the capacity to make the decision for themselves?
- Does the person understand what decision they need to make and why they need to make it?
- Can they understand information about the decision? Can they retain it, use it and weigh it to make the decision?
- Be aware that the fact that a person agrees with you or assents to what is proposed does not necessarily mean that they have capacity to make the decision.

What other factors might affect an assessment of capacity?

4.46 It is important to assess people when they are in the best state to make the decision, if possible. Whether this is possible will depend on the nature and urgency of the decision to be made. Many of the practical steps suggested in chapter 3 will help to create the best environment for assessing capacity. The assessor must then carry out the two stages of the test of capacity (see paragraphs 4.11–4.25 above).

4.47 In many cases, it may be clear that the person has an impairment or disturbance in the functioning of their mind or brain which could affect their ability to make a decision. For example, there might be a past diagnosis of a disability or mental disorder, or there may be signs that an illness is returning. Old assumptions about an illness or condition should be reviewed. Sometimes an illness develops gradually (for example, dementia), and it is hard to know when it starts to affect capacity. Anyone assessing someone's capacity may need to ask for a medical opinion as to whether a person has an illness or condition that could affect their capacity to make a decision in this specific case.

Scenario: Getting a professional opinion

Mr Elliott is 87 years old and lives alone. He has poor short-term memory, and he often forgets to eat. He also sometimes neglects his personal hygiene. His daughter talks to him about the possibility of moving into residential care. She decides that he understands the reasons for her concerns as well as the risks of continuing to live alone and, having weighed these up, he has the capacity to decide to stay at home and accept the consequences.

Two months later, Mr Elliott has a fall and breaks his leg. While being treated in hospital, he becomes confused and depressed. He says he wants to go home, but the staff think that the deterioration in his mental health has affected his capacity to make this decision at this time. They think he cannot understand the consequences or weigh up the risks he faces if he goes home. They refer him to a specialist in old age psychiatry, who assesses whether his mental health is affecting his capacity to make this decision. The staff will then use the specialist's opinion to help their assessment of Mr Elliott's capacity.

4.48 Anyone assessing someone's capacity must not assume that a person lacks capacity simply because they have a particular diagnosis or condition. There must be proof that the diagnosed illness or condition affects the ability to make a decision when it needs to be made. The person assessing capacity should ask the following questions:

- Does the person have a general understanding of what decision they need to make and why they need to make it?
- Do they understand the likely consequences of making, or not making, this decision?
- Can they understand and process information about the decision? And can they use it to help them make a decision?

In borderline cases, or where there is doubt, the assessor must be able to show that it is more likely than not that the answer to these questions is 'no'.

4.49 Anyone assessing someone's capacity will need to decide which of these steps are relevant to their situation.

- They should make sure that they understand the nature and effect of the decision to be made themselves. They may need access to relevant documents and background information (for example, details of the person's finances if assessing capacity to manage affairs). See chapter 16 for details on access to information.
- They may need other relevant information to support the assessment (for example, healthcare records or the views of staff involved in the person's care).
- Family members and close friends may be able to provide valuable background information (for example, the person's past behaviour and abilities and the types of decisions they can currently make). But their personal views and wishes about what they would want for the person must not influence the assessment.
- They should again explain to the person all the information relevant to the decision. The explanation must be in the most appropriate and effective form of communication for that person.

- Check the person's understanding after a few minutes. The person should be able to give a rough explanation of the information that was explained. There are different methods for people who use non-verbal means of communication (for example, observing behaviour or their ability to recognise objects or pictures).
- Avoid questions that need only a 'yes' or 'no' answer (for example, did you understand what I just said?). They are not enough to assess the person's capacity to make a decision. But there may be no alternative in cases where there are major communication difficulties. In these cases, check the response by asking questions again in a different way.
- Skills and behaviour do not necessarily reflect the person's capacity to make specific decisions. The fact that someone has good social or language skills, polite behaviour or good manners doesn't necessarily mean they understand the information or are able to weigh it up.
- Repeating these steps can help confirm the result.

4.50 For certain kinds of complex decisions (for example, making a will), there are specific legal tests (see paragraph 4.32 above) in addition to the two-stage test for capacity. In some cases, medical or psychometric tests may also be helpful tools (for example, for assessing cognitive skills) in assessing a person's capacity to make particular decisions, but the relevant legal test of capacity must still be fulfilled.

When should professionals be involved?

4.51 Anyone assessing someone's capacity may need to get a professional opinion when assessing a person's capacity to make complex or major decisions. In some cases this will simply involve contacting the person's general practitioner (GP) or family doctor. If the person has a particular condition or disorder, it may be appropriate to contact a specialist (for example, consultant psychiatrist, psychologist or other professional with experience of caring for patients with that condition). A speech and language therapist might be able to help if there are communication difficulties. In some cases, a multi-disciplinary approach is best. This means combining the skills and expertise of different professionals.

4.52 Professionals should never express an opinion without carrying out a proper examination and assessment of the person's capacity to make the decision. They must apply the appropriate test of capacity. In some cases, they will need to meet the person more than once – particularly if the person has communication difficulties. Professionals can get background information from a person's family and carers. But the personal views of these people about what they want for the person who lacks capacity must not influence the outcome of that assessment.

4.53 Professional involvement might be needed if:

- the decision that needs to be made is complicated or has serious consequences
- an assessor concludes a person lacks capacity, and the person challenges the finding
- family members, carers and/or professionals disagree about a person's capacity
- there is a conflict of interest between the assessor and the person being assessed
- the person being assessed is expressing different views to different people – they may be trying to please everyone or telling people what they think they want to hear
- somebody might challenge the person's capacity to make the decision – either at the time of the decision or later (for example, a family member might

challenge a will after a person has died on the basis that the person lacked capacity when they made the will)

- somebody has been accused of abusing a vulnerable adult who may lack capacity to make decisions that protect them
- a person repeatedly makes decisions that put them at risk or could result in suffering or damage.

Scenario: Involving professional opinion

Ms Ledger is a young woman with learning disabilities and some autistic spectrum disorders. Recently she began a sexual relationship with a much older man, who is trying to persuade her to move in with him and come off the pill. There are rumours that he has been violent towards her and has taken her bankbook.

Ms Ledger boasts about the relationship to her friends. But she has admitted to her key worker that she is sometimes afraid of the man. Staff at her sheltered accommodation decide to make a referral under the local adult protection procedures. They arrange for a clinical psychologist to assess Ms Ledger's understanding of the relationship and her capacity to consent to it.

4.54 In some cases, it may be a legal requirement, or good professional practice, to undertake a formal assessment of capacity. These cases include:

- where a person's capacity to sign a legal document (for example, a will), could later be challenged, in which case an expert should be asked for an opinion[12]
- to establish whether a person who might be involved in a legal case needs the assistance of the Official Solicitor or other litigation friend (somebody to represent their views to a court and give instructions to their legal representative) and there is doubt about the person's capacity to instruct a solicitor or take part in the case[13]
- whenever the Court of Protection has to decide if a person lacks capacity in a certain matter
- if the courts are required to make a decision about a person's capacity in other legal proceedings[14]
- if there may be legal consequences of a finding of capacity (for example, deciding on financial compensation following a claim for personal injury).

Are assessment processes confidential?

4.55 People involved in assessing capacity will need to share information about a person's circumstances. But there are ethical codes and laws that require professionals to keep personal information confidential. As a general rule, professionals must ask their patients or clients if they can reveal information to somebody else – even close relatives. But sometimes information may be disclosed without the consent of the person who the information concerns (for example, to protect the person or prevent harm to other people).[15]

4.56 Anyone assessing someone's capacity needs accurate information concerning the person being assessed that is relevant to the decision the person has to make. So professionals should, where possible, make relevant information available. They should make every effort to get the person's permission to reveal relevant information. They should give a full explanation of why this is necessary, and they should tell the person about the risks and consequences of revealing, and not revealing information. If the person is unable to give permission, the professional might still be allowed to provide information that will help make an accurate assessment of the person's capacity to make the specific decision. Chapter 16 has more detail on how to access information.

What if someone refuses to be assessed?

4.57 There may be circumstances in which a person whose capacity is in doubt refuses to undergo an assessment of capacity or refuses to be examined by a doctor or other professional. In these circumstances, it might help to explain to someone refusing an assessment why it is needed and what the consequences of refusal are. But threats or attempts to force the person to agree to an assessment are not acceptable.

4.58 If the person lacks capacity to agree or refuse, the assessment can normally go ahead, as long as the person does not object to the assessment, and it is in their best interests (see chapter 5).

4.59 Nobody can be forced to undergo an assessment of capacity. If someone refuses to open the door to their home, it cannot be forced. If there are serious worries about the person's mental health, it may be possible to get a warrant to force entry and assess the person for treatment in hospital – but the situation must meet the requirements of the Mental Health Act 1983 (section 135). But simply refusing an assessment of capacity is in no way sufficient grounds for an assessment under the Mental Health Act 1983 (see chapter 13).

Who should keep a record of assessments?

4.60 Assessments of capacity to take day-to-day decisions or consent to care require no formal assessment procedures or recorded documentation. Paragraphs 4.44–4.45 above explain the steps to take to reach a 'reasonable belief' that someone lacks capacity to make a particular decision. It is good practice for paid care workers to keep a record of the steps they take when caring for the person concerned.

Professional records

4.61 It is good practice for professionals to carry out a proper assessment of a person's capacity to make particular decisions and to record the findings in the relevant professional records.

- A doctor or healthcare professional proposing treatment should carry out an assessment of the person's capacity to consent (with a multi-disciplinary team, if appropriate) and record it in the patient's clinical notes.
- Solicitors should assess a client's capacity to give instructions or carry out a legal transaction (obtaining a medical or other professional opinion, if necessary) and record it on the client's file.
- An assessment of a person's capacity to consent or agree to the provision of services will be part of the care planning processes for health and social care needs, and should be recorded in the relevant documentation. This includes:
  - Person Centred Planning for people with learning disabilities
  - the Care Programme Approach for people with mental illness
  - the Single Assessment Process for older people in England, and
  - the Unified Assessment Process in Wales.

Formal reports or certificates of capacity

4.62 In some cases, a more detailed report or certificate of capacity may be required, for example,

- for use in court or other legal processes
- as required by Regulations, Rules or Orders made under the Act.

How can someone challenge a finding of lack of capacity?

4.63 There are likely to be occasions when someone may wish to challenge the results of an assessment of capacity. The first step is to raise the matter with the person who carried out the assessment. If the challenge comes from the individual who is said to lack capacity, they might need support from family, friends or an advocate. Ask the assessor to:

- give reasons why they believe the person lacks capacity to make the decision, and
- provide objective evidence to support that belief.

4.64 The assessor must show they have applied the principles of the Mental Capacity Act (see chapter 2). Attorneys, deputies and professionals will need to show that they have also followed guidance in this chapter.

4.65 It might be possible to get a second opinion from an independent professional or another expert in assessing capacity. Chapter 15 has other suggestions for dealing with disagreements. But if a disagreement cannot be resolved, the person who is challenging the assessment may be able to apply to the Court of Protection. The Court of Protection can rule on whether a person has capacity to make the decision covered by the assessment (see chapter 8).

NOTES

1. Undue influence in relation to consent to medical treatment was considered in *Re T (Adult: Refusal of Treatment)* [1992] 4 All ER 649, 662 and in financial matters in *Royal Bank of Scotland v. Etridge* [2001] UKHL 44.
2. See for example *Re MB (Medical Treatment)* [1997] 2 FLR 426, CA; *Re A (Male Sterilisation)* [2000] 1 FLR 549; *Re S (Sterilisation: Patient's Best Interests)* [2000] 2 FLR 389; *Re F* (Adult Patient: Sterilisation) [2001] Fam 15
3. This issue has been considered in a number of court cases, including *Re MB* [1997] 2 FLR 426; *R v. Collins and Ashworth Hospital Authority ex parte Brady* [2001] 58 BMLR 173
4. This was demonstrated in the case *Re AK (Adult Patient) (Medical Treatment: Consent)* [2001] 1 FLR 129
5. For details, see British Medical Association & Law Society, *Assessment of Mental Capacity: Guidance for Doctors and Lawyers* (Second edition) (London: BMJ Books, 2004)
6. *Banks* v *Goodfellow* (1870) LR 5 QB 549
7. *Re Beaney* (deceased) [1978] 2 All ER 595
8. *Boughton v Knight* (1873) LR 3 PD 64
9. *Masterman-Lister* v *Brutton & Co and Jewell & Home Counties Dairies* [2003] 3 All ER 162 (CA)
10. *Sheffield City Council* v *E & S* [2005] 1 FLR 965
11. See for example, British Medical Association & Law Society, *Assessment of Mental Capacity: Guidance for Doctors and Lawyers* (Second edition) (London: BMJ Books, 2004); the Joint Royal Colleges Ambulance Service Liaison Committee Clinical Practice Guidelines (JRCALC, available online at www2.warwick.ac.uk/fac/med/research/hsri/emergencycare/jrcalc_2006/clinical_guidelines_2006.pdf) and British Psychological Society, *Guidelines on assessing capacity* (BPS, 2006 available online at www.bps.org.uk)
12. *Kenward* v *Adams*, *The Times*, 29 November 1975

13. Civil Procedure Rules 1998, r 21.1
14. *Masterman-Lister* v *Brutton & Co and Jewell & Home Counties Dairies* [2002] EWCA Civ 1889, CA at 54
15. For example, in the circumstances discussed in *W* v. *Egdell and others* [1990] 1 All ER 835 at 848; *S* v. *Plymouth City Council and C*, [2002] EWCA Civ 388) at 49

Court of Protection

C.1 INTRODUCTION

The origins of the Court of Protection are to be found in the Middle Ages, when the Crown assumed responsibility for managing the estates of the 'mentally ill and mentally handicapped'. In the more recent past, the Court of Protection was an office of the Supreme Court, deriving its statutory powers from Part VII of the Mental Health Act 1983 and the Enduring Powers of Attorney Act 1985. Its jurisdiction was limited to matters relating to the property and affairs of a patient within its jurisdiction.

As of 1 October 2007, the Mental Capacity Act 2005 established a new Court of Protection as a superior court of record,[1] having all the powers of the High Court. As such, it is able to establish precedent, i.e. it can set examples for future cases.

C.2 JURISDICTION AND POWERS

The jurisdiction of the Court and its powers were also dramatically increased as of 1 October 2007. In exercising those powers, the Court must have regard to the provisions of the MCA, in particular to s.1 (the principles) and s.4 (best interests) (see **Chapter 3**).

Test of capacity

The old Court of Protection operated a general test of incapacity to manage property and affairs. The new Court must be satisfied that the person lacks capacity to make the specific decision or decisions in question, applying the statutory test of capacity set out in MCA,[2] before it has jurisdiction to make any relevant decision(s) or declaration(s).

Powers

The powers of the Court of Protection granted by the MCA provide that the Court can make declarations as to:

- whether a person has or lacks capacity to make a decision specified in the declaration;
- whether a person has or lacks capacity to make decisions on such matters as are described in the declaration;
- the lawfulness or otherwise of any act done, or yet to be done, in relation to that person.[3]

In respect of a person lacking capacity to make specific decisions, the Court can also:

- by making an order, make the decision or decisions on that person's behalf in relation to the matter or matters, or

- appoint a deputy to make decisions on the person's behalf in relation to the matter or matters.[4]

Where there is doubt about the person's capacity to make a relevant decision, or about the Court's jurisdiction concerning the matter in question, the MCA provides powers for the Court to make interim orders or directions while the doubt is resolved.[5] The Court has said that the 'gateway' test for using these powers is lower than what is normally required to rebut the presumption of capacity. In such cases, the test in the first instance is whether there is evidence giving good cause for concern that the person may lack capacity in some relevant regard. Once that is raised as a serious possibility, the court then moves on to the second stage to decide what action, if any, it is in the person's best interests to take before a final determination of capacity can be made.[6]

Deputies

Where there is an on-going need for decisions to be made on behalf of a person lacking capacity to make such decisions, the Court may appoint a deputy with authority to make specific decisions. Deputies appointed by the Court of Protection are, in broad terms, the equivalent to receivers previously appointed under Part VII Mental Health Act 1983. Receivers appointed before the MCA came into effect are treated under the new regime as property and affairs deputies appointed by the Court of Protection.[7] Court appointed deputies can be given wide powers by the Court and, importantly, can be appointed to make decisions both in respect of property and financial affairs and also in respect of the welfare of the patient. However, the Court is required where possible to make a single decision in preference to the appointment of a deputy,[8] so the appointment of welfare deputies is rare.

C.3 STRUCTURE

The Court of Protection is presided over by a president and a vice-president. The role formerly performed by the Master in the old Court of Protection is now taken by the Senior Judge. Judges entitled to sit as Court of Protection judges include:

- all High Court judges in the Family and Chancery Divisions;
- designated circuit judges; and
- designated district judges.

The Court has a central registry (currently at Archway Tower, 2 Junction Road, London N19 5SZ) where the Senior Judge and five district judges are based. All applications are sent to and processed at the central registry. Cases can be heard in any location, and are allocated by the Senior Judge to the appropriate level of judge. Serious welfare or healthcare matters and complex cases will generally be referred to a High Court judge, while district judges at the central registry and in the regions will deal with most property and affairs cases and some welfare issues.

Initially, the administration of the Court of Protection was handled by the Office of the Public Guardian (OPG). However, in April 2009, the administration of the Court was transferred to Her Majesty's Court Service, to underpin the separation of the Court's judicial powers from the administrative and supervisory role of the OPG.

Office of the Public Guardian

The functions given to the Public Guardian under the MCA[9] include:

- maintaining the registers of Lasting Powers of Attorney (LPAs) and court appointed deputies;

- supervising the role of court appointed deputies;
- directing visits by a Court of Protection Visitor;
- receiving reports from donees of LPAs and deputies;
- reporting to the Court on any matters as required by the Court;
- dealing with representations and complaints about the conduct of both donees of LPAs and deputies.

Court of Protection Visitors

The Court of Protection can appoint Visitors to provide independent advice to the Court and to the Public Guardian as to how anyone given power under the MCA is, or should be, carrying out their duties and responsibilities.[10] Visitors are either General or Special, in which latter case they are registered medical practitioners with relevant expertise.

C.4 APPLICATIONS TO THE COURT OF PROTECTION

It is important to note that the Court of Protection is intended to be a judicial forum of last resort. To this end, the MCA Code of Practice sets out a list of alternatives to recourse to the Court, including the use of advocates, mediation, and formal complaints procedures.[11] However, an order of the Court will usually be necessary to deal with the property and financial affairs of a person lacking capacity to make financial decisions, unless they have previously made an EPA or LPA giving a donee authority to manage those affairs (see **Chapter 5**).

In the majority of cases, applications can only be brought with the permission of the Court, unlike applications for declaratory relief in the High Court in 'best interests' cases. Exceptions to this rule are provided for in the MCA and in the Court of Protection Rules made under the Act.[12]

Applications to the Court of Protection must be made on the forms specified by the Court (available from **www.hmcs.gov.uk**).

C.5 PARTIES

For cases concerning major decisions relating to medical treatment, the NHS Trust or other organisation responsible for the patient's care will usually make the application.

Where the concern arises from non-medical social welfare issues, the relevant local authority should usually make the application. However, it is also possible for applications to be brought by persons properly concerned as to the welfare of the person, including family members.[13]

For decisions about the property and affairs of someone who lacks capacity to manage their own affairs, the applicant will usually be the person who needs specific authority from the court to deal with the individual's money or property (for example, family carer).

If the applicant is the person who is alleged to lack capacity, that person will always be a party to the court proceedings. In all other cases, the court will decide whether the person who lacks, or is alleged to lack, capacity should be involved as a party to the case. Where the person is a party to the case, the court may appoint the Official Solicitor to act for them (upon the Official Solicitor so consenting, see **Appendix E**).

C.6 COMMENCING PROCEEDINGS

Applications other than deprivation of liberty cases

A first application to the Court must be made on Form COP1. Except where permission is not required, an application must include a COP2 Permission form. The application must also include a COP3 Assessment of capacity form (see **Appendix G**), in which a medical practitioner addresses the question of the person's capacity. If it is not possible to obtain medical evidence to complete such a form, the applicant should provide witness evidence in a COP24 Witness statement form, explaining why it has not been possible to provide a COP3 form and setting out in the fullest detail possible why they believe the person lacks capacity to make the decision(s) in question. In such cases, the Court may direct a Special Visitor to see the person and prepare a report for the Court. It may also be possible for the Court to make an interim order or direction while the issue of capacity is decided (see section C.2 above).

Deprivation of liberty cases

As part of the introduction of the new regime to authorise deprivations of liberty (see **Chapter 15**), the Court of Protection introduced a dedicated procedure for deprivation of liberty cases.[14] The procedure (including dedicated forms) is intended to ensure that such cases are brought urgently before a judge, with a first hearing within five working days of the date of issue of the application.[15]

C.7 THE CONDUCT OF PROCEEDINGS

The Court of Protection has its own set of procedural rules and Practice Directions, which set down in considerable detail the conduct of proceedings before it (see **www.hmcs.gov.uk**).

Where relevant, the Court will consider the question of permission, either on paper or at an oral hearing. If permission is granted (or is not needed), directions will then be made for the future conduct of the application.

In personal welfare applications, these directions will usually include directions for the obtaining of suitable expert reports from independent psychiatrists and/or social workers. Assuming that there is sufficient evidence of a lack of capacity to give it jurisdiction, the Court can make interim declarations as to the best interests of the person to whom the application relates, and will often make such declarations relating to contact, residence and care arrangements.

Further applications can be made during the course of proceedings (and do not require the permission of the Court). Depending on their nature, they will either be determined on the papers or at an oral hearing.

C.8 APPEALS

An appeal against either an interim or a final decision of the Court will lie either to a more senior judge of the Court of Protection or, in some circumstances, to the Court of Appeal.[16]

NOTES

1. Mental Capacity Act 2005, s.45(1).
2. The statutory test in sections 2 and 3 of the Mental Capacity Act 2005, having regard to the principles set out in s.1. See also **Chapter 3**.
3. Mental Capacity Act 2005, s.15.
4. Ibid: s.16. Further explanation is given as to how the Court may exercise these powers in respect of personal welfare matters (s.17) and property and affairs matters (s.18).
5. Ibid: s.48.
6. *Re F* [2009] COP 11649371 (unreported). See **www.wikimentalhealth.co.uk**
7. Mental Capacity Act 2005, Schedule 5.
8. Ibid: s.16(4).
9. Ibid: s.58(1).

10. Ibid: s.61.
11. Department of Constitutional Affairs (2007) *Mental Capacity Act 2005 Code of Practice*, TSO, Chapter 15.
12. The Court of Protection Rules 2007 (SI 2007/1744).
13. It is currently unclear whether an application brought by an incapacitated person through a litigation friend (other than the Official Solicitor) requires the permission of the Court of Protection.
14. Court of Protection (Amendment) Rules 2009 (SI 2009/582); and Court of Protection Practice Direction 10A Deprivation of Liberty Applications. (Supplements Part 10A of the Court of Protection Rules 2007 (SI 2007/1744)).
15. Court of Protection Practice Direction 10A Deprivation of Liberty Applications. (Supplements Part 10A of the Court of Protection Rules 2007 (SI 2007/1744)). Paragraph 8.2. This Practice Direction gives detailed guidance as to what is required for bringing an application under this procedure.
16. Mental Capacity Act 2005, s.52; Court of Protection Rules 2007 (SI 2007/1744), Part 20.

Court of Protection Practice Direction 9E: Applications relating to serious medical treatment

PRACTICE DIRECTION – HOW TO START PROCEEDINGS

This practice direction supplements Part 9 of the Court of Protection Rules 2007

PRACTICE DIRECTION E – APPLICATIONS RELATING TO SERIOUS MEDICAL TREATMENT

General

1. Rule 71 enables a practice direction to make additional or different provision in relation to specified applications.

Applications to which this practice direction applies

2. This practice direction sets out the procedure to be followed where the application concerns serious medical treatment in relation to P.

Meaning of 'serious medical treatment' in relation to the Rules and this practice direction

3. Serious medical treatment means treatment which involves providing, withdrawing or withholding treatment in circumstances where:

   (a)   in a case where a single treatment is being proposed, there is a fine balance between its benefits to P and the burdens and risks it is likely to entail for him;
   (b)   in a case where there is a choice of treatments, a decision as to which one to use is finely balanced; or
   (c)   the treatment, procedure or investigation proposed would be likely to involve serious consequences for P.

4. 'Serious consequences' are those which could have a serious impact on P, either from the effects of the treatment, procedure or investigation itself or its wider implications. This may include treatments, procedures or investigations which:

   (a)   cause, or may cause, serious and prolonged pain, distress or side effects;
   (b)   have potentially major consequences for P; or
   (c)   have a serious impact on P's future life choices.

Matters which should be brought to the court

5. Cases involving any of the following decisions should be regarded as serious medical treatment for the purpose of the Rules and this practice direction, and should be brought to the court:

(a) decisions about the proposed withholding or withdrawal of artificial nutrition and hydration from a person in a permanent vegetative state or a minimally conscious state;

(b) cases involving organ or bone marrow donation by a person who lacks capacity to consent; and

(c) cases involving non-therapeutic sterilisation of a person who lacks capacity to consent.

6. Examples of serious medical treatment may include:

(a) certain terminations of pregnancy in relation to a person who lacks capacity to consent to such a procedure;

(b) a medical procedure performed on a person who lacks capacity to consent to it, where the procedure is for the purpose of a donation to another person;

(c) a medical procedure or treatment to be carried out on a person who lacks capacity to consent to it, where that procedure or treatment must be carried out using a degree of force to restrain the person concerned;

(d) an experimental or innovative treatment for the benefit of a person who lacks capacity to consent to such treatment; and

(e) a case involving an ethical dilemma in an untested area.

7. There may be other procedures or treatments not contained in the list in paragraphs 5 and 6 above which can be regarded as serious medical treatment. Whether or not a procedure is regarded as serious medical treatment will depend on the circumstances and the consequences for the patient.

Consultation with the Official Solicitor

8. Members of the Official Solicitor's staff are prepared to discuss applications in relation to serious medical treatment before an application is made. Any enquiries about adult medical and welfare cases should be addressed to a family and medical litigation lawyer at the Office of the Official Solicitor, 81 Chancery Lane, London WC2A IDD, ph: 020 7911 7127, fax: 020 7911 7105, email: enquiries@offsol.gsi.gov.uk.

Parties to proceedings

9. The person bringing the application will always be a party to proceedings, as will a respondent named in the application form who files an acknowledgment of service.[1] In cases involving issues as to serious medical treatment, an organisation which is, or will be, responsible for providing clinical or caring services to P should usually be named as a respondent in the application form (where it is not already the applicant in the proceedings).

(Practice direction B accompanying Part 9 sets out the persons who are to be notified that an application form has been issued.)

10. The court will consider whether anyone not already a party should be joined as a party to the proceedings. Other persons with sufficient interest may apply to be joined as parties to the proceedings[2] and the court has a duty to identify at as early a stage as possible who the parties to the proceedings should be.[3]

Allocation of the case

11. Where an application is made to the court in relation to:

(a)   the lawfulness of withholding or withdrawing artificial nutrition and hydration from a person in a permanent vegetative state, or a minimally conscious state; or

(b)   a case involving an ethical dilemma in an untested area,

the proceedings (including permission, the giving of any directions, and any hearing) must be conducted by the President of the Court of Protection or by another judge nominated by the President.

12.   Where an application is made to the court in relation to serious medical treatment (other than that outlined in paragraph 11) the proceedings (including permission, the giving of any directions, and any hearing) must be conducted by a judge of the court who has been nominated as such by virtue of section 46(2)(a) to (c) of the Act (i.e. the President of the Family Division, the Chancellor or a puisne judge of the High Court).

Matters to be considered at the first directions hearing

13.   Unless the matter is one which needs to be disposed of urgently, the court will list it for a first directions hearing.
      (Practice direction B accompanying Part 10 sets out the procedure to be followed for urgent applications.)

14.   The court may give such directions as it considers appropriate. If the court has not already done so, it should in particular consider whether to do any or all of the following at the first directions hearing:

(a)   decide whether P should be joined as party to the proceedings, and give directions to that effect;

(b)   if P is to be joined as a party to the proceedings, decide whether the Official Solicitor should be invited to act as a litigation friend or whether some other person should be appointed as a litigation friend;

(c)   identify anyone else who has been notified of the proceedings and who has filed an acknowledgment and applied to be joined as a party to proceedings, and consider that application; and

(d)   set a timetable for the proceedings including, where possible, a date for the final hearing.

15.   The court should also consider whether to give any of the other directions listed in rule 85(2).

16.   The court will ordinarily make an order pursuant to rule 92 that any hearing shall be held in public, with restrictions to be imposed in relation to publication of information about the proceedings.

Declarations

17.   Where a declaration is needed, the order sought should be in the following or similar terms:

•   That P lacks capacity to make a decision in relation to the (proposed medical treatment or procedure).
    E.g. 'That P lacks capacity to make a decision in relation to sterilisation by vasectomy'; and

•   That, having regard to the best interests of P, it is lawful for the (proposed medical treatment or procedure) to be carried out by (proposed healthcare provider).

18. Where the application is for the withdrawal of life-sustaining treatment, the order sought should be in the following or similar terms:

   - That P lacks capacity to consent to continued life-sustaining treatment measures (and specify what these are); and
   - That, having regard to the best interests of P, it is lawful for (name of health-care provider) to withdraw the life-sustaining treatment from P.

NOTES

1. Rule 73(1).
2. Rule 75.
3. Rule 5(2)(b)(ii).

APPENDIX E

The Official Solicitor

The need for representation of a vulnerable person who may be unable to conduct legal proceedings for themselves has long been recognised by the state. The Office of Official Solicitor to the Senior Courts dates back to 1875. The Official Solicitor is an office holder of the Senior Court appointed by the Lord Chancellor under section 90 of the Senior Courts Act 1981. The duties of the Official Solicitor are carried out pursuant to statute, rules of court, direction of the Lord Chancellor, at common law, or in accordance with established practice.

The function and purpose of the Office of the Official Solicitor is to act where there is no other suitable person (such as an appropriate relative or friend) willing and able to act on behalf of someone who is vulnerable because of their age (children under 18) or because of lack of mental capacity, or where for some other reason failure to act would result in an injustice. The Official Solicitor's role in relation to children is beyond the scope of this book, apart from those cases where the Official Solicitor agrees to act for young people whose lack of capacity is likely to persist beyond their 18th birthday. In relation to adults, the work of the Office of the Official Solicitor includes:

- Acting as last resort litigation friend, and in some cases as solicitor, for adults (known as 'protected parties'[1]) in a wide range of court proceedings because they lack the mental capacity to conduct the proceedings.
- Acting as advocate to the court providing advice and assistance to the court; and making enquiries on behalf of the court.[2]
- Acting as last resort administrator of estates and trustee.
- Acting as last resort financial deputy in relation to Court of Protection clients.
- Reviewing all committals to prison for contempt of court and taking such action as he considers necessary.

Litigation friend of last resort

Before the Official Solicitor accepts an appointment as litigation friend, he must be satisfied that:

1. there is cogent evidence that the adult lacks capacity to conduct the proceedings (and is therefore a 'protected party') or that the court has determined that the adult lacks capacity to conduct the proceedings;
2. there is nobody else suitable and willing to act as litigation friend; and
3. there is provision for the costs of legal representation he will incur whether by way of legal aid or otherwise.

If there is a conflict in the evidence relating to an adult party's capacity to conduct the proceedings then the Official Solicitor will not accept appointment unless or until that conflict is resolved either by the experts arriving at a consensus, or by determination of the court. When the Official Solicitor acts in this representative capacity, he fulfils the same role as any other person appointed to act as litigation friend.

There is limited formal guidance with regard to the role of the litigation friend. It has always been accepted that the Official Solicitor's duty is to fairly and competently conduct the proceedings in the best interests of the protected party (or 'P' if the proceedings are taking place at the Court of Protection proceedings).

The types of court proceedings in which the Official Solicitor may be invited to act include:

- disputes about the personal welfare of a protected person (such as residence or contact matters);
- cases involving decisions about serious medical treatment or disputes about healthcare (see **Appendix D** for the Court of Protection Practice Direction 9E);
- cases in the Court of Protection (including property and affairs cases) where the person lacking capacity is made a party to the proceedings;
- court proceedings (such as care or adoption proceedings, residence or contact disputes) concerning the children of parents who lack capacity to represent themselves;[3]
- where a protected person is involved in proceedings relating to divorce, nullity of marriage, judicial separation or for the dissolution or nullity of a civil partnership;
- other civil proceedings, including personal injury claims, possession actions, applications in connection with the ownership of property, claims for appropriate provision from a deceased's estate, and applications to displace a nearest relative under the Mental Health Act 1983.

The Official Solicitor does not charge for acting as last resort litgation friend but may make his involvement in proceedings conditional upon an undertaking to meet his legal costs where there is otherwise no provision to cover his costs of acting. Undertakings to meet costs will not be required for cases involving declaratory proceedings in respect of medical treatment, where his involvement is a matter of necessity[4], or where the other party is legally aided. The Official Solicitor may seek the authority of the Court of Protection to recover his costs from the person lacking capacity who is the subject of the proceedings where that person has the funds to pay.

Where the person on whose behalf the Official Solicitor is invited to act is eligible to apply for financial assistance by a scheme funded by the Legal Services Commission, the Official Solicitor will apply on the person's behalf if it is in the interests of that person to do so.

There is nothing to prevent the Official Solicitor seeking his costs in the same way as any other successful litigant. In medical treatment cases, the Official Solicitor will usually ask for one half of his costs.[5]

Provision is made as to the costs of the Official Solicitor in proceedings in respect of a person's property and affairs before the Court of Protection in Part 19 of the Court of Protection Rules 2007 and in particular rule 156 which provides that the general rule in such proceedings is that the costs of the proceedings shall be paid by the person or charged to his estate.

NOTES

1. The definition of a 'protected party' is a party, or an intended party, who lacks capacity (within the meaning of MCA 2005) to conduct the proceedings CPR 21.1 (2) and FPR 9.1(1).
2. *Harbin* v. *Masterman* (1896) 1 Ch 351.

3. The Court of Appeal has examined the role of the Official Solicitor in acting for a parent in care proceedings, where that parent is said to be a protected party: see *RP* v. *Nottingham City Council and the Official Solicito*r [2008] EWCA Civ 462. The policy of the Official Solicitor is helpfully set out at the end of the judgment.
4. *Re F (Mental Patient: Sterilisation)* [1990] 2 AC 1.
5. *A Hospital* v. *SW and A PCT* [2007] EWHC 425 (Fam).

Certificate as to capacity to conduct proceedings (Official Solicitor)

CERTIFICATE AS TO CAPACITY
TO CONDUCT PROCEEDINGS

* You should read the whole of this form and the attached notes for guidance before completing this form.

Please answer all questions as fully as you can.

Name of person concerned:

Date of birth:

The proceedings are ... ... **(and see paragraph 3 below)**

Insert your full name and address (including postcode) Give your professional qualifications	**I** **of**
	1. Nature of your professional relationship with the person concerned: ■ I have acted as practitioner for the person concerned since ... ... and last assessed him/her on ... ... **or** ■ I assessed the person concerned on ... ... following a referral from ... ...

For a definition of 'a person who lacks capacity' see note 2 attached	**AND in my opinion** . . . . ■ **is capable** (within the meaning of the Mental Capacity Act 2005) of conducting the proceedings* **or** ■ **lacks capacity** (within the meaning of the Mental Capacity Act 2005) to conduct the proceedings* (**strike through as appropriate**) **If in your opinion** . . . . . . **is a person who lacks capacity to conduct the proceedings please answer questions 2–8 below**

2. The person concerned has the following impairment of, or disturbance in the functioning of, the mind or brain (see note 2):

this has lasted since: . . . .

3. As a result, the person concerned is incapable of conducting the proceedings described below and/or in the attached letter of instructions.

because (please tick as many boxes as apply)

☐   he or she is unable to understand the following relevant information (please give details):

and/or

☐   he or she is unable to retain that information (please give details)

and/or

☐   he or she is unable to use or weigh the following information as part of the process of making the decisions in the conduct of the proceedings:

or

☐ for cases where the person can in fact understand, retain and use / weigh the information he or she is unable to communicate his or her decisions by any means at all (please give details):

4. Do you consider that the person concerned might regain or develop capacity to conduct the proceedings in the future –

    ☐ Yes – please state why and give an indication of when this might happen
    ☐ No – please state why

5. Is the person concerned capable of discussing the proceedings with my representative or with a solicitor instructed by me?

☐ **YES**   ☐ **NO**

Please comment

6. If so, is such discussion likely to affect him/her detrimentally and if so, in what way?

☐ **YES**   ☐ **NO**

Please comment

7. Has the person concerned made you aware of any views that he / she has in relation to the proceedings?

8. Any additional comments

Statement of Truth:

I confirm that insofar as the facts stated in this certificate are within my own knowledge I have made clear which they are and I believe them to be true and that the opinions I have expressed represent my true professional opinion.

Signed

_____

Dated

_____

Please read these notes before completing the Certificate

GUIDANCE NOTES

1. Where a person who is involved in legal proceedings lacks capacity (within the meaning of the Mental Capacity Act 2005) to conduct the proceedings, their interests must be protected by the appointment of a 'litigation friend' who will conduct the proceedings on their behalf. In some proceedings the litigation friend is known as a 'next friend' or 'guardian ad litem'. The Official Solicitor is usually approached in cases where there is no other suitable person who is willing to act. Evidence is required to establish whether the person lacks capacity (within the meaning of the Mental Capacity Act 2005) to conduct the proceedings. A person who lacks capacity to conduct proceedings is referred to as the 'protected party' within the proceedings.

Capacity to conduct proceedings

2. The Mental Capacity Act 2005 (section 2(1)) provides that a person lacks capacity if, at the time a decision needs to be made, he or she is unable to make or communicate the decision because of an 'impairment of, or a disturbance in the functioning of, the mind or brain'.

    The Act contains a two-stage test of capacity which has diagnostic and functional elements:

    1. Is there an impairment of, or disturbance in the functioning of, the person's mind or brain?
    2. If so, is the impairment or disturbance such that the person lacks the capacity to make decisions in relation to the proceedings.

239

Please refer to the information set out in your instructions and any accompanying letter for details of the proceedings and relevant information about the circumstances of the person

The assessment of capacity must be based on the person's ability to conduct the proceedings and not on his/her ability to make decisions in general. It does not matter therefore if the lack of capacity is temporary, or the person retains the capacity to make other decisions, or if the person's capacity fluctuates.

To have capacity to conduct the proceedings the person must have capacity to understand, absorb and retain information (including advice) relevant to the issues on which his consent or decisions are likely to be necessary in the course of the proceedings, sufficiently to enable him or her to make decisions based upon such information. This includes the ability to weigh information (and advice) in the balance as part of the process of making decisions within the proceedings and the ability to communicate his decision (whether by talking, using sign language or any other means).

A lack of capacity cannot be established merely because of a person's age or appearance or his condition or an aspect of his behaviour. Similarly a person is not be treated as being unable to make a decision merely because he or she has made an unwise decision.

Practitioners are required to have regard to the statutory principles set out in section 1 of the Mental Capacity Act 2005 and to the Code of Practice, in particular Chapters 2, 3 and 4, when assessing capacity.

The statutory principles provide that:

Section 1 . . . . .

'(2) *A person must be assumed to have capacity unless it is established that he lacks capacity.*

(3) *A person is not be treated as unable to make a decision unless all practicable steps to help him to do so have been taken without success.*

(4) *A person is not to be treated as unable to make a decision merely because he makes an unwise decision.*

(5) *An act done, or decision made, under this Act for or on behalf of a person who lacks capacity must be done, or made, in his best interests.*

(6) *Before the act is done, or the decision is made, regard must be had to whether the purpose for which it is needed can be as effectively achieved in a way that is less restrictive of the person's rights and freedom of action'.*

3. The Code of Practice is available on line at *www.publicguardian.gov.uk*.
4. If it is your opinion that the person does have capacity to conduct the proceedings, there is no need for you to give grounds for that opinion. However, if you are of the opinion that the person lacks capacity to conduct the proceedings, the Official Solicitor's certificate requires you to state in paragraphs 2 and 3 the grounds for that opinion.
5. It may assist you to know that particularly in cases of periodic remission, the Official Solicitor will ensure that the protected party's condition is regularly reassessed for the purpose of the legal proceedings. In an appropriate case the Official Solicitor will take immediate steps for his removal as guardian ad litem, next friend or litigation friend to enable the protected party to resume personal conduct of the proceedings.
6. This certificate relates only to the proceedings in which the protected party is currently involved. A separate certificate may be required if any application is made to the Court of Protection. Similarly, separate considerations apply to any

question whether the person is subject to compulsory detention under the Mental Health Act 1983: in some cases the person concerned is liable to compulsory detention but may have capacity to conduct proceedings, and in many other cases the person concerned lacks capacity to conduct proceedings but is not liable to compulsory detention.

COP3 Assessment of Capacity and Guidance Notes

COP 3 Court of Protection
04.09 **Assessment of capacity**

For office use only
Date received
Case no.

Full name of person to whom the application relates
(this is the name of the person who lacks, or is alleged to lack, capacity)

Please read first

- If you are applying to start proceedings with the court you must file this form with your COP1 application form. The assessment must contain current information.

- You must complete Part A of this form.

- You then need to provide the form to the practitioner who will complete Part B. The practitioner will return the form to you or your solicitor for filing with the court.

- The practitioner may charge a fee for completing the form. Please ask the practitioner about the amount they will charge.

- The practitioner may be a registered medical practitioner, psychologist or psychiatrist who has examined and assessed the capacity of the person to whom the application relates. In some circumstances it might be appropriate for a registered therapist, such as a speech therapist or occupational therapist, to complete the form.

- When the form has been completed, its contents will be confidential to the court and those authorised by the court to see it, such as parties to the proceedings.

- Please continue on a separate sheet of paper if you need more space to answer a question. Write your name, the name and date of birth of the person to whom the application relates, and number of the question you are answering on each separate sheet.

- There are additional guidance notes at the end of this form.

- If you need help completing this form please check the website, www.hmcourts-service.gov.uk, for further guidance or information, or contact Customer Services on 0845 330 2900.

- Court of Protection staff cannot give legal advice. If you need legal advice please contact a solicitor.

- This form has been prepared in consultation with the British Medical Association, the Royal College of Physicians and the Royal College of Psychiatrists.

Part A - To be completed by the applicant

Section 1 - Your details (the applicant)

1.1   Your details   ☐ Mr.   ☐ Mrs.   ☐ Miss   ☐ Ms.   ☐ Other _____

First name

Middle name(s)

Last name

1.2   Address
(including
postcode)

Telephone no.	Daytime	
	Evening	
	Mobile	

E-mail address

1.3   Is a solicitor representing you?   ☐ Yes   ☐ No

If Yes, please give the solicitor's details.

Name

Address
(including
postcode)

Telephone no.		Fax no.	
DX no.			
E-mail address			

1.4   To which address should the practitioner return the form when they have completed Section 2?

☐ Your address

☐ Solicitor's address

☐ Other address (please provide details)

Section 2 - The person to whom the application relates (the person to be assessed by the practitioner)

2.1   ☐ Mr.   ☐ Mrs.   ☐ Miss   ☐ Ms.   ☐ Other _____

First name

Middle name(s)

Last name

Address (including postcode)

Telephone no.

Date of birth   ☐ Male   ☐ Female

Section 3 - About the application

3.1   Please state the matter you are asking the court to decide. **(see note 1)**

3.2   What order are you asking the court to make?

3.3   How would the order benefit the person to whom the application relates?

3.4   What is your relationship or connection to the person to whom the application relates?

Section 4 - Further information

Please provide any further information about the circumstances of the person to whom the application relates that would be useful to the practitioner in assessing his or her capacity to make any decision(s) that is the subject of your application. **(see note 2)**

Now read note 3 about what you need to do next.

Part B - To be completed by the practitioner

Section 5 - Your details (the practitioner)

5.1 ☐ Mr. ☐ Mrs. ☐ Miss ☐ Ms. ☐ Dr. ☐ Other _____

First name

Middle name(s)

Last name

Address
(including
postcode)

Telephone no.

E-mail address

5.2 Nature of your professional relationship with the person to whom the application relates
(e.g. general practitioner, psychiatrist or other)

5.3 Professional qualifications

Section 6 – Sensitive information

If there is information that you do not wish to provide in this form because of its sensitive nature you can provide the information directly to the court.

6.1   Are you providing any sensitive information separately to the court?   ☐ Yes   ☐ No

Please provide it in writing to:
        Court of Protection
        Archway Tower
        2 Junction Road
        London N19 5SZ

Please include your name and contact details, and the name, address and date of birth of the person to whom the application relates on any information you provide separately to the court.

Section 7 - Assessment of capacity

7.1   The person to whom the application relates has the following impairment of, or disturbance in the functioning of, the mind or brain: **(see note 4)**

```



```

This has lasted since:

```

```

As a result, the person is unable to make a decision for themselves in relation to the following matter(s) in question:

```



```

7.2   The person to whom the application relates is unable to make a decision in relation to the relevant matter because: **(see note 5)**

☐ he or she is unable to understand the following relevant information (please give details);

```



```

and/or

☐ he or she is unable to retain the following relevant information (please give details);

```



```

and/or

☐ he or she is unable to use or weigh the following relevant information as part of the process of making the decision(s) (please give details);

```



```

or

☐ for cases where he or she can in fact understand, retain and use/weigh the information but is unable to communicate his or her decision(s) by any means at all (please give details).

```



```

7.3   My opinion is based on the following evidence of a lack of capacity:

```




```

7.4   Please answer either (a) **or** (b).

(a) I have acted as a practitioner for the person to whom the application

relates since [ ][ ][ ][ ][ ][ ][ ][ ]   and last assessed

him or her on [ ][ ][ ][ ][ ][ ][ ][ ]

(b) I assessed the person to whom the application

relates on [ ][ ][ ][ ][ ][ ][ ][ ]

following a referral from:

```




```

7.5   Has the person to whom this application relates made you aware of any views they   ☐ Yes   ☐ No
have in relation to the relevant matter?

If Yes, please give details.

```



```

7.6   Do you consider there is a prospect that the person to whom the application relates might regain or
acquire capacity in the future in respect of the decision to which the application relates? **(see note 6)**

☐ Yes – please state why and give an indication of when this might happen.

☐ No – please state why.

```



```

7.7   Are you aware of anyone who holds a different view regarding the capacity of the   ☐ Yes   ☐ No
person to whom the application relates?

If Yes, please give details.

```



```

7.8   Do you, your family or friends have any interest (financial or otherwise) in any matter concerning the person to whom the application relates?   ☐ Yes   ☐ No

If Yes, please give details.

7.9   Do you have any general comments or any other recommendations for future care? **(see note 7)**

Signed

Name   **Date**

Now read note 8 about what you need to do next.

251

GUIDANCE NOTES

Note 1   About the application

These questions are repeated on the COP1 application form. Please copy your answers from the COP1 form so that the information on both forms is the same.

Note 2   Further information

Please provide any further information about the circumstances of the person to whom the application relates that would be relevant in assessing their capacity. For example, if your application relates to property and financial affairs, it would be useful for the practitioner to know the general financial circumstances of the person concerned. This information will help the practitioner evaluate the decision-making responsibility of the person to whom the application relates and may help to inform the practitioner's view on whether that person can make the decision(s) in question.

Note 3   What you need to do next

Please provide this form to the practitioner who will complete Part B.

The practitioner will return the form to you or your solicitor when they have completed Part B. You will then need to file the form with the court together with the COP1 application form and any other information the court requires. See note 8 on the COP1 form for further information.

Note 4   Assessing capacity

For the purpose of the Mental Capacity Act 2005 a person lacks capacity if, at the time a decision needs to be made, he or she is unable to make or communicate the decision because of an impairment of, or a disturbance in the functioning of, the mind or brain.

The Act contains a two-stage test of capacity:

1. Is there an impairment of, or disturbance in the functioning of, the person's mind or brain?
2. If so, is the impairment or disturbance sufficient that the person lacks the capacity to make a decision in relation to the matter in question?

Please refer to Part A of this form where the applicant has set out details of the application and relevant information about the circumstances of the person to whom the application relates. In particular, section 3.1 sets out the matter the applicant is asking the court to decide.

The assessment of capacity must be based on the person's ability to make a decision in relation to the relevant matter, and not their ability to make decisions in general. It does not matter therefore if the lack of capacity is temporary, if the person retains the capacity to make other decisions, or if the person's capacity fluctuates.

Under the Act, a person is regarded as being unable to make a decision if they cannot:

- understand information about the decision to be made;
- retain that information;
- use or weigh the information as part of the decision-making process; or
- communicate the decision (by any means).

A lack of capacity cannot be established merely by reference to a person's age or appearance or to a particular condition or an aspect of behaviour. A person is not to be treated as being unable to make a decision merely because they have made an unwise decision.

The test of capacity is not the same as the test for detention and treatment under the Mental Health Act 1983. Many people covered by the Mental Health Act have the capacity to make decisions for themselves. On the other hand, most people who lack capacity to make decisions will never be affected by the Mental Health Act.

Practitioners are required to have regard to the Mental Capacity Act 2005 Code of Practice. The Code of Practice is available online at **www.publicguardian.gov.uk**. Hard copies are available from The Stationery Office (TSO), for a fee, by:

- phoning 0870 600 5522;
- emailing customerservices@tso.co.uk; or
- ordering online at www.tsoshop.co.uk.

For further advice please see (for example):

- Making Decisions: A guide for people who work in health and social care (2nd edition), Mental Capacity Implementation Programme, 2007.
- Assessment of Mental Capacity: Guidance for Doctors and Lawyers (2nd edition), British Medical Association and Law Society (London: BMJ Books, 2004)

Note 5   Capacity to make the decision in question

Please give your opinion of the nature of the lack of capacity and the grounds on which this is based. This requires a diagnosis and a statement giving clear evidence that the person to whom the application relates lacks capacity to make the decision(s) relevant to the application. It is important that the evidence of lack of capacity shows how this prevents the person concerned from being able to take decision(s).

Note 6   Prospect of regaining or acquiring capacity

When reaching any decision the court must apply the principles set out in the Act and in particular must make a determination that is in the best interests of the person to whom the application relates. It would therefore assist the court if you could indicate whether the person to whom the application relates is likely to regain or acquire capacity sufficiently to be able to make decisions in relation to the relevant matter.

Note 7   General comments

The court may make any order it considers appropriate even if that order is not specified in the application form. Where possible, the court will make a one-off decision rather than appointing a deputy with on-going decision making power. If you think that an order other than the one being sought by the applicant would be in the best interests of the person to whom the application relates, please give details including your reasons.

Note 8   What you need to do next

Please return the completed form to the applicant or their solicitor, as specified in section 1.4. You are advised to keep a copy for your records.

Sample letter to a GP requesting evidence of testamentary capacity

Note: The information that is relevant to the test of capacity depends on the subject area. This example uses testamentary capacity. Please refer to the relevant chapter for details of the specific test of capacity to make other types of decisions.

Dear Dr [*name*]

RE: CLIENT'S NAME [X] DATE OF BIRTH [. . .] AND SOLICITOR'S REFERENCE [. . .]

I am instructed on behalf of [X] who wishes me to prepare a will on his/her behalf. As you may be aware, the courts have advised that wills that are drawn up for an elderly person or for someone who is seriously ill should be witnessed or approved by a medical practitioner. In accordance with good practice I am therefore writing to request that you assess [X]'s capacity to make a will and prepare a report which may be used in evidence in the event that there is any subsequent legal challenge.

I attach evidence of [X]'s consent for you to disclose medical information for the purpose of this report.

As you may know, under the Mental Capacity Act 2005, we are required to presume that [X] has capacity to make specific decisions unless there is proof that s/he does not and also to take steps to enable him/her to make decisions. In relation to making a will, I have seen [X] personally and have explained the legal consequences of the wishes s/he would like to be put into effect in the will. The fact that [X] has made choices that others may think are unwise does not, by itself, indicate that s/he lacks capacity.

You may wish to note that you need only show on the balance of probabilities whether [X] has or does not have testamentary capacity, in other words, that it is more likely than not. I also request that you pay particular attention to the following points, and indicate whether [X] understands them.

- The nature of the act of making a will. This involves understanding that s/he will die and that when s/he does the will comes into operation. Further, s/he can change or revoke the will before his/her death, but only for as long as s/he has the mental capacity to do so.
- The effect of making a will. This includes the appointment of executors, deciding who receives what, whether the gifts are outright or limited or conditional in some way, the consequences of a depleted estate, that a beneficiary may pre-decease him/her, the effect on any previous will, and the reasonably foreseeable consequences of making or not making a will at this time.
- The extent of the estate. This includes the amount of property or money or investments s/he holds (although not necessarily the exact value) and the fact that some

may be jointly owned, whether s/he has any debts, that some benefits may be payable only on his/her death irrespective of his/her will, and that the estate may change during his/her lifetime.

- The possible claims of others. This involves the ability to distinguish between individuals who may have some claim on the estate and to reach some kind of moral judgement in relation to them. Beneficiaries may be left out because they are otherwise well provided for, or because of personal reasons or preferences. [X] must be aware of these reasons and the possibility that these could be challenged.

I attach details of [X]'s estate for your reference along with a draft will which s/he has agreed to disclose.

As you may be aware, a diagnosis of mental disorder does not necessarily mean that [X] lacks capacity. It would be helpful therefore to include in your report details of any impairment of, or disturbance in the functioning of, [X's] mind or brain and whether that has any effect on his/her ability to make decisions concerning the will. I would be grateful if you would also include reference to [X]'s physical state in so far as it is relevant to this report.

I have requested you prepare this report because [X] informs me that you have been his/her family doctor for a number of years. If, however, in the course of taking a psychiatric history and conducting a mental state examination you consider a specialist report is required (for example from a psychiatrist or psychologist), please let me know.

If you are of the opinion that [X] has the capacity to make a valid will, I would be grateful if you would agree to act as one of the witnesses when the time comes for him/her to sign it.

I confirm that we have agreed the sum of [£ . . .] for the purposes of the examination and preparation of this report. In the unlikely event that you are required to give evidence at court a further fee will be negotiated. Please mark your invoice with the reference stated at the top of this letter.

If you require any further information or clarification on any points please do not hesitate to contact me.

Yours sincerely

Addresses

Action on Elder Abuse
PO Box 60001
Streatham
London SW16 9BY
Tel 020 8835 9280
URL **www.elderabuse.org.uk**
Email enquiries@elderabuse.org.uk

**Age Concern Cymru and Help
the Aged in Wales**
Ty John Pathy
13/14 Neptune Court
Vanguard Way
Cardiff CF24 5PJ
Tel 029 2043 1555
URL **www.accymru.org.uk**
Email enquiries@accymru.org.uk

Age Concern England and Help the Aged
Astral House
1268 London Road
London SW16 4ER
Tel 020 8765 7200

York House
207-221 Portonville Road
London N1 9UZ
Tel 020 7278 1114
URL **www.ageconcern.org.uk**
      www.helptheaged.org.uk

Alzheimer's Society
Devon House
58 St. Katherine's Way
London E1W 1JX
Tel 020 7423 3500
URL **www.alzheimers.org.uk**
Email enquiries@alzheimers.org.uk

**Association of Directors of Adult Social
Services**
ADSS Business Unit
Local Government House
Smith Square
London SW1P 3HZ
Tel 020 7072 7433
URL **www.adass.org.uk**

British Association of Social Workers
16 Kent Street
Birmingham B5 6RD
Tel 0121 622 3911
URL **www.basw.co.uk**
Email info@basw.co.uk

British Bankers' Association
Pinners Hall
105–108 Old Broad Street
London EC2N 1EX
Tel 020 7216 8800
URL **www.bba.org.uk**

**British Institute of Learning Disabilities
(BILD)**
Campion House
Green Street
Kidderminster
Worcestershire DY10 1JL
Tel 01562 723 010
URL **www.bild.org.uk**
Email enquiries@bild.org.uk

British Medical Association (BMA)
BMA House
Tavistock Square
London WC1H 9JP
Tel 020 7387 4499 (switchboard)
    020 7383 6286 (medical ethics)
URL **www.bma.org.uk**
E-mail ethics@bma.org.uk

British Psychological Society
St Andrews House
48 Princess Road East
Leicester LE1 7DR
Tel 0116 254 9568
URL **www.bps.org.uk**
E-mail enquiries@bps.org.uk

Care UK
Connaught House
850 The Crescent
Colchester Business Park
Colchester
Essex C04 9QB
Tel 01206 752552
URL **www.careuk.com**

Carers UK
20 Great Dover Street
London SE1 4LX
Tel 020 7378 4999
URL **www.carersuk.org**
Email info@carersuk.org

Counsel and Care
Twyman House
16 Bonny Street
London NW1 9PG
Tel 020 7241 8555 (general enquiries)
URL **www.counselandcare.org.uk**

Court of Protection
Archway Tower
2 Junction Road
London N19 5SZ
Tel 0845 330 2900 (contact centre)
URL **www.hmcourts-service.gov.uk**

Depression Alliance
212 Spitfire Studios
63-71 Collier Street
London N1 9BE
Tel 0845 123 2320
URL **www.depressionalliance.org**

Down's Syndrome Association
2A Langdon Park
Teddington
Surrey TW11 9PS
Tel 0845 230 0372 (helpline)
URL **www.downs-syndrome.org.uk**
Email info@downs-syndrome.org.uk

General Medical Council
Regent's Place
350 Euston Road
London NW1 3JN
Tel 020 7189 5404 (standards and ethics
    enquiries)
    0845 357 8001 (general enquiries)
URL **www.gmc-uk.org**

Headway (the brain injury association)
7 King Edward Court
King Edward Street
Nottingham NG1 1EW
Tel 0115 924 0800
URL **www.headway.org.uk**

**Institute of Mental Health Act
Practitioners**
1a Phelps House
133a St Margarets Road
Twickenham
Surrey TW1 1RG
Tel 0845 2300105
URL **www.imhap.org.uk**

Law Society of England and Wales
113 Chancery Lane
London WC2A 1PL
Tel 020 7242 1222
    0870 606 2522 (Practice Advice
    Service)
URL **www.lawsociety.org.uk**

Liberty
21 Tabard Street
London SE1 4LA
Tel 020 7403 3888
URL **www.liberty-human-rights.org.uk**

Medical Defence Union
MDU Services Limited
230 Blackfriars Road
London SE1 8PJ
Tel 08444 20 20 20 (general enquiries)
URL **www.the-mdu.com**

Medical Protection Society
33 Cavendish Square
London W1G 0PS
Tel 020 7399 1300
URL **www.medicalprotection.org**

Medical Research Council
Medical Research Council
20 Park Crescent
London W1B 1AL
Tel 020 7636 5422
URL **www.mrc.ac.uk**

Mencap
123 Golden Lane
London EC1Y 0RT
Tel 020 7454 0454
URL **www.mencap.org.uk**
Email information@mencap.org.uk

Mental Health Alliance
C/o SCMH
134-138 Borough High Street
London Se1 ILB
Tel 020 7827 8353
URL **www.mentalhealthalliance.org.uk**

Mental Health Foundation
9th Floor, Sea Containers House
20 Upper Ground
London SE1 9QB
Tel 020 7803 1100
URL **www.mentalhealth.org.uk**

Mind
15–19 Broadway
Stratford
London E15 4BQ
Tel 020 8519 2122
URL **www.mind.org.uk**
Email contact@mind.org.uk

Mind Cymru
3rd Floor, Quebec House
Castlebridge
5–19 Cowbridge Road East
Cardiff CF11 9AB
Tel 029 2039 5123
URL **www.mind.org.uk**
Email contact@mind.org.uk

National Patient Safety Agency
4–8 Maple Street
London W1T 5HD
Tel 020 7927 9500
URL **www.npsa.nhs.uk**
Email enquiries@npsa.nhs.uk

Nursing and Midwifery Council
23 Portland Place
London W1B 1PZ
Tel 020 7333 9333 (registrations and pro-
fessional advice)
URL **www.nmc-uk.org**

National Autistic Society
393 City Road
London EC1V 1NG
Tel 020 7833 2299
URL **www.autism.org.uk**
Email nas@nas.org.uk

Office of the Public Guardian
PO Box 15118
Birmingham B16 6GX
Tel 0300 456 0300
URL **www.publicguardian.gov.uk**
Email customerservices@public
guardian.gsi.gov.uk

Official Solicitor
81 Chancery Lane
London WC2A 1DD
Tel 020 7911 7127
URL **www.officialsolicitor.gov.uk**
Email enquiries@offsol.gsi.gov.uk

Patients Association
PO Box 935
Harrow
London HA1 3YJ
Tel 0845 608 4455 (helpline)
020 8423 9111 (general enquiries)
URL **www.patients-association.com**
Email helpline@patients-
association.com

Principal Registry of the Family Division
First Avenue House
42–49 High Holborn
London WC1V 6NP
Tel 020 7947 6000
URL **www.hmcourts-service.gov.uk**

RADAR
12 City Forum
250 City Road
London EC1V 8AF
Tel 020 7250 3222
www.radar.org.uk

Rethink
15th Floor,
89 Albert Embankment
London SE1 7TP
Tel 0845 456 0455 (general enquiries)
URL **www.rethink.org**

Royal College of General Practitioners
14 Princes Gate
Hyde Park
London SW7 1PU
Tel 0845 456 4041
URL **www.rcgp.org.uk**

Royal College of Nursing
20 Cavendish Square
London W1G ORN
Tel 020 7409 3333
URL **www.rcn.org.uk**

Royal College of Physicians
11 St Andrews Place
Regent's Park
London NW1 4LE
Tel 020 7224 1539
URL **www.rcplondon.ac.uk**

Royal College of Psychiatrists
17 Belgrave Square
London SW1X 8PG
Tel 020 7235 2351
URL **www.rcpsych.ac.uk**

Royal Courts of Justice
Strand
London WC2A 2LL
Tel 020 7947 6000
URL **www.hmcourts-service.gov.uk**

Royal College of Speech and Language Therapists
2 White Hart Yard
London SE1 1NX
Tel 020 7378 1200
URL **www.rcslt.org**

Royal Hospital of Neuro-disability
West Hill
Putney
London SW15 3SW
Tel 020 8780 4500
URL **www.rhn.org.uk**
Email info@rhn.org.uk

SANE
1st Floor Cityside House
40 Adler Street
London E1 1EE
Tel 020 7375 1002
    0845 767 8000 (SANEline)
URL **www.sane.org.uk**
Email info@sane.org.uk

SignHealth
5 Baring Road
Beaconsfield
Buckinghamshire
HP9 2NB
Tel 01494 687626
URL **www.signhealth.org.uk**

Sainsbury Centre for Mental Health
134-138 Borough High Street
London SE1 LLB
Tel 020 7827 8300
URL **www.scmh.org.uk**

Social Care Institute for Excellence
Goldings House
2 Hay's Lane
London SE1 2HB
Tel 020 7089 6840
URL **www.scie.org.uk**

Solicitors for the Elderly
Room 17, Conbar House
Mead Lane
Hertford
Herts SG13 7AP
Tel 0870 067 0282
URL **www.solicitorsfortheelderly.com**

Stroke Association
Stroke House
240 City Road
London EC1V 2PR
Tel 020 7566 0300
URL **www.stroke.org.uk**

The Treasury Solicitor's Department
One Kemble Street
London WC2B 4TS
Tel 020 7210 3000
URL **www.tsol.gov.uk**

Turning Point
Standon House
21 Mansell Street
London E1 8AA
Tel 020 7841 7600
URL **www.turningpoint.co.uk**

Values in Action
Oxford House
Derbyshire Street
London E2 6HG
Tel 020 7729 5436
URL **www.viauk.org**

VOICE UK
Rooms 100–106, Kelvin House
RTC Business Centre
London Road
Derby DE24 8UP
Tel 01332 291042
URL **www.voiceuk.org.uk**
Email voice@voiceuk.org.uk

World Health Organization
Avenue Appia 20
1211 Geneva 27
Switzerland
Tel +41 22 791 21 11
URL **www.who.int**

APPENDIX J

Further reading

1. LEGAL

1.1 Principal Statutes

See **www.opsi.gov.uk** and **www.tsoshop.co.uk**

Mental Capacity Act 2005 (as amended by the Mental Health Act 2007)
Mental Health Act 1983 (as amended by the Mental Health Act 2007)

1.2 Code of Practice

See **www.publicguardian.gov.uk** and **www.dh.gov.uk** and **www.tsoshop.co.uk**

Ministry of Justice (2008) *Mental Capacity Act 2005: Deprivation of Liberty Safeguards. Code of Practice to supplement the main Mental Capacity Act 2005 Code of Practice*, TSO.
Department of Health (2008) *Mental Health Act 1983 Code of Practice*, TSO.
Department for Constitutional Affairs (2007) *Mental Capacity Act 2005 Code of Practice*, TSO.

1.3 Background to the MCA 2005

See **www.lawcom.gov.uk** and **www.tsoshop.co.uk** and **www.parliament.uk**

Joint Committee on Human Rights (2004) *Scrutiny of Bills: Final Progress Report. Twenty-third Report (HL Paper 210 / HC 1282)* Houses of Parliament (see **www.parliament.uk**).

Mental Capacity Bill 2004.

Joint Committee on the Draft Mental Incapacity Bill (2003) *First Report on the Draft Mental Incapacity Bill 2003* Houses of Parliament (see **www.parliament.uk**).

Draft Mental Incapacity Bill 2003.

Lord Chancellor's Department (1999) *Making Decisions: The government's proposals for making decisions on behalf of mentally incapacitated adults* (Cm 4465) TSO.

Lord Chancellor's Department (1997) *Who Decides? Making Decisions on behalf of Mentally Incapacitated Adults* (Cm 3903) TSO.

Law Commission (1995) *Mental Incapacity* (Law Com No.231) TSO.

Law Commission (1993) *Mentally Incapacitated Adults and Decision-Making: Medical Treatment and Research* (Law Com 124) TSO.

Law Commission (1993) *Mentally Incapacitated and other Vulnerable Adults: Public Law Protection* (Law Com 130) TSO.

Law Commission (1993) *Mentally Incapacitated Adults and Decision-Making: A new jurisdiction?* (Law Com No.128) TSO.

Law Commission (1991) *Mentally Incapacitated Adults and Decision-Making: An overview* (Law Com 119) TSO.

1.4 Relevant Statutory Instruments

See **www.opsi.gov.uk** and **www.tsoshop.co.uk**

Civil Procedure Rules (SI 1998/3132)
Family Proceedings Rules (SI 1991/1247)
Insolvency Rules (SI 1986/1925)
Court of Protection (Amendment) Rules 2009 (SI 2009/582)
Court of Protection Fees (Amendment) Order 2009 (SI 2009/513)
Court of Protection Fees Order 2007 (SI 2007/1745)
Court of Protection Rules 2007 (SI 2007/1744)
Public Guardian (Fees etc) (Amendment) Regulations 2007 (SI 2007/2616)
Public Guardian (Fees etc) Regulations 2007 (SI 2007/2051)
Public Guardian Board Regulations 2007 (SI 2007/1770)
The Mental Capacity (Deprivation of Liberty: Appointment of Relevant Person's Representative) (Amendment) Regulations 2008 (2008/2368)
The Mental Capacity (Deprivation of Liberty: Standard Authorisations, Assessments and Ordinary Residence) Regulations 2008 (SI 2008/1858)
Mental Capacity (Deprivation of Liberty: Appointment of Relevant Research Person's Representative) Regulations 2008 (SI 2008/1315)
Mental Capacity Act 2005 (Independent Mental Capacity Advocates) (Expansion of Role) Regulations 2006 (SI 2006/2883)
Mental Capacity Act 2005 (Appropriate Body) (England) Regulations (SI 2006/2810)
Mental Capacity Act 2005 (Independent Mental Capacity Advocate) (General) Regulations 2006 (SI 2006/1832)
Mental Capacity Act 2005 (Appropriate Body) (Wales) Regulations 2007 (SI 2007/883)
Mental Capacity Act 2005 (Independent Mental Capacity Advocate) (Wales) Regulations 2006 (SI 2007/852)
Mental Capacity Act 2005 (Loss of Capacity During Research) (Wales) Regulations 2007 (SI 2007/837)

Mental Capacity Act 2005 (Loss of Capacity During Research) (England) Regulations 2007 (SI 2007/679)

Mental Capacity Act 2005 (Commencement No.2) Order 2007 (SI 2007/1031)

Mental Capacity Act 2005 (Transitional and Consequential Provisions) Order 2007 (SI 2007/1898)

Mental Capacity Act 2005 (Transfer of Proceedings) Order 2007 (SI 2007/1899)

Lasting Powers of Attorney, Enduring Powers of Attorney and Public Guardian (Amendment) Regulations 2007 (SI 2007/2161)

Lasting Powers of Attorney, Enduring Powers of Attorney and Public Guardian Regulations 2007 (SI 2007/1253)

Lasting Powers of Attorney, Enduring Powers of Attorney and Public Guardian (Amendment) Regulations 2009 (SI 2009/1884)

The Mental Health Act 2007 (Commencement No.10 and Transitional Provisions) Order 2009 (SI 2009/139)

The Medicines for Human Use (Clinical Trials) Amendment (No.2) Regulations 2006 (SI 2006/2984)

Medicines for Human Use (Clinical Trials) Amendment Regulations 2006 (SI 2006/1928)

Medicines for Human Use (Clinical Trials) Regulations 2004 (SI 2004/1031)

Human Tissue Act 2004 (Persons who lack capacity to consent and transplants) Regulations 2006 (SI 2006/1659)

1.5 European and International Conventions and Protocols

Council of Europe: Committee of Experts on Family Law (2009) *Draft Recommendation on Principles Concerning Continuing Powers of Attorney and Advance Directives for Incapacity [and its explanatory memorandum] (CJ-FA(2009) 2 rev)* Council of Europe.

Council of Europe: Committee of Ministers (2006) *Recommendation of the Committee of Ministers to Member States on the Council of Europe Action Plan to promote the rights and full participation of people with disabilities in society: improving the quality of life of people with disabilities in Europe 2006–2015 (Rec (2006)5)* Council of Europe (see **www.coe.int**).

Council of Europe (2005) *Additional Protocol to the Convention on Human Rights and Biomedicine, Concerning Biomedical Research* Council of Europe (see **http:// conventions.coe.int**).

United Nations (2006) *Convention on the Rights of Persons with Disabilities and its Optional Protocol* The United Nations (see **www.un.org/disabilities**).

Hague Conference on Private International Law (2000) *Hague Convention on the International Protection of Adults* HCCH (see **www.hcch.net**).

Council of Europe Committee of Ministers (1999) *Recommendation on Principles Concerning the Legal Protection of Incapable Adults (No. R(99)4)* Council of Europe (see **www.coe.int**).

Council of Europe (1997) *Convention for the Protection of Human Rights and Dignity of the Human Being with regard to the Application of Biology and Medicine: Convention on Human Rights and Biomedicine ('the Oviedo Convention')* Council of Europe (see **http://conventions.coe.int**).

United Nations (1991) *The protection of persons with mental illness and the improvement of mental health care (Resolution 46/119, 17 December 1991)* United Nations (see **www.un.org**).

World Medical Association (1964) *Declaration of Helsinki: Ethical Principles for Medical Research Involving Human Subjects* World Medical Association (last amended 2008) (see **www.wma.net**).

Council of Europe (1950) *Convention for the Protection of Human Rights and Fundamental Freedoms (as amended)* Registry of the European Court of Human Rights (see **www.echr.coe.int**).

1.6   Other Relevant Statutes

See **www.opsi.gov.uk**

Adults with Incapacity (Scotland) Act 2000
Children Act 1989
Data Protection Act 1998
Health and Social Care Act 2001
Health and Social Care Act 2008
Human Rights Act 1998
Human Tissue Act 2004
Human Fertilisation and Embryology Act 2008
Human Fertilisation and Embryology Act 1990
Powers of Attorney Act 1971
Representation of the People Act 1983
Representation of the People Act 2000
Sexual Offences Act 2003

1.7   Court of Protection Practice Directions

See **www.hmcourts-service.gov.uk** and **Appendix D**

4A	Court documents
4B	Statements of truth
6A	Service
7A	Notifying P
8A	Permission
9A	The application form
9B	Notification of other persons that an application form has been issued
9C	Responding to an application
9D	Applications by currently appointed Deputies, Attorneys, and Donees in relation to P's property and affairs
9E	Applications relating to serious medical treatment
9F	Applications relating to statutory wills, codicils, settlements and other dealings with P's property
9G	Applications to appoint or discharge a trustee
9H	Applications relating to the registration of Enduring Powers of Attorney
10A	Applications within proceedings
10B	Urgent and interim applications
11A	Human rights
12A	Court's jurisdiction to be exercised by certain judges
12B	Procedure for disputing the Courts jurisdiction
13A	Hearings (including reporting restrictions)
14A	Written evidence
14B	Depositions
14C	Fee for examiners of the Court
14D	Witness summons
14E	Section 49 reports
15A	Expert evidence
17A	Litigation friend
18A	Change of solicitor

19A Costs in the Court of Protection
20A Appeals
21A Contempt of Court
22A Transitional provisions
22B Transitory provisions
22C Appeals against decisions made under Part 7 of the Mental Health Act 1983 or under the Enduring Powers of Attorney Act 1985 which are brought on or after commencement
23A Request for directions where notice of objection prevents the Public Guardian from registering an Enduring Power of Attorney
23B Where P ceases to lack capacity or dies

1.8 The Public Guardian

See **www.publicguardian.gov.uk**

The Office of the Public Guardian (2009) *LPA109 – Office of the Public Guardian Registers – Registers of Lasting Power of Attorney, Register of Enduring Power of Attorney, Register of Court Orders Appointing Deputies* The Office of the Public Guardian. (This is a booklet to accompany Form OPG100 Application for a search of the Public Guardian Registers.)

The Office of the Public Guardian (2009) *LPA107 – Lasting Powers of Attorney: A Guide for Certificate Providers and Witnesses* The Office of the Public Guardian.

National Care Association (2009) *OPG603 – Making Decisions: A guide for people who work in health and social care* 4th edition Mental Capacity Implementation Programme (MCIP) and the Office of the Public Guardian.

Speaking Up (2007) OPG606 – *Making decisions: The Independent Mental Capacity Advocate (IMCA) Service* 2nd edition Mental Capacity Implementation Programme (MCIP) and the Office of the Public Guardian.

1.9 The Law Society's Practice Notes

See **www.lawsociety.org.uk**

Law Society (2009) *Making Gifts of Assets Practice Note,* The Law Society.
Law Society (2009) *Representation Before Mental Health Tribunals,* The Law Society.
Law Society (2008) *Lasting Powers of Attorney Practice Note,* The Law Society.

1.10 The Solicitors Regulation Authority

See **www.sra.org.uk**

Solicitors Regulation Authority (June 2009) *Solicitors Code of Conduct 2007: Including SRA Recognised Bodies Regulations 2009,* The Law Society.

1.11 Other Publications on Mental Capacity

Aldridge T (2007) *Powers of Attorney* 10th edition, Sweet and Maxwell.
Ashton G, Letts P, Marin M, Oates L, Terrell M, (2009) *Court of Protection Practice 2009,* Jordan Publishing.
Ashton G, Letts P, Oates L, Terrell M (2006) *Mental Capacity: The new law,* Jordan Publishing.
Bartlett P (2008) *Blackstone's Guide to the Mental Capacity Act 2005* 2nd edition, Oxford University Press.
Bartlett P (2007) *Mental Health Law: Policy and Procedure* 3rd edition, Oxford University Press.

Bielanska C and Terrell M (2004) *Elderly Client Handbook* 3rd edition, Law Society.

British Bankers' Association (2007) *Banking for people who lack capacity to make decisions*, British Bankers' Association (see **www.bba.org.uk**).

Dew R, Marina O, Bedworth G (2009) *Trust and Estate Practitioner's Guide to Mental Capacity*, Lexis Nexis.

Fennell P (2007) *Mental Health: The New Law*, Jordans Publishing.

Francis R and Johnston C (2009) *Medical Treatment Decisions and the Law* 2nd edition, Bloomsbury Professional.

Greaney N, Morris F, Taylor B (2008) *Mental Capacity Act 2005: A guide to the new law* 2nd edition, Law Society.

Hockton A. (2001) *The Law of Consent to Medical Treatment*, Sweet and Maxwell (a 2nd edition is due in 2010).

Jacoby R, Oppenheimer C, Denning T, Thomas A (2008) *Oxford Textbook of Old Age Psychiatry*, Oxford University Press.

Jones R (2008) *Mental Capacity Act Manual* 3rd edition, Sweet and Maxwell.

Jones R (2009) *Mental Health Act Manual* 12th edition, Sweet and Maxwell.

Law Society and BMA (2009) *Assessment of Mental Capacity* 3rd edition, Law Society.

Lush D, Bielanska C, Margrave J (2009) *Elderly Clients: Precedent Manual* 3rd edition, Jordans Publishing.

Lush D (2009) *Cretney and Lush on Lasting and Enduring Powers of Attorney*, Jordans Publishing.

Krish J and Taylor C, with Farnham F (2009) *Advising Mentally Disordered Offenders* 2nd *edition*, Law Society.

Terrell M (2009) *A Practitioner's Guide to the Court of Protection* 3rd edition, Bloomsbury Professional.

Thurston J (2007) *A Practitioner's Guide to Powers of Attorney* 6th edition, Bloomsbury Professional.

Ward C (2008) *Lasting Powers of Attorney: A Practical Guide*, Law Society.

Whitehouse C (2009) *Finance and Law for the Older Client*, Lexis Nexis in association with STEP.

2. MEDICAL

2.1 British Institute of Learning Disabilities (BILD)

See **www.bild.org.uk**

Hardie E and Brooks L (2009) *Brief Guide to the Mental Capacity Act 2005*, British Institute of Learning Disabilities.

2.2 British Medical Association (BMA)

See **www.bma.org.uk**

British Medical Association (2009) *Access to Medical Reports: Guidance from the BMA Medical Ethics Department,* British Medical Association.

British Medical Association (2009) *End-of-Life Decisions: Views of the BMA,* British Medical Association.

British Medical Association (2009) *Ethics of Caring for Older People* 2nd edition, Wiley Blackwell.

British Medical Association (2009) *The Mental Capacity Act 2005: Guidance for health professionals.* British Medical Association.

British Medical Association (2008) *Mental Capacity Act 2005 Tool Kit*, British Medical Association.

British Medical Association (2008) *Consent Tool Kit* 4th edition, British Medical Association.

British Medical Association (2008) *Confidentiality and disclosure of health information tool kit*, British Medical Association.

British Medical Association (2007) *Advance Decisions and Proxy Decision-Making in Medical Treatment and Research*, British Medical Association.

British Medical Association (2007) *Medical Ethics Today: The BMA's Handbook of Ethics and Law* 2nd edition, British Medical Association.

British Medical Association (2007) *Withholding and Withdrawing Life-Prolonging Medical Treatment: Guidance for Decision Making* 3rd edition, Wiley Blackwell.

British Medical Association (October 2007) *Decisions relating to cardiopulmonary resuscitation: A joint statement from the British Medical Association, the Resuscitation Council and the Royal College of Nursing*, British Medical Association, Resuscitation Council (UK), Royal College of Nursing.

British Medical Association (2007) *Expert Witness Guidance*, British Medical Association.

British Medical Association (2005) *Guidance for doctors preparing professional reports and giving evidence in court*, British Medical Association.

2.3   British Psychological Society

See **www.bps.org.uk**

Joyce T (2008) *Best Interests: Guidance on determining the best interests of adults who lack the capacity to make a decision (or decisions) for themselves [England and Wales]*, British Psychological Society.

British Psychological Society's Expert Witnesses Working Party (2007) *Psychologists as Expert Witnesses: Guidelines and Procedures for England and Wales*, British Psychological Society.

Dobson C (2008) *Conducting research with people not having the capacity to consent to their participation*, British Psychological Society.

The Assessment of Capacity Guidelines Group (2006) *Assessment of Mental Capacity in Adults: Interim Guidance for Psychologists*, British Psychological Society.

2.4   Department of Health

See **www.dh.gov.uk** and **www.wales.nhs.gov.uk/hcsw**

Department of Health (2009) *Reference guide to consent for examination or treatment* 2nd edition, Department of Health.

Department of Health and Welsh Assembly Government (2009) *Arrangements under paragraph 183(4) of Schedule A1 to the Mental Capacity Act 2005 between the Secretary of State and the Welsh Ministers*, Department of Health.

Department of Health (2009) *Approved mental health professionals, approved clinicians and best interests assessors – guidance on changes to qualifying requirements for psychologists from 1 July 2009*, Department of Health.

Department of Health (2009) *Making Decisions: The Independent Mental Capacity Advocate (IMCA) Service*, Department of Health.

Department of Health (2009) *Deprivation of Liberty Safeguards: A guide for primary care trusts and local authorities*, Department of Health.

Department of Health (2009) *Deprivation of Liberty Safeguards: A guide for hospitals and care homes*, Department of Health.

Department of Health (2009) *Deprivation of Liberty Safeguards: A guide for relevant person's representatives*, Department of Health.

Department of Health (2008) *Mental Capacity Act 2005 and consent for research*, Department of Health.

Department of Health (2008) *What are the Mental Capacity Act Deprivation of Liberty Safeguards?* Department of Health.

Department of Health (2008) *Guidance on Nominating a Consultee for Research Involving Adults Who Lack Capacity to Consent*, Department of Health.

University of Central Lancashire and Social Care Workforce Research Unit (King's College London) (2007) *Mental Capacity Act 2005: Training materials*, Department of Health

Department of Health (2007) *Mental Capacity Act – Transitional provisions for existing advance decisions to refuse life-sustaining treatment*, Department of Health.

Department of Health (2007) *NHS Information Governance – Guidance on legal and professional obligations*, Department of Health.

Department of Health (2005) *Research governance framework for health and social care* 2nd edition, Department of Health.

Department of Health (2003) *Confidentiality: NHS Code of Practice*, Department of Health.

Department of Health (2002) *Guidance on restrictive physical interventions for people with learning disability and autistic spectrum disorder, in health, education and social care settings*, Department of Health.

Department of Health (2000) *No Secrets: Guidance on developing and implementing multi-agency policies and procedures to protect vulnerable adults from abuse*, Department of Health.

2.5 General Medical Council

See www.gmc-uk.org

Note: Any current guidance from the General Medical Council published before 2005 should be read in conjunction with the Mental Capacity Act 2005 Code of Practice.

General Medical Council (2009) *Confidentiality: guidance for doctors*, general Medical Council.

General Medical Council (2009) *Draft End of Life Treatment and Care: Good practice in treatment and care*, General Medical Council. (**Note:** this guidance is currently in draft form for consultation.)

General Medical Council (2008) *Consent: Patients and doctors making decisions together*, General Medical Council.

General Medical Council (2008) *Acting as an Expert Witness*, General Medical Council.

General Medical Council (2007) *0–18: Guidance for all doctors*, General Medical Council.

General Medical Council (2006) *Good Medical Practice* General Medical Council.

General Medical Council (2002) *Research: The role and responsibilities of doctors*, General Medical Council. (**Note:** an initial consultation was carried out in June-August 2008 and a second consultation in July-September 2009. The GMC intend to publish revised guidance in due course).

General Medical Council (2002) *Withholding and withdrawing life-prolonging treatments: good practice in decision-making*, General Medical Council.

General Medical Council (2002) *Making and using visual and audio recordings of patients*, General Medical Council. (**Note:** an initial consultation was carried out in July-September 2009. The GMC intend to publish revised guidance in due course.).

2.6 Joint Royal Colleges Ambulance Liaison Committee (JRCALC)

See **www.jrcalc.org.uk**

JRCALC (2006) *UK Ambulance Service Clinical Practice Guidelines*, JRCALC.

2.7 Medical Defence Union

See **www.the-mdu.com**

Medical Defence Union (2002) *Consent to Treatment*, Medical Defence Union.

2.8 Medical Protection Society

See **www.medicalprotection.org**

Medical Protection Society (2008) *MPS Guide to Consent in the UK*, Medical Protection Society.

2.9 Medical Research Council

See **www.mrc.ac.uk**

Medical Research Council (2007) *MRC Ethics Guide – Medical research involving adults who cannot consent*, Medical Research Council.
Medical Research Council (2000) *Personal Information in Medical Research*, Medical Research Council.

2.10 National Patient Safety Agency

See **www.nres.npsa.nhs.uk**

National Research Ethics Service (2007) *Critieria for approving research under section 34 of the Mental Capacity Act*, National Patient Safety Agency.
National Research Ethics Service (2007) *Critieria for approving research under sections 30–33 of the Mental Capacity Act*, National Patient Safety Agency.
National Research Ethics Service (2008) *Medicines for Human Use (Clinical Trials Regulations) 2004: Informed Consent in Clinical Trials*, National Patient Safety Agency.
National Research Ethics Service (2007) *Research involving adults unable to consent for themselves version 2*, National Patient Safety Agency.
National Research Ethics Service (2009) *Mental Capacity Act – Questions and answers*, National Patient Safety Agency.

2.11 Nursing and Midwifery Council

See **www.nmc-uk.org**

Nursing and Midwifery Council (2009) *Confidentiality Advice Sheet*, Nursing and Midwifery Council.
Nursing and Midwifery Council (2009) *Record Keeping: Guidance for nurses and midwives advice sheet*, Nursing and Midwifery Council.
Nursing and Midwifery Council (2008) *The Code: Standards of conduct, performance and ethics for nurses and midwives*, Nursing and Midwifery Council.

Nursing and Midwifery Council (March 2009) *Guidance for the care of older people*, Nursing and Midwifery Council.

Nursing and Midwifery Council (May 2008) *Consent Advice Sheet*, Nursing and Midwifery Council.

2.12 Royal College of Nursing

See **www.rcn.org.uk**

Royal College of Nursing (2007) *Mental Health Nursing of Adults with Learning Disabilities: RCN Guidance*, Royal College of Nursing.

Royal College of Nursing (2007) *Research ethics. RCN guidance for nurses*, Royal College of Nursing.

Royal College of Nursing (2006) *Meeting the Health Needs of People with Learning Disabilities: Guidance for nursing staff*, Royal College of Nursing.

2.13 Royal College of Physicians

See **www.rcplondon.ac.uk**

Conroy S, Fade P, Fraser A, Schiff R (2009) *Advance Care Planning: National Guidelines*, Royal College of Physicians.

2.14 Royal College of Psychiatrists

See **www.rcpsych.ac.uk**

Royal College of Psychiatrists (2000) *Guidelines for researchers and for research ethics committees on psychiatric research involving human participants (Council Report CR82)*, Royal College of Psychiatrists.

2.15 Royal Hospital for Neuro-Disability (RHN)

See **www.rhn.org.uk**

The Institute of Neuropalliative Rehabilitation (2008) *Mental Capacity Act 2005: The Management of People with Complex Neurological Disabilities*. Royal Hospital for Neuro-disability.

The Institute of Neuropalliative Rehabilitation (2008) *Mental Capacity Act 2005: Research Involving People with Complex Neurological Disabilities*. Royal Hospital for Neuro-disability.

2.16 World Health Organization

See **www.who.int**

World Health Organization (2007) *International Statistical Classification of Diseases and Related Health Problems 10th revision*, World Health Organization.

Index